To D

May this book stretch
your mind and expand
your understanding of
the Word of God.

Kenneth Upshegrove

Dawning: The Next Great Move Of God

Bringing The Church To:
— Spiritual Awakening —
— Spiritual Power —
— Spiritual Victory —

Kenneth Uptegrove

ISBN: 1-4107-3645-8 (e-book)
ISBN: 1-4107-4011-0 (Paperback)

This book is printed on acid free paper.

1stBooks - rev. 09/09/03

Dawning: The Next Great Move of God
— A Vision of Recovery —
Copyright © 1999 by Kenneth Uptegrove
ArkHaven Publications
Springdale, Arkansas 72764

Fourth Printing
Printed in the United States of America
Uptegrove, Kenneth, 1936 —
Dawning: The Next Great Move of God: A Vision of Recovery/
Kenneth Uptegrove
p. cm.
Includes bibliographical references
1. Christianity, 2. Revivals, 3. Evangelism, 4. Gifts, Spiritual,
5. Church Renewal. I. Title
BT876.U67 2002

Correspondence is encouraged. Email: ken@arkhaven.org. Website:
http://www.arkhaven.org.
Scripture, unless otherwise noted, taken from the New American
Standard Bible ®, 1960, 1962, 1963, 1968, 1971, 1972, 1973, 1975, 1977,
© Copyright the Lockman Foundation. Used by permission.
(www.Lockman.org)

Cover design by Kenneth Uptegrove
Graphic technicians: Nancy Spiegelberg and Alpha Graphics
Interior design by Kenneth Uptegrove
Editors: Jody El-Assadi & Julie Turner.

Contents

Preface

I have known Ken Uptegrove for over twenty years and have seen him develop from a serious Bible student into a serious Bible researcher. He has great depth of insight into the Word of God. He cares about the local church and the Church Universal. He is committed to the truth and will go to great lengths to see it revealed.

This book is a culmination of years of research into church history, Christian theology, and Christian apologetics: research done in order to help make clear the important things of God's kingdom. He is careful to be sensitive to all, but will not step on truth to please them. He has consulted me, and others, because he wanted things not only to be clear but correct.

Ken Uptegrove is a prophet and a visionary, not a prophet like Isaiah or Jeremiah, but one who can still be called a seer. He is a person who is able to see the kind of kingdom that God has for His people. Ken's prophetic vision of recovery is best described by Wellington Boone where, in reference to Joel 2:28, he said:

> The Lord has a vision, and by the Holy Spirit, He is pouring out His vision and His dreams upon his people. When we dream, we are dreaming that which is in the heart of God for His people as a part of the last day outpouring. God is achieving His visions, plans, sights, and goals through a people whom He has sensitized to Himself. He is achieving them through a people whose hearts He has touched and who are embracing His purposes, a people who burn for Him so intensely that they do not want to live for anything other than to see the will of God fulfilled. They have gone even beyond wanting to just see it fulfilled out in the earth. They want to be involved in the fulfillment of the ages, and the culmination of God's visions and dreams.
>
> — Wellington Boone[1]

This book demonstrates Ken's involvement in the prophetic vision described by Wellington Boone.

Ken challenges us to be overcomers in the Kingdom and dares us to stretch our faith as far as we can. At the present time I am not able to meet his challenge, and the challenge of many others, to fast for forty days. Even so, I pray it may happen in my life. It is an attainable goal.

Too many times teachers and other church leaders have called for overcomers. They have said that overcomers are a special class of Christians — far ahead of the rest of us. Consequently, many of us in the church feel like second-class citizens. I think you and I will be encouraged to hear Ken's definition of an overcomer in this book: "The overcomers are not some special breed or class. They are simply people from every generation who overcame the shortcomings found in each of the seven churches. Because they overcame these short-comings they were promised wonderful privileges that are not prom-ised to other Christians."

I recommend this book as a must for all Christians as we seek the Lord before His Second Coming.

May God continue to bless you, my brother,

Charles A. Schism, M. Div., Th. D.

Footnote:
1. Excerpt from *Visions and Dreams*, an article by Welling-ton Boone, published in *The Morning Star Journal*, Char-lotte, NC, Vol. 9, No. 3, 1999.

Foreword

This book contains answers for Christians who are hungry for greater insight into what God is doing today to bring forth a great end time harvest. The question we must all ask ourselves is, just how hungry are we? Are we truly *growing* in God's wisdom and truth, or are we *stagnating* in the status quo?

By virtue of being human, we live in — and frequently are subject to — the flesh. But to grow is to take the risk of muddling around in both error and truth, and not always knowing the difference. To not grow spiritually is to stagnate, which leads to death. Either way the risk is real — a closed loop — and risk is unavoidable so long as we live.

Those who take the growth route are "seekers of wisdom and truth." Those who take what is considered the safe route are in fact taking the route to stagnation. The middle ground between growth and stagnation could be called the conservative or traditionalist route.

A traditionalist is often a minimalist; i.e., one who holds to well established standards set in place by the founders of their tradition without variance or consideration. Minimalists lean towards Murphy's Law that states: Whatever *can* go wrong *will* go wrong — and Satan always wins the lion's share. In the end God wins, but He will have only *the pitiful, picked over, unavoidable minimum* to show for His narrow victory — according to Murphy's Law.

But God's law is radical, and says just the opposite of Murphy's Law. God is absolutely victorious. Victory is another aspect of who God is — He is perpetually and absolutely victorious. His victory is unceasingly on schedule and is all encompassing. And the Lion of Judah takes the lion's share! Amen!

Before God created our universe He already had foreknowledge of every human and bird and flower that would exist on Earth during human history. Because He is omnipotent, omnipresent, and omniscient in space and time, He was perfectly able to foreknow before the creation that Adam would fall, and that every human would fall short of the glory of God. This also explains how He was able to write all those names in the Lamb's book of life (Rev. 21: 27). Isn't it wonderful that He made provision for our salvation through Jesus Christ before creating our universe?

But what is foreknowledge?

Time is God's will in motion. To God there is no future or past. He is the mighty *I AM* who lives in the eternal *present tense*. For God the present was, the present is, and the present will be — simultaneously. He predetermined the beginning, world history, and the end of all events eons before the events transpire. He is able to be "the Alpha and the Omega" because His foreknowledge is part of being omnipotent, omniscient, and omnipresent in all of time and space.

That is why — before creating anything — He was able to record in the Bible all that will ever happen on earth. To us that is prophecy of future events. But for God, He is already there and has already done that — present tense. So, for Him, foreknowledge is (as He told Moses) summed up in His name — *I AM THAT I AM.*

When someone talks about God doing "a quick work," we must remember that He knew before the foundation of the world the exact day that He would do that "quick work." All that He will ever do is as much an established fact in His mind as the fall of Adam was before the foundation of the world.

That means He is precisely on time and is absolutely in control, and never has to rush. He may release some events in rapid succession, but He is never pressured or persuaded to react to anything.

So, God's foreknowledge comes out of His omnipresence in all of time. And with this divine foreknowledge comes His ability to hold the future in His absolute, omniscient power. He is **THE** epitome, **THE** definition of "absolute victory."

Perhaps this understanding of God's omnipresence in time will help dispel the poorly thought out Deist notion that says, "God doesn't have foreknowledge of everything, but is dependent, in part, upon our choices and actions."

When we take a second look at the Jonah epic we can see that Jonah still could have chosen to <u>not</u> deliver God's message to Nineveh even after being belched up by that "great fish." God allowed both

Jonah's will and His will to be fulfilled. But if Jonah had lain on that beach, reeking of vomit, and still refused to go, God would have sent another prophet. God chooses whom He chooses, but His will is inevitably done.

Omnipresence in time is beyond our comprehension, but maybe a chess game scenario will help our human perspective. Consider what would happen if you could look into the future and watch the next game with your chess opponent. Even if you lost that future game, you then know in advance what your opponents moves will be, and you can prepare to counter them before the game is played in the present tense.

However, your opponent may be able to counter your new strategy. So you would have to replay that scene over and over again so as to see every possible move of your opponent before allowing the future to evolve into the present and past tense.

When we add God's omnipotence to His omnipresence we can see that His ways are far above our ways. In fact, they are so far above our ways that even our best explanations of how He is able to write history in advance is beyond our comprehension.

As one commentator put it, "History is His Story — prophecy is history in the making."

This concept of God as omnipotent, omnipresent, and omniscient in space and time leads me to suspect that this I AM'ness of God transcends all human theologies. Specifically, this concept transcends Calvinism and Arminianism. It even transcends our concept of "the sovereignty of God." God is always beyond our definitions.

But before someone has decided that I have invented a new school of theology, and names it Uptegroveism, let me point out that I don't understand what I just said. This concept transcends human thinking. But man never ceases to endeavor to place God in a box. That is what doctrines and theologies are all about. But Christianity is bigger than just doctrines, isn't it? When my sons were three years old they were not capable of understanding their father, but they loved me nonetheless. And I loved them *passionately*, despite their immaturity. We can have that relationship with our Heavenly father, can't we?

Does this help you gain a larger concept of God?

The Bible describes a life of virtue, glory, privilege, and **VICTORY** for us — in Christ Jesus. Many Christians mouth the words in that old gospel song, *"Victory in Jesus,"* without understanding or believing in victory for ourselves or for His church.

Now, back to the subject of "seekers of wisdom and truth," or choosing the growth route versus the traditionalist or minimalist route.

Those who take the **growth** route are ***"seekers of wisdom and truth."*** Those who take what is considered to be the traditional ***minimalist*** route are — in reality — ***"seekers of confirmation of the status quo."*** One is a Berean and the other is Pharisaic. One preserves, protects, defends the traditions of the elders and condemns all who don't agree with what some have already determined to be ***the*** truth. The Bereans repeatedly and consistently shake and test every opinion presented to them to see if it holds up to the Word of God. It was not the conservative traditionalists that brought about the Reformation — it was the risk-taking Bereans.

Martin Luther believed that the Reformation was to be an ongoing process — culminating in the Second Coming. Although Luther was wrong about some doctrinal issues, he was right to take the huge God-inspired risk that changed the world. So must we. As A.W. Tozer said, "No revival is without reformation.

There will forever be only one man whose message was perfect — Jesus. There is only one book that is infallible — the Bible. None of us agree with anybody 100%. Therefore, neither anyone quoted in this book nor I will be found infallible. Even so, if any of my assertions are to be proven wrong, let it be by the Berean method. I believe that this message is on time and critical for our generation.

It is my hope that you will find this book to be a unique work that deserves the attention of all serious Bible students. Whether you agree or disagree with something I say, this book will inform, encourage, challenge, and motivate you in your daily Christian walk. You will be stretched and enriched. ♦

Kenneth Uptegrove

Section One

Spiritual Awakening

The Church is awakening, rising up, from her spiritual slumber into an on-going synergism of simultaneous restoration, power, and victory.

I proclaim to you new things for this time, Even hidden things which you have not known. (Isaiah 48:6b)

Scripture Reading For Section One

No one puts new wine into old wineskins; otherwise the new wine will burst the skins and it will be spilled out, and the skins will be ruined. But new wine must be put into fresh wineskins. And no one, after drinking old wine wishes for new; for he says, "The old is good enough." (Luke 5: 37-39)

By this we know that we have come to know Him, if we keep His commandments. The one who says, "I have come to know Him," and does not keep His commandments, is a liar, and the truth is not in him; but whoever keeps His word, in him the love of God has truly been perfected. By this we know that we are in Him: the one who says he abides in Him ought himself to walk in the same manner as He walked. (1 John 2:3-6)

Chapter 1

A Vision of Recovery

Is God doing something new as we enter a new millennium? Is He bringing change into the church today? Yes! He always is!

God is perfect and is eternally the same, but He is eternally up to something different in every generation (Mal. 3:6). His ways and methods stay fresh, and are forever fresh and unpredictably new. We can count on this.

It is through our personal relationship with Jesus Christ that God promotes change and freshness in our lives. Therefore, what He is doing in the church today may seem, in our limited perspective, to be new and creative, but to Him it is all part of His plan for our progression towards perfection in Christ Jesus. Hasn't that been His plan all along? Take a look from a millennial perspective and you will find this "new" thing that is coming is not really new, but rather an embracing of radical, biblical Christianity.

> Forgetting what lies behind and reaching forward to what lies ahead, I press on toward the goal for the prize of the upward call of God in Christ Jesus. (Philippians 3:13b-14)

Today, most evangelical groups anticipate the next revival — a great movement of God to *far exceed* any revival in the past. Therefore, it stands to reason that the *preparation* preceding the next great revival will have to far exceed anything God has required in past revivals. After all, if our present level of faith, works, and understanding could accomplish God's great commission, America and the world would have been won to Christ long ago.

3

God has revealed all in His Son, Jesus Christ! We just never seem to walk in all of that revelation at any given time. The good news is that the church now appears to be entering into a more complete and balanced insight of old revelation.

CATCHING THE VISION

I believe that the reformation, restoration movement that God started through Martin Luther in A.D. 1520 is an on-going process. Nearly every flame of truth established by Christ and His apostles was dampened during the Dark Ages; but with the Reformation, those smoldering embers were rekindled.

Biblical truths are being restored one at a time, a recovery process that will continue until, and culminate at, the Second Coming of Jesus Christ. In fact, Martin Luther said (in reference to Rev. 19:7), "We can expect God to restore truths to His church until we become a Bride acceptable to the Bridegroom." "An ever reforming church" was the cry of our reformation fathers.[1]

Even so, Lord Jesus, reform and restore quickly!

Reform means *to change the form*, and this is about to happen.

In the Biblical sense of the word, *reformation* is a call to repent of disobedience to God's word. It always involves getting rid of things that are not biblical. *Restoration* is a restoring of obedience to God's will and a return to all things biblical.

Remember this! When we pray for God's blessings, we are praying against the status quo and for God's reformation/restoration process that incessantly conforms us to the image of Christ.

Now is the time to rid ourselves of unbiblical understandings of the Church based upon preference or past traditions. It is our duty to return to the mission of the New Testament church as stated by Jesus and recorded in Acts 1:8.

Have we Evangelicals reformed? Have we repented of our sin and error? Do we have that first century zeal, fire, and anointing? If not, we need a vision of recovery! It is no wonder that revival hasn't started yet.

Spiritual vision originates with God and focuses on Christ. Such *vision* captures an understanding of Christ's role in the Kingdom of God.

Solomon said, **"Where there is no vision, the people are unrestrained"** (NASB), **". . . *and* perish"** (KJV) (Proverbs 29:18). Ryrie's Bible Commentary on this verse says, **"Without prophetic revelation from God, people are unrestrained and fall under judgment."**

If we are not submitting to God's supernatural mandate, we are busy doing good works; we are building a church franchise; we are heading towards judgment — towards a lack of vision.

Paul gives us a clear picture of what personal sacrifice may involve. He exemplified what American Christians would call radical and fanatical Christianity, but he considered his walk with the Lord *normal* . . . for an apostle. Paul also instructed us to follow his example, and the example that Jesus set.

> For whom He foreknew, He also predestined to become conformed to the image of His Son. (Romans 8:29)

Consider how many times Paul was stoned, whipped, shipwrecked, and thrown out of many towns, cold, poor, and hungry. We may not ever experience any of these hardships, but the question is: are we committed to God's Kingdom or to our personal comfort? Loving our personal comfort can be a symptom of loving *self* more than Christ and His church. We may have to lay down some of our comforts in order to pick up our cross and do *whatever is necessary* to fulfill the great commission.

When I speak of building a New Testament Church, or of God restoring the Church to first century standards, many leaders look askance at me. I like the way Arthur Wallis expresses it in his book, ***The Radical Christian.***[2]

> To many, what has been written in this book regarding God's way for His church will be dismissed as idealistic, impractical, or super-spiritual. They will tell us that institutionalized Christianity is too well established.
>
> A New Testament Church today is a pipe dream. No leader of any stature would entertain it. In a word, it can never be.

5

Then let us remember God's word to Sarah when, in her unbelief, she too laughed off God's promise to her as impossible: "Is anything too hard for the Lord?"

Most Christian books are written on what God has done in the past and on what we can learn from those visitations. There are also many books devoted to various needs, issues, and problems confronting the church today as well as methodologies to address them. However, there is too little published on what the Lord is ***currently*** speaking to the church. By God's grace that is what I have attempted to do in this book.

What has been restored so far, and what is yet to be restored before a worldwide revival can begin in earnest? At this time, probably very few people can answer that with very much detail or authority. But perhaps a working model, based on Bible prophecy, can be presented in this book for your prayerful consideration.

> **Time will test this radical statement. Brethren, I believe the dozen or so compelling new insights presented in this book are but a mild prelude to the discussions and decisions that will confront us all in the not too distant future. Most assuredly, this is the time for "reaching forward to what lies ahead."**

Please hear my heart. By my thinking, the reformation/restoration vision of recovery presented in this book is decidedly mainstream Evangelical.

Even so, I am not trying to establish doctrine here. I'm trying to propose fresh insights, and plead for openness to what the Holy Spirit is doing in the church today.

My intent is to briefly state the results of my years of research, prayers, and meditation on these pages, and submit them for discussion and correction by the brethren. ♦

Chapter 2

The Next Great Move of God

What many Christians are calling revival is actually a harvest. Revival is
bringing back to life what was dying;
harvest is reaping of souls. Therefore,
the church must first be revived before she can participate in a great
harvest of souls.

The Great Harvest that is yet to come must wait until the church
submits to the process of revival. Many prominent leaders in the body
of Christ are fasting and praying for God to do whatever it takes to
revive His church in these last days. This should be our cry to the
Lord: *Oh Lord here are your people; we will do whatever it takes...*
whatever it takes! We will be zealous, obedient, whatever the cost!
Now is the time to draw a great line in the sand and make our stand!

The word *revival* means:

1. *Restoration* or *renewal* to vigor and activity
2. Bringing, or coming back to life, or consciousness
3. Bring back into use, operation, or attention
4. To come or bring to mind again

When we pray for revival, we are admitting that we are backslid-
den. That means (to some degree) our ministry is inactive, our services are lifeless; we are unequipped for effective ministry, and we
have forgotten our marching orders. Very little has been done to break

us out of the frustrating cycle of being revived, followed by backsliding, and the need for being revived and renewed again.

Unless we understand all that is involved in revival, we cannot understand what God is doing in the Church today. God has the Church in His hands and is beginning to breathe His resurrection life into it. That is revival!

Revival involves repentance and a return to our first love for God. In the process of reviving His church, God is cleansing and empowering it. If we misunderstand this work of the Holy Spirit — which can sometimes be painful — we may perceive that this pruning process brings defeat and loss — not revival.

While we certainly do not want to unnecessarily offend the members of our church or even unbelievers, still, we must remain faithful to Jesus' agenda even if it means having a temporary "backdoor revival." That is, an exodus of people who do not desire all that Jesus wants to give them.

Perhaps losing the half-hearted and uncommitted — though they be long-standing members — would have a divine "purging effect" on all parties concerned! Remember, John reports that when Jesus did not water down the truth, "Many of His disciples walked no more with Him" (John 6:60-66).

After His resurrection, Jesus ". . . appeared to more than 500 brethren at one time . . ." (1 Cor. 15:6). Yet on the day of Pentecost there were only 120 brethren present. It makes one wonder why more were not present. I wonder how many would-be disciples left the Upper Room the day before Pentecost. It must have been discouraging as night after night passed, and the promise didn't materialize. They weren't told how long to wait, just wait . . . *until*.

What a frustrating directive: to wait for an undetermined period for an unknown sign. For 2,000 years the church has been asked to wait for an undetermined period for the culmination of all things. You and I must wait . . . *until*.

Presently we are waiting for the Church in our generation to be pruned and revived, then harvest will be imminent. In that harvest, the Church will celebrate over a great gathering of souls for Jesus.

We must keep foremost in our minds and hearts during these days of restoration that we are not seeking revival;

we are seeking Jesus Christ! Our emphasis and focus is always to be on Christ; not revival, not a harvest, not the rapture — but JESUS, our Lord and Savior!

Revival is a result of repentance, right relationships, and exalting Jesus to His rightful place in our hearts and in our churches. We must seek that right relationship with Him and allow Him to work His perfect will in our midst.

IS THE CHURCH READY?

A church can be engrossed for months in prayer, fasting, weeping, supplications, begging, and beseeching God to move in a mighty way — and yet still not be ready for God to move mightily in their midst.

It is necessary to search God's Word to find out how His people prepared themselves in ancient times. Actually, God has given you and me many biblical promises that are "on call" — or — are ready to be fulfilled. Brethren, I believe He is simply waiting on a people who will prepare themselves to accept these promises. A lot of church members who are singing "Standing on the Promises" are just sitting on the premises.

This is comparable to a package under the Christmas tree that has your name on it. You do not fast, pray, or beg for it. You didn't even know you were going to receive a present, but it is yours for the taking. You simply pick it up, rejoice over it, and give thanks to the giver. That Christmas package was an "on call" promise to you!

The way to release these promises is to seek the face of the giver, not His hand. If we will but shower Him with our genuine love, He will shower us with His heavenly presents. A small child doesn't just say "thanks" to her father for the present, she runs over and showers him with a barrage of kisses and hugs.

Of course, God is sovereign and can bring a great harvest to anyone He chooses. However, God also gives us a biblical pattern that shows us His standard and way: **He works through a prepared people who love Him!**

That raises a question. Do you love God?

JUDGMENT STARTS AT THE HOUSEHOLD OF GOD

First, due to America's terrible moral landslide, God has no option left but judgment. When we look at what God did to Noah's generation, and to Sodom and Gomorrah, we can't help but conclude that America is ripe for destruction! I often pray, ***Oh, God — if You destroyed them, how can You spare us? Why have Your fierce judgments been held back from America?***

A number of Christians have been saying (in agreement with Billy Graham), "If God does not bring judgment to America, He will have to apologize to Sodom and Gomorrah."

Who would deny that our nation has fallen into sharp decline and decadence, and is in the throes of judgment? One of the first steps to real revival is to recognize that we are in a state of decline. This isn't an easy task in our professed prosperity, but we need to say, "We're in decline; we're not in the best of times." Ironically, we find ourselves in the odd situation of matching the famous line from ***A Tale of Two Cities*** by Charles Dickens, "It was the best of times, it was the worst of times."[1] It might be the best of times economically, but on the whole, today's church is not riding a wave of spiritual prosperity.

Judgment starts at the household of God. Most of our social, economic, and political ailments began when the church "turned off and dropped out" of the world in order to evangelize the world. As the old saying goes, "we became so heavenly minded that we were of no earthly good." There was a time when most holders of public office were required to be church members in good standing, but that ceased in the early 1900's. Most schools and universities were founded by Christians — but we let them go. That doesn't make sense, does it? Now we want back what was ours, and we can't get it back.

How can we be ready for revival if we believe that all hope is gone; that we have sinned away our day of grace and there is nothing left but judgment?

Brethren, we can't have faith for another great move of God until we are convinced that God still wants to pour out His blessing upon us one more time.

Why hasn't America been judged yet? Why hasn't Jesus come yet? For many years a multitude of Christians have been repenting for the sins of the church and our nation and asking for God to temper His wrath with mercy. I believe He has.

If we are going to compare the United States to Sodom, then the church should be compared to Abraham. Indeed, as Francis Frangipane said, "If we take the judgmental premise to its conclusion, we will have to add the counterbalance that: If the Lord does not rebuke judgmental Christians, He will have to apologize to Abraham!"

When Abraham was confronted with the imminent possibility of Sodom's destruction, he did not jump on the "destroy Sodom" bandwagon. Instead, he went before the Lord and prayed for mercy for the city.

Abraham's prayer, and the Lord's response, is an amazing study on the effect a mercy-motivated intercessor has on the heart of God. It tells us that the Lord is actually looking for a spark of hope, a reason for mercy, to justify delaying His wrath.

There is another reason why God's judgment has not fallen on us — a great harvest is still ahead! And God is " . . . not willing that any should perish, but that all should come to repentance" (2 Peter 3:9). Won't you pray to Abba Father that He will hear our plea for mercy and visit us with a great harvest?

THE HINDRANCES

What hindrances stand in the way of the next great move of God? Some of our major hindrances today are our traditions that we consider to be an integral part of acceptable, contemporary Western Christianity. Words such as "tradition" or "mind-set" come to mind. The problem is, we are too comfortable! We — the collective Western church — are lukewarm and unchallenged.

Is God starting a new move today? Yes, of course He is! But the bigger question is this: who will follow the pillar of fire by night and the pillar of smoke by day?

Some Christians will, some Christians won't (Luke 12:47-48).

I believe that the Holy Spirit is saying to this generation something to this effect: "Choose this day what you will follow — the last move of God or the new move of God!"

11

My study of church history shows that many Christians who were praying for revival rejected it when it came.

Why? Because even though they were dissatisfied with what they had, they were convinced that it was the only way God moves. The new didn't look like what they had, so they rejected it. In other words,

The last move of God is always the enemy of the next move of God.

Romans 3:11 tells us why…

10. As it is written, There is none righteous, no, not one:

11. There is none that understandeth, there is none that seeketh after God.

12. They are all gone out of the way, they are together become unprofitable; there is none that doeth good, no, not one.

13. Their throat is an open sepulcher; with their tongues they have used deceit; the poison of asps is under their lips:

14. Whose mouth is full of cursing and bitterness:

15. Their feet are swift to shed blood:

16. Destruction and misery are in their ways:

17. And the way of peace have they not known:

18. There is no fear of God before their eyes.

19. Now we know that what things soever the law saith, it saith to them who are under the law: that every mouth may be stopped, and all the world may become guilty before God.

20. Therefore by the deeds of the law there shall no flesh be justified in his sight: for by the law is the knowledge of sin.

21. But now the righteousness of God without the law is manifested, being witnessed by the law and the prophets;

22. Even the righteousness of God which is by faith of Jesus Christ unto all and upon all them that believe: for there is no difference:

> 23. For all have sinned, and come short of the glory of God;
>
> 24. Being justified freely by his grace through the redemption that is in Christ Jesus:
>
> 25. Whom God hath set forth to be a propitiation through faith in his blood, to declare his righteousness for the remission of sins that are past, through the forbearance of God. (Romans 3 KJV)

Men in the Bible, such as Moses at the burning bush, disqualified themselves from any calling on their lives because of their carnal feelings of inadequacy, unworthiness, and sinfulness. In turn, **God rebuked them for what amounts to false humility**, and pointed out that they were to stop disqualifying themselves because of their own unworthiness and look to His righteousness instead.

We can never make ourselves into who we should be. When we are used, it is because of who Jesus is, not who we are. We must trust Jesus to make us who we should be, and that is a life-long process.

Dealing with our sin nature and finding victory in Christ Jesus will be a reoccurring theme throughout this book. Part of maturing in Christ is learning how to deal with our sin nature, and not allowing it to hinder us from becoming a part of the next great move of God.

OH TO BE FOOLS FOR CHRIST

We have filled our churches in this generation with people who, for all practical purposes, are Biblically illiterate. Yet, the Bible says:

> Study to show thyself approved unto God, a workman that needeth not to be ashamed, rightly dividing the word of truth. (2 Timothy 2:15 KJV)

The Laodicean church represents the last age of the church because (to some theologians) it was the last of the seven churches that Jesus wrote to. This is a prophetic description of the church of our day; and raises the question: "Have we become lukewarm?"

> 14. And to the angel of the church in Laodicea write: The Amen, the faithful and true Witness, the Beginning of the creation of God, says this:

13

15. I know your deeds, that you are neither cold nor hot; I would that you were cold or hot.

16. So because you are lukewarm, and neither hot nor cold, I will spit [vomit] you out of My mouth. (Revelation 3)

20. Behold, I stand at the door and knock; if anyone hears My voice and opens the door [of the church in Laodicea], I will come in to him, and will dine with him, and he with Me. (Revelation 3)

We must rightly divide the Word of truth. The text "Behold, I stand at the door and knock" (Rev. 3:20), has nothing to do with sinners and a waiting Savior. No! Here is the tragic picture of our Lord at the door of His own Laodicean Church trying to get in. Imagine it!

Again, in the majority of prayer meetings, what text is more used than 'Where two or three are gathered together in My Name, there am I in the midst?' But too often He is not in the midst; He is at the door! We sing His praise, but shun His person!

— Leonard Ravenhill[2]

Max Lucado, another orator, confirmed Ravenhill's exhortation when he said:

There is never a time during which Jesus is not speaking. Never. There is never a place in which Jesus is not present. Never. There is never a room so dark . . . a lounge so sensual . . . an office so sophisticated . . . that the ever present, ever pursuing, relentless tender Friend is not there, tapping gently on the doors of our hearts — waiting to be invited in. Few hear His voice. Fewer still open the door.

Although much of the modern church goes into denial and tries to explain away the possibility of Jesus standing at the door of the last generation church — there *is* good news.

The bad news is that too many end-time Christians **will not open the door** to Jesus and let Him in when two or three are gathered together in His name — **but not in His presence.** The good news is that many will. Revelation 3:21 says "He who overcomes . . . ." just as the letter to all the other six churches did. **This means there are overcomers in every church age.** We end-time Christians have a challenge and a choice. Will you and I choose to be lukewarm Christians, or overcoming Christians?

> Wisdom says: "Make a careful study of what an overcomer is, and become one, no matter what the cost!"

It would appear that many Evangelical Christians think they have fulfilled all their religious obligations. After all, they have done everything they have been taught to do. They answered an altar call to get saved. They repeated everything they were asked to repeat and filled out a card. Then they were baptized, and they joined the church. What else is there?

> Oh in comparison with the New Testament Church we are so sub-apostolic, so substandard! Sound doctrine has put most believers sound asleep, for the letter plus the Spirit which 'giveth life.' A sound sermon in faultless English and flawless interpretation can be as tasteless as a mouthful of sand.
>
> — Leonard Ravenhill[3]

This is the age of non-commitment! Ask any pastor what the major problem is in his congregation, and the vast majority will say: "My people are not committed to Kingdom work and Kingdom ways. They try to worship Jesus and the world at the same time, but the two just don't mix." We can get enthused about everything under God's heaven except God himself. At a worldly Saturday night ball game we can yell ourselves hoarse — and not have an ounce of enthusiasm for God on Sunday morning.

The word "fan" is a colloquialism that was derived from the word "fanatic." Brethren, total commitment is nothing short of being overzealous and unreasonably enthusiastic!

Paul said he was a fool for Christ (2 Cor. 11:23: 12:11). Personally, I would rather be a fool for the Creator of the Universe than for a group of large physical specimens contending over an inflated animal skin. In the 1950s, I was an all-conference center, and I still love to play basketball; but today I trust that my enthusiasm, my commitment, and my focus is on Jesus, the greatest champion of all time!

THE NEED FOR PERSECUTION

According to Rick Joyner (and others), persecution may be the catalyst that brings this new level of spiritual maturity. Joyner says:

> The Scriptures make it clear that the end of the age will be marked both by an increase in the supernatural quality of Christianity and an increase in persecution — two of the very things that characterized the church in Acts. Church leaders since the first century have understood these to be *'the former rain, and the latter rain'* (Joel 2:23 NKJV). We also see this in Peter's quote (in Acts 2) from the book of Joel.
>
> Opposition can never hurt the truth; it can only help to purify the truth and make it stronger. During the times of persecution, there were no false conversions! And because leaders became special targets, those who accepted leadership positions were not motivated by selfish ambition, but only by a sincere love for the Lord and His people.
>
> Many of the petty issues that can cause division in the church in times of peace could find no place for producing discord in the persecuted church. Persecution was the fire that consumed the wood, hay, and stubble, and that purified the gold, silver, and precious stones.
>
> When viewing the procession of the church throughout history, it is apparent that persecution is the "normal" state of people whose faith is genuine.
>
> **Persecution has a way of stripping away all the facades and pretenses, in order to reduce our faith and our life to what we truly believe and hold essential.**
>
> Those who really believe the truth of the gospel will not compromise it, even if that means giving up their lives.[4]

Many church historians estimate that approximately 50 million Christians were martyred for their faith from the first through the twentieth century. In the twentieth-first century, another estimated 50 million were martyred.

The acceleration is obvious, more Christians have been martyred in the last 100 years than in all the other 1,900 years combined.

Based on this history lesson, we can anticipate that many more will be martyred before the Second Coming.

Joyner continues to say:

> Throughout much of the world today, Christians are under the continual threat of official, government-endorsed or led, persecution. During the past ten years, Christianity has experienced the greatest percentage of growth in nations where the persecution is the worst. In most of the world, Christianity is under assault.
>
> It is estimated that one third of all the people who have come to Christ throughout church history have been saved during the past 10 years!
>
> It can be said of Christianity as it was said of Israel, *"The more they afflicted them, the more they multiplied"* (Ex. 1:12).[5]

I have heard that 150,000 people per day came to the Lord in 1988. Then, in 1999, 180,000 per day. And in the year 2000, between 200,000 to 400,000 converts per day were expected. Around the world Christianity is making great advances.

In Central and South America, there are countries where people are being born again at a rate four times faster than children are being born. In Asia, new believers are coming into the kingdom at a rate of between 20,000 and 40,000 per day. Statistics show that in the last twelve years more people have given their lives to Jesus Christ than in the entire church history. Truly the next great move of God is dawning!

Does this give you hope that — eventually — billions of the world's population will be professing Christians? According to Pat

Robertson, there are already 1.8 billion Christians in the world at the time of this writing.

Contrary to popular belief (and post-modern sociological determinism), most of these conversions are among non-western and non-white people.

YOU GET WHAT YOU GET READY FOR

All the wondrous things God is about to loose in *The Next Great Move of God* will not be seen until we do first things first. An item by item outline for the divine order that God has called us to — I believe — is found in Isaiah 58:6-14. It starts out with a discourse on fasting and repentance and ends with the rewards of the obedient. This Scripture is a systematic plan to prepare for success and for being on the cutting edge of what God is doing in this last generation. Let the following Scriptures be our guide for this book.

> 6. Is not this the fast that I have chosen: to loose the bonds of wickedness, to undo the bands of the yoke, and to let the oppressed go free, and that ye break every yoke?
> 7. Is it not to deal thy bread to the hungry, and that thou bring the poor that are cast out to thy house? when thou seest the naked, that thou cover him; and that thou hide not thyself from thine own flesh?
> 8. Then shall thy light break forth as the morning, and thy healing shall spring forth speedily; and thy righteousness shall go before thee; the glory of Jehovah shall be thy rear guard.
> 9. Then shalt thou call, and Jehovah will answer; thou shalt cry, and he will say, Here I am. If thou take away from the midst of thee the yoke, the putting forth of the finger, and speaking wickedly;
> 10. and if thou draw out thy soul to the hungry, and satisfy the afflicted soul: then shall thy light rise in darkness, and thine obscurity be as the noonday;
> 11. and Jehovah will guide thee continually, and satisfy thy soul in dry places, and make strong thy bones;

and thou shalt be like a watered garden, and like a spring of water, whose waters fail not.

12. And they that shall be of thee shall build the old waste places; thou shalt raise up the foundations of many generations; and thou shalt be called the repairer of the breach, the restorer of paths to dwell in.

13. If thou turn away thy foot from the sabbath, from doing thy pleasure on my holy day; and call the sabbath a delight, and the holy of Jehovah honorable; and shalt honor it, not doing thine own ways, nor finding thine own pleasure, nor speaking thine own words:

14. then shalt thou delight thyself in Jehovah; and I will make thee to ride upon the high places of the earth; and I will feed thee with the heritage of Jacob thy father: for the mouth of Jehovah hath spoken it. (Isaiah 58:6-14 ASV)

37. Jesus said unto him, Thou shalt love the Lord with all thy heart, and with all thy soul, and with all thy mind.

38. This is the first and great commandment.

39. And the second is like unto it, Thou shalt love thy neighbor as thyself. (Matthew 22:37-39 KJV)

If we want to see a great revival in our land we must delight ourselves in Jehovah and obey His great commandment. If we do, we will fast and repent of the sins of the church and meet human needs. We have not paid the price, and for that reason we have not seen what we think is our hearts desire.

HASTENING THE DAY

What sort of people ought you to be in holy conduct and godliness, looking for and hastening the coming of the day of God. (2 Peter 3:11b-12a)

Amazing as it may seem — according to Peter — we can hasten "the coming of the day of God." Since Peter says this is so, evidently our lack of sensitivity and obedience to God's perfect plan can also

19

delay the harvest. Obviously, delaying the coming revival, the next great move of God, would also delay "the coming of the day of God."

God forbid that any Christian would try to obstruct God's divine will!

Every time God moves in fresh new ways, revealing new dimensions of His person, opposition arises from "Christians" seeking to preserve their old traditions, earnestly arguing that they already have all the truth — that "the old is good enough." This attitude has been fairly constant throughout church history.

> No one puts new wine into old wineskins: otherwise the new wine will burst the skins, and it will be spilled out, and the skins will be ruined. But new wine must be put into fresh wineskins. And no one, after drinking old wine wishes for new; for he says, The old is good enough. (Luke 5:37-39)

In this parable the new wine comes ***every*** season, not just once. If we are fortunate enough to witness more than one "new wine" season in our life, we must have the wisdom and flexibility to use "new wineskins" that will hold each new move of God.

Will you pay the price? Many have! Many are! And the glorious harvest is upon us! ◆

Chapter 3

The Coming
Glorious Harvest

God's promises are prophetic! They
will be fulfilled! But the generation
that sees this prophecy fulfilled may
be the only generation that will understand the promise.

You are about to examine a prophetic promise that is found all the
way through the Bible, from Genesis through Revelation. I am pro-
posing here that this prophetic promise was made to our generation,
and is therefore worthy of your inspection (1 Cor. 14:29). Specifically, this promise says we may possibly see an end-time harvest of
hundreds of millions of souls — perhaps even billions!

**God promised Abraham that his descendants would be
as numerous as the stars in the heavens and the sand on
the seashore, which — if taken literally — numbers in the
astronomical billions.**

Here is that promise:

*Indeed I will greatly bless you, and I will greatly multiply
your seed as the stars of the heavens, and as the sand
which is on the seashore; and your seed shall possess
the gate of their enemies, and in your seed all the na-*

tions of the earth shall be blessed, because you have obeyed My voice. (Genesis 22:17-18)

ACCELERATION OF WORLD POPULATION

The only constraint to just how large Abraham's lineage can possibly be is set by the total population of planet Earth in these end-times.

In the year our Lord was born, the world population is estimated to have been 200 million. Contrast that to the 6.2 billion world population in January of the year 2000. As incredible as it may seem, the world population has multiplied at least 31 times since the first century. And the growth will continue. The world population is supposed to increase to 8.5 billion by the year 2025. You can confirm these figures in any encyclopedia under "world population."

Here is another time snapshot:

Between the years 1965 & 2000, more people populated planet earth than in all the prior 6,000 years of world history combined — multiplying over 31 times! That is a staggering statistic! However, it shows us the magnitude of the potential harvest.

PARALLEL ACCELERATION OF THE HARVEST

Because of a wider emphasis today on the power of God in preaching the gospel, and because of technological advances (such as television, satellites, video, and audio media) there has been a further shortening of the season between sowing and reaping. It is an ever-accelerating trend.

Worldwide, as many people became Christians between 1988 and 1998, as were saved from the time of Christ's ascension to 1988! But, in America, the number of Christians has remained the same percentage wise (from 1963 through 1998) since the assassination of John F. Kennedy.

America is no longer the number one nation in the world for sending out missionaries. South Korea is now the leader. We rejoice for

South Korea, and we desire that many more nations will surpass us — but we weep for our nation.

> Behold, days are coming, declares the Lord, when the plowman will overtake the reaper and the treader of grapes him who sows seeds. (Amos 9:13)

Not only will working the field and grain become overwhelming, but there will also be essentially no season between sowing and reaping. Such a great harvest would appear to be an impossible task!

THE WORLD JEWRY POPULATION

Today the world Jewry population is estimated to be 13.8 million, but God has promised that, *someday*, **ALL** Israel — **ALL** of those 13.8 million — shall be saved! (Rom. 11:26). It is estimated that there are already over one million Messianic Jews in the world today — a wonderful beginning!

Based on this 13.8 million count, it seems evident that in all of world history the total number of Jews falls short of God's promise to Abraham. We still have to account for the rest.

In Genesis 22:17 God said, *"I will greatly multiply your **seed** as the stars."* Then in Galatians 3:29 Paul said *"If ye be Christ's, then are ye Abraham's **seed**, and heirs according to the promise"* [that God made to Abraham]. And, as the song says: "Everything He has said He will do, because He is faithful and true."

THE TWO ISRAELS

So, where will this multitude come from? Here is a clue.

> Jesus said to them, "Did you never read in the Scriptures, 'THE STONE WHICH THE BUILDERS REJECTED, THIS BECAME THE CHIEF CORNER STONE; THIS CAME ABOUT FROM THE LORD, AND IT IS MARVELOUS IN OUR EYES'? Therefore I say to you, the Kingdom Of God will be taken away from you, and be given to a nation producing the fruit of it." (Matthew 21:42, 43)

The nation Jesus spoke of in this verse was *taken away from* the Jews and *given to* the Church — Abraham's seed. At this point in history, this Jewish nation was Judea, but earlier in history, Judea was part of Israel.

Since there are some diverse views on this subject, I need to digress a little in order to build my case as to who Abraham's seed is today.

Both the Old and New Testaments make clear that there are two Israels — a natural Israel, which exists on earth, and a spiritual Israel. We see this truth demonstrated in the Old Testament through Jacob's two names — his natural, fleshly name (Jacob) and his regenerate, spiritual name (Israel).

We also see two Israels mentioned in the New Testament. According to Paul, one of these is an "Israel after the flesh" (see 1 Cor. 10:18). This refers to the literal nation of Israel — people who are Jewish by virtue of birth, natural lineage, and ethnic heritage.

By contrast Paul says, there is another Israel, one that he calls "the Israel of God" (Gal. 6:16). The Jews referred to here couldn't be just natural Jews, because in this context Paul is speaking of a people who had become new creatures in Christ (see Gal. 6:15). To underscore this difference, Paul writes, **"For they are not all Israel, which are of Israel"** (Rom. 9:6). This is to say that not everyone who is literally born into the nation of Israel is one of God's spiritual children. Remember what Paul says:

> They which are the children of the flesh, these are not the children of God: but the children of the promise are counted for the seed [of Abraham]. (Romans 9:8)

Only those who come to God by faith in Christ are truly the children of Abraham. We see a type of this in the life of Jacob, who received his regenerate, or spiritual, name *Israel* only by faith in God's grace.

> I know ye therefore that they which are of faith, the same are the children of Abraham. (Galatians 3:7)

The children of Abraham are those who by faith have received Jesus Christ as king and Lord in their lives. And God makes special promises to this "spiritual seed" of Abraham that are not promised to the natural seed.

THE SPIRITUAL JEW

Because there are two kinds of Israel, there are also two kinds of Jews — Jews of the flesh and spiritual Jews. Paul says the spiritual Jew is recognized as the recipient of God's Zion promises. He writes,

> For he is not a Jew which is one outwardly; neither is that circumcision, which is outward in the flesh: but he is a Jew which is one inwardly; and circumcision is that of the heart, in the spirit, and not in the letter; whose praise is not of men, but of God. (Romans 2:28-29)

Because of the work of Christ, this "spiritual Jew" can receive the glorious promises of God. Of course, natural Israel still has its covenants of future blessings, but all of those blessings still depend on returning to the true Messiah, Jesus Christ. No true Christian gives up hope for natural Israel. God still has a plan of restoration for the Israel of the flesh!

If you daily trust Jesus as your Lord and Savior, resting in Him by faith, then you are the seed of Abraham. Certainly, this covenant reaches us today. The Bible says:

> He hath remembered His covenant forever, the word which He commanded to a thousand generations. Which covenant He made with Abraham, and His oath unto Isaac. And confirmed the same unto Jacob for a law, and to Israel for an everlasting covenant. (Psalms 105:8-10)

Now, here is the punch line. When Gentile Christians (the wild olive branches) could be "grafted" into Abraham's lineage along with Jews (the original olive branches) by way of Spiritual rebirth in Jesus Christ, the number in Abraham's lineage jumped dramatically (Rom. 11:17-24; Gal. 3:6-9; John 1:12).

MINIMALIST VS MAXIMUM METAPHOR

Since there are more than six billion stars, and sand granules numbers in the trillions, we know that being as numerous as the stars and the sand is figurative — a metaphor — and has to mean a number that was huge and mind-boggling to Moses who wrote the book of

Genesis. We are talking about the potential for billions! Billions of born-again saints of God! In addition, let's be honest, in no way can we define "outnumbering the stars" to mean a *small* number — metaphor or not. The apostle John seems to confirm this.

> After these things I looked, and behold, a great multitude, which no one could count, from every nation and {all} tribes and peoples and tongues, standing before the throne and before the Lamb, clothed in white robes, and palm branches (were) in their hands. (Revelation 7:9)

"A great multitude, which no one could count, from every nation and tribes and peoples and tongues . . ." sounds as numerous as "the stars of the heavens, and sand on the seashore." Clearly this "great multitude" is no longer a "remnant" or a "little flock."

The word "remnant" primarily means, "what is left over," and secondarily "a small amount." Therefore, we cannot force the word "remnant" to mean "a little flock," every time "remnant" is used. For instance, if you cut one shirt out of a twenty-foot bolt of cloth, the fifteen feet left over is the remnant.

On the other hand, in Luke 12:32, our Lord describes His Church as being a "little flock." The word "little" used here, is the Greek word *mikros*, from which we get microbe and microscope. *Mikros* means "distinctly and obviously small," not just "small in comparison." There is no way we can force this verse to mean something big. Yet, at the same time, we have quoted verses that can in no way be taken to mean something small.

So, how do we handle this apparent discrepancy — the small vs. the large harvest?

Scripture never contradicts itself, we just misunderstand it sometimes. Yes, the church was a little flock way back in the first century when the earth's population was also very small — but today it is not. And in those ancient times, it could be said of that audience: only a few would find life. However, the number of Christians today outnumbers the entire *world population* in the first century, and the number continues to increase daily by the hundreds of thousands.

Even so, God's promise to Abraham has not yet been completed. Myriad millions must come into the fold first. Therefore, God's promise to Abraham must happen sometime in the future. This is one reason that I believe there will be a massive harvest — possibly in our generation.

If this multitude seen in Revelation 7:9 can't be counted using our modern technology and experience with crowds, just how huge is this multitude? And how can such an unprecedented harvest be Biblical, prophetic, and probable?

Here is a simple but profound spiritual law. If anything is of God, it is because God is doing it, with or without our involvement.

Since the Church — the Kingdom of God — is His work and His responsibility, He will complete it. Our responsibility is merely to be faithful, to work alongside His people. We are simply His instruments who bind Satan, and loose God's will in Jesus' name.

THE TWO TEMPLES

The same passage in Scripture that speaks of the falling away also speaks of the man of sin who will be revealed.

> 3. Let no man deceive you by any means: for that day shall not come, except there come a falling away first, and that man of sin be revealed, the son of perdition;
> 4. Who opposeth and exalteth himself above all that is called God, or that is worshiped; so that he as God sitteth in the temple of God, showing himself that he is God. (2 Thessalonians 2 KJV)

Whatever future fulfillment this 2nd Thessalonians warning still carries in its mysterious folds, the fact is that numerous times throughout Israel's turbulent history the Holy Place was already desecrated and taken over by pagan powers and false messiahs who sought domination of the known world.

Most scholars tell us that this temple in verse 4 is Herod's Temple. But since it was destroyed in A.D. 70, these scholars say it will have to be rebuilt in the future so "that man of sin" can set in it and declare himself to be God.[1]

These same scholars also tell us that every individual believer, and all believers collectively, constitute "the temple of the Holy Spirit."

> Know ye not that ye are the temple of God, and that the Spirit of God dwelleth in You? (1 Corinthians 3:16 KJV)

This verse can just as easily be understood to say: "Don't you know that individually you are a temple of God, and that the omnipresent Spirit of God dwells in every believer, collectively and simultaneously?"

> In whom ye also are builded together for an habitation of God through the Spirit. (Ephesians 2:22 KJV)

What we are seeing here is the Old Testament temple and the New Testament temple being contrasted. These Scriptures show us that (in context) the temple can be interpreted to be either physical or spiritual.

Solomon built the original temple for God's presence, but God's plan was to dwell directly with His people apart from any temple. The temple was symbolic, and sometimes God's presence was manifested there. But the temple was not to be looked upon as **THE** dwelling place of God.

In 1 Chronicles, chapters 17, 22, and 28 we see that God did not tell King David to build Him a temple, it was David's desire to do that. God was satisfied with the tent that David built to house the ark, but He gave David permission to have Solomon build the temple, but with the understanding that God would have another descendent of the Davidic dynasty build the house that God would dwell in. Acts 15: shows a prophecy in Amos concerning the temple.

> After this I will return, and will build again the tabernacle of David, which is fallen down; and I will build again the ruins thereof, and I will set it up: that the residue of men might seek after the Lord, and all the Gentiles, upon whom my name is called, saith the Lord, who doeth all these things. (Acts 15:16, 17 KJV)

Here is a prophecy concerning Jesus as the last and eternal king in David's linage.

> And it shall come about when your days are fulfilled that you must go to be with your fathers, that I will set up one of your descendants after you, who shall be of your sons; and I will establish his kingdom. He shall build for Me a house, and I will establish His throne forever. I will be His father, and He shall be My son... (I Chronicles 17:11,13)

The New King James says in verse 12, "He (Jesus) is the one who will build a house for me."

If we believe that God is "omnipresent," then we believe that He is everywhere, and a temple can't contain Him. In Isaiah 66:1 God said, ***"Thus saith the Lord, The heaven is my throne, and the earth is my footstool: where is the house that ye build unto me?"***

Since the falling away and the man of sin are mentioned in the same sentence, we get the impression that these two events can be a one-and-the-same event — or at least related.

WHY GOD DESTROYED THE TEMPLE

Why did God want the temple destroyed?

Some scholars make the point that Jesus declared Himself to be the temple.[2] They argue that when Jesus was telling the Samaritan woman about the coming destruction of the temple, He was telling her that He was the temple (John 4:21-24; 2:19-21). Even a cursory search of the word "temple" in the Bible will begin to show us that these scholars are probably right.

It was the Temple issue that came up with decisive force during the Lord's mock trial.

> Now the chief priests and the whole Council kept trying to obtain false testimony against Jesus, in order that they might put Him to death; and they did not find any, even though many false witnesses came forward. But later on two came forward, and said, 'this man stated, 'I am able to destroy the temple of God and to rebuild it in three days.' (Matthew 26:59-61 NAS)

This was the real issue! The danger which Jesus' life and words brought against the religious system with the Temple in its heart gave

29

judicial opening to the final blow: **"...tell us whether you are the Christ, the Son of God"** (Matthew 26:63 NAS).

It was the "Jesus versus Temple" case that brought the Son of God to stand accused before a human court; and it was the question of His divine life in contrast to the Temple's emptiness that drove Him to the cross.

Without a temple the Pharisees and Sadducees had no authority to rule. If you have never read Josephus's account of the destruction of Jerusalem and the temple, you should. As unbelievable as it may seem, a war was going on inside the city between three different Jewish factions while the Romans besieged it from without. Fellow Jews murdered most of the priests right on the temple grounds. With no priests and no temple, there was no authority and therefore no religion.

God brought the religion, the city, and the nation that crucified Jesus to an end. Jerusalem ceased to exist as a city for centuries. And Judea (Israel) ceased to exist as a nation from A.D. 70 to A.D. 1948.

In the Old Covenant days, God manifested His presence first in the wilderness temple, and then in Solomon's Temple. There is no reference to God's manifesting Himself in the two subsequent temples, Zerubbabel's and Herod's, and the ark of the covenant was never present in either of them.[3] But, starting on the day of Pentecost, God's Holy Spirit came to reside in Christians — the temple of the Holy Spirit. Since He now had a new residence, He no longer needed the old one. By obliterating Herod's temple, He made this abundantly clear, and made known to all He no longer dwelt there.

The stone temple had served its purpose and was replaced by living stones that — accumulatively — make up the spiritual church of Christ.

> **The next great move of God is simply going to be God moving. The Lord is going to suddenly come into His temple, and the whole world will know it.**
> **— Rick Joyner**

A DOUBLE MEANING

Pulling all of this together, there may well be a double meaning to the act of the "man of sin" who will sit in the temple of God, showing himself to be God. This man of sin may plan to sit in the physical temple, but even more than that, he wishes to enthrone himself in all Christians — the spiritual temple — and show that he is God, or a substitute for Christ.

From the time of the early church fathers, it was understood that the primary objective of this Anti-Christ was to gain dominance in the church. Because Christ also means "the anointed," it was also understood that the spirit of Anti-Christ would always oppose, or seek to supplant, the anointing.

I believe that Satan's enthronement in Christians will be so subtle that his victims will not be aware of it. You will be able to spot them because they are self-serving and lack the fruit of the Spirit. These lukewarm believers will be 90 percent Christian and 10 percent worldly. Jesus Christ is more of a Sugar Daddy to them than a Bridegroom.

I also believe most Christians today think they are immune to deception. But the Bible says that Satan can disguise himself as "an angel of light" and his disciples can masquerade as "servants of righteousness" (2 Cor. 11:14-15).

Christian are most likely to be deceived by a pious, smooth-talking person who can quote a Scripture for anything and everything. And, the deceiver may well be right in about 90 percent of what he or she is teaching. It's that 10 percent that can be deadly.

The point is that we must watch for the ones who seek to gain authority in the church through a spirit of lawlessness.

ROMANTIC BUT FOOLISH

There are those in the Lord's Church who have such a romantic view of Israel that they are sending money to help prepare the 3rd Temple to be rebuilt.[4]

Obviously, God reserves the right to bring this mystery to full light in His own way and in His own time. Yet, powerful forces are literally "pushing" in this direction, aggressively attempting to fulfill these prophecies by the strength of man. Some are doing so ignorantly, others sincerely trying to thus "expedite" the Lord's return. They are moving ahead in their preparations and are attracting some well meaning, though misguided, Christian support and funding.

For example, on July 29, 2001, a group of well meaning zealots carried out a symbolic ceremony of cornerstone laying in a parking lot next to the Western Wall in Jerusalem.

That four and a half ton marble stone was to symbolize the beginning of the third Temple construction and prophetically point in its direction. Fortunately, the Israeli government did not permit this ceremony to take place on top of Temple Mount as was originally requested by the sponsors, thus avoiding an all out eruption of violent sentiments throughout the Muslim world.

Mere human attempts to have the physical Temple rebuilt in Jerusalem prior to the Lord's second coming are in danger of assisting the spirit and agenda of the anti-Christ.

RADICALLY SAVED

There are those who call for a radical salvation. They say Jesus wants every bit of you — or nothing. As my favorite evangelist, Craig Miller, says:

If Jesus is not Lord and Master of your life, then He is not your Savior. Because with salvation comes change. If you are what you were, then you ain't.[5]

That's poor English, but you get the point.

Our churches are full of professing Christians (in name only) who acknowledge Jesus as Savior, but have never repented of their sins and have never made Jesus Lord of their life. These are the kind of false Christians who fall away from their religion when enough pressure falls on them, because they were never saved in the first place.

This has been possible because too many preachers and evangelists today present a cheap salvation. They tell the lost to accept Jesus as Savior but never mention or emphasize repentance and Lordship. Since these converts are told that they are now saved, they believe it and go on with self — Satan — on the throne of their lives.

This "easy-ism" must be spoken against in the clearest and harshest of terms NOW, in order to bring correction and true Salvation to these precious souls that have been lied to. And they need to hear this message before the pressure cooker starts heating up and we witness a huge falling away.

Here is what Paul said to Timothy about such teachers and preachers:

> Correct and rebuke your people when they need it, encourage them to do right, and all the time be feeding them patiently with God's Word. For there is going to come a time when people won't listen to the truth, but will go around looking for teachers who will tell them just what they want to hear. They won't listen to what the Bible says but will blithely follow their own misguided ideas. (*2 Timothy 4:2b-4 LB*)

God will sovereignly increase His grace as He reaches out to all mankind in a final great demonstration of love and mercy before the day of His wrath and judgment comes. This grace, which reveals the love and compassion of Jesus, is where our hope should be focused.

> Therefore, gird up your minds for action, keep sober in spirit, fix your hope completely on the grace to be brought to you at the revelation of Jesus Christ. (1 Peter 1:13)

THE POWER OF A MAJORITY

We attribute more power and authority to the National Day of Prayer, when millions are praying for our nation, than we do to the prayers of a Sunday school class. On the National Day of Prayer we frequently quote this Scripture:

> If my people, who are called by my name, shall humble themselves, and pray, and seek my face, and turn from their wicked ways, then will I hear from heaven and will forgive their sin, and will heal their land. (2 Chronicles 7:14)

When God made this promise to those He called "My people," He was speaking to the spiritual descendants of Israel [Jacob], and not the physical real estate named after him. You will recall that God renamed Jacob, the grandson of Abraham, "Israel" (Gen. 32:28). God

33

made promises to both the spiritual Israel and the land itself, and we must take care to keep track of the difference between these two Israels. This Scripture therefore applies to all Christians, because the lineage of Abraham was grafted in by way of Salvation. Therefore, if the major part of a nation — any nation — becomes grafted into Abraham's lineage, they become an extension of spiritual Israel — the Kingdom of God.

As a result, when the great harvest is just about gathered, can you imagine the healing, the forgiveness that God will release upon nations unified in such a prayer? Oh, to witness the power of prayer on such a massive scale!

I know this sounds wild and crazy, and I know this is a very big "IF," but even so, help me decide if this is not a logical continuum of thought?

If **EVERY** nation on earth were to pray this prayer found in second Chronicles, and if **EVERY** "land" were to be healed, then the whole planet would be healed. If this were to happen, the whole curse would be removed, and Eden would be restored. That sounds like . . . Dare I say it? The Second Coming? The millennium?

WHAT IS HOLDING BACK REVIVAL?

I heard a Christian song that said, "We can make a difference. We can make a change. We can make the world a better place." That's true, isn't it? But that is also thinking with small, human-sized faith. For instance, in the Lord's Prayer, Jesus prayed to the Father: "Thy will be done on earth as it is in heaven" (Matt. 6:9-13).

Because Jesus' prayers are all prophetic, we can declare with faith and confidence that God's will is, in fact, taking place in our personal life, our family, our church, our nation, and in the entire world, even as it is in heaven.

Let's proclaim our faith in God's Word and speak out with the authority of Jesus' name, and make disciples of all nations! Not to make the world a better place for us, but to fill the Kingdom of God for His pleasure.

What is holding back the revival? It is not Satan, because he was defeated at the cross. It is not the world, because Christ has overcome the world. It is the lack of an army of spiritual revolutionaries with the character of Jesus.

— Wellington Boone

But what will be characteristic of these "spiritual revolutionaries with the character of Jesus"? Like Abraham (as described in Romans 4) these revolutionaries simply need to be ready and full of humility, transparency, vulnerability, hunger, and brokenness, so they do not tear apart when the weight of the presence of the Lord touches them.

Is Jesus telling us that He will pour out His Spirit on **ALL** the nations and **ALL** ethnic groups as a sovereign act? Is He fulfilling His promise to Abraham? Is He saying that we will inherit the glorious task of discipleship for these brand-new converts — this harvest? If we are, we need to be preparing right now to disciple this coming multitude. For instance, what would your church do with 3,000 new converts *in one day,* as happened to Peter on the day of Pentecost?

THE GREAT COMMISSION IS ANOTHER PROPHECY

Can you see that the great commission is a prophecy, and not just wishful thinking on Jesus' part? After all, Jesus has **ALL** power and authority to empower His church to disciple **ALL** nations. The word "disciple" means: adherence to, or follower of a teacher. By the power and authority in His name He sent us out to fulfill the commission He gave us as if it were a prophecy that would be fulfilled. Jesus said:

> All authority has been given to Me in heaven and earth. Go therefore and make disciples of all the nations, baptizing them in the name of the Father and the Son and the Holy Spirit. (Matthew 28: 18,19)

To make disciples of born again, water baptized multitudes in every nation is a command, a promise, a prophecy; something Jesus spoke into existence — a done deal! Let us be prepared in advance to "go therefore

and make disciples of all the nations" when the time is full.

Currently, about 25% of the world has not even heard of Jesus Christ, even as an historical figure. And, even among those who are familiar with Jesus' life, very few have actually "witnessed" the power of the "gospel of the kingdom."

What most Christians have experienced is the gospel of grace. There is a difference, brethren, between the gospel of grace and the gospel of the kingdom of heaven. The gospel of grace introduces us to Jesus. When we hear of His sacrifice, His death on the cross, we are assured of a place in heaven. The gospel of the kingdom includes the good news of God's favor, but also brings us into the spiritual reality of heaven.

We are born again from above; a new heavenly life, born of the Holy Spirit, beings aligning our hearts with the life and power of heaven. Indeed, as we actually become disciples and study Christ's words, we cannot help but realize:

> Jesus did not come simply to bring us to heaven when we die; He came to bring heaven to where we live.
> — Francis Frangipane

This chapter has proven from the Bible that God's promise to Abraham is going to result in a great end-time harvest. So, how does the great commission play into God's promise to Abraham?

> When Jesus spoke of "THIS gospel," He was talking about His message! HIS message comes with corresponding signs, wonders and miracles, authenticating its divine source. Please recall that this is how Jesus sent His disciples in the first century. The main message of this book is captured in this paragraph and in Matthew 28:18-19. You will see this message unfold in the preceding pages. ♦

Chapter 4

The Coming Sovereign Manifestations of God

When does the end of the age occur? I believe that we are on the brink of the end of the age right now. We are — in all probability — in the last generation.

The New Testament indicates that *the end of the age* is another expression for *the last days,* which (as we will show in chapter 13) began on the day of Pentecost and ends at the Second Coming (1 Cor. 10: 11; Heb. 9: 26).

> If we are in the generation that is to see the Second Coming, then we are also in the generation that will see the harvest that Jesus said will immediately precede it.

> Keep in mind that this last generation is at least thirty-one times more populous than the first generation, and the world population has more than doubled since 1950. Which explains why there can and will be such a large harvest in "these last days."

We have answered the "*when*"; the question now is "*how*?" How is God going to bring about this massive harvest? The answer may be in the familiar parable of the tares.

THE PARABLE OF THE TARES

Observe how these following two Scripture readings confirm each other on who "the gathered out" are.

> 37. (Jesus said), "The one who sows the good seed is the Son of Man,
>
> 38. And the field is the world; and as for the good seed, these are the sons of the kingdom; and the tares are the sons of the evil one;
>
> 39. And the enemy who sowed them is the devil, and <u>the harvest is the end of the age</u>; and the reapers are angels.
>
> 40. Therefore, just as the tares are gathered up and burned with fire, so shall it be <u>at the end of the age</u>.
>
> 41. The Son of Man will send forth His ANGELS, and they will <u>gather out of His Kingdom</u> all stumbling blocks, and those who commit lawlessness,
>
> 42. And will cast them into the furnace of fire; in that place there shall be weeping and gnashing of teeth.
>
> 43. Then the RIGHTEOUS WILL SHINE FORTH AS THE SUN in the kingdom of their Father. He who has ears, let him hear. (Matthew 13:37-43)

> 37. For the coming of the Son of Man will be just like the days of Noah.
>
> 38. For as in those days which were before the flood THEY were eating and drinking, THEY were marrying and giving in marriage, until the day that Noah entered the ark,
>
> 39. and THEY did not understand until the flood came and <u>took THEM all away</u>, so shall the coming of the Son of Man be. (Matthew 24:37-39)

Let me point out the obvious. The phrases "gather out of" (in vs. 41) and "took them all away" (in vs. 39 & 48) are saying the same thing about the same kind of people, and refers to the same event — the Second Coming. Verses 47 through 50 really clench this point.

When the Lord speaks of removing the rebellious from His Kingdom, He means He will remove them from the face of His planet —

which also belongs to His people. Those rebellious ones simply do not belong in His holy presence (Matt. 5: 5).

GATHERING THE TARES

Keep in mind that we are the generation that will see the gathering of the tares.

There will be those who are deceived and unaware they are not born-again, who will remain in the midst of the Church. Jesus warns us against trying to root them out, especially since it is not always possible to discern other people's hearts. In an effort to destroy these tares, we might offend one of Christ's "little ones" and cause his or her profession of faith to waver. Or, we might uproot a potential convert — a tare converting into wheat for God's Kingdom.

That is why the motivation — the spirit — behind the Crusades and the Inquisition was so ungodly, so much like the Antichrist. Like the Pharisees, these medieval religionists thought they were the hand of God when, in their spiritual delusion, they were the fist of Satan — usurpers of God's mandate to His angels. What's more, this group still has not repented of those despicable deeds.

We are left then, with the question: What should the Church do about false Christians who temporarily look like true believers? The answer, given in the second parable, is to leave them alone until the end of the age when the Lord Himself will judge (Matt. 13:30).

As the Church comes closer to its final days before Christ's return, God will miraculously cover His good wheat with His mighty hand (as He did Noah and his family in the ark) while He obliterates . . . sweeps away Satan's tares . . . just as He did in the flood.

MINISTRY OF ANGELS

Matthew 13:39 says, ". . . the reapers are the angels." And in Matthew 13:30 Jesus says, "I will say to the reapers, gather ye together first the tares, and bind them in bundles to burn them: but gather the wheat into my barn." Now I ask you . . .

Can we humans burn the tares? Of course not! Nor can we gather the wheat into His barn. That is the work of

39

the angels. The church must never try to usurp the mandate God has given His angels. [1]

THE CLINCHER!

These verses in Revelation 14 actually give us a still-frame of the angel harvest in action!

> 6. And I saw another angel flying in midheaven, having an eternal gospel to preach to those who live on the earth, and to every nation and tribe and tongue and people;
> 7. And he said with a loud voice, "Fear God, and give Him glory, because the hour of His judgment has come; and worship Him who made the heaven and the earth and sea and springs of waters."
> 14. And I looked, and behold, a white cloud, and sitting on the cloud was one like a son of man, having a golden crown on His head, and a sharp sickle in His hand.
> 15. And another angel came out of the temple, crying out with a loud voice to Him who sat on the cloud, "Put in your sickle and reap, because the harvest of the earth is ripe."
> 16. And He who sat on the cloud swung His sickle over the earth; and the earth was reaped. (Revelation 14)

Some will say the scene in verses 6 and 7 is a literal angel harvest. Others will say it means the angels will be behind the scenes, prompting Christians in a worldwide proclamation of the Gospel. But why does it have to be an either/or choice? Since Scripture clearly supports both, so do I.

In verse 14, the *"one like a son of man, sitting on a white cloud"* is either Jesus or a very powerful angel. While the scholars debate these issues, I will stick my neck out and defend the view that this *"one sitting on a cloud"* is an angel.

Thus, through this worldwide angelic messenger, every
man, woman, and child will have heard the gospel of

Christ before Jesus catches away His Bride, and destroys the wicked at the end of the age.

Regardless of how effective or ineffective our missionary effort may be, God's own angelic messenger will preach the gospel to every nation and tribe and tongue and people, *"and then the end shall come"* (Matt. 24:14).

THE HARVEST SEASON

Wheat does not become ripe for the harvest through any efforts of the harvesters. They have to wait for the season of ripening to come. But, if the harvesters do not bring the ripened grain into storehouses, it will fall to the ground and become worthless to the field's owner.

Again, anything that is of God is a supernatural act, only He and His angels are able to burn the tares or gather the wheat — not us. That compels me to wonder . . .

Will the ministry of angels again be commonplace, perhaps even more so than in the early church? After all, the world population is now over thirty-one times what it was in the first century.

THE LONG HAUL HARVEST

For balance, we need to consider another harvest quote from Jesus:

Do not say, there are yet four months, and then comes the harvest? Behold, I say to you, lift up your eyes and look on the fields, that they are white for harvest. (John 4:35)

Our Lord and Savior is telling us that the mission fields are ripe and waiting for harvesters. In this case, I think the harvesters are Christians, whether they are missionaries, evangelists, or ordinary Christians like you and me. This has been our Lord's commission to His Church for 2,000 years, but not long from now we will see a ministry team of both human and angel harvesters. As the Lord said, "the harvest is the end of the age" (Matt. 13:39).

41

THE PAULINE PRECEDENT

Most (but not all) of these hundreds of millions of converts will not be brought to Christ through our evangelizing, preaching, or witnessing, but by visitations, dreams, and visions. These will be sovereign manifestations of God. Just as Jesus confronted Paul (Saul) on the road to Damascus, He can likewise appear to thousands . . . to millions . . . to billions . . . if He wishes — can He not?

God is omnipresent, and He so loved the whole world that He gave His only begotten Son, that whoever believes in Him should not perish, but have eternal life. So, why resist, why oppose or restrain Him with our unbelief and small thinking?

A CONFIRMATION TESTIMONY

Unprecedented evidence from sources, such as Bill Bright and others, is already available, confirming my assertion. Bill Bright's (first fruits) report reminds me of those who were resurrected with Jesus (Matt. 27:52-53).

Here is an excerpt from a fundraising letter, dated August 1995. Bill Bright says:

> The evidence is powerful . . . it is extremely compelling!
>
> Our director, who leads Campus Crusade for Christ's work in the Middle East and the Muslim nations of North Africa, directs a radio program that is being broadcast to this entire region. He reports an astounding phenomenon. His office has received thousands of letters from Muslims. Many tell of a dream they had: 'I saw Jesus. He declared to me "I am the way."' Moved by this compelling dream, they are writing the Campus Crusade's Middle East office to find out just who Jesus is. Once they know, they freely respond!
>
> In Algeria, a number of people discovered they had the very same dream. They began to talk with one another and discovered each had experienced the same dream. The details were the same, and even the words Jesus said

to them were the same. On their own, they have formed a Bible study and are following Christ!

A fanatical Muslim woman had spent four years in prison for her political activities. While there, Jesus appeared to her in her cell. He personally explained redemption and the gospel. She is now on our Campus Crusade staff, totally sold out to reaching her Muslim people for her Savior!

I could tell you other stories — miraculous, incredible stories of visions. Muslims are seeing the risen Christ! Can there be any doubt? Our great, wonderful Lord is calling the Muslim world to Himself! Praise His Holy name.

THE JESUS FILM PROJECT

Now for more unprecedented evidence from the same source. The following is a fundraising letter (dated July 1998) from Paul Eshleman, director of The JESUS Film Project, a ministry of Campus Crusade for Christ International. I removed the paragraphs that pertained to fundraising and left only the testimony for your amazement.

Eshleman begins:

Dear partner in reaching the world for Christ . . .

God is still performing signs and wonders around the world. He is working marvelously through the powerful, evangelistic film 'JESUS.' This is the most biblically accurate film ever produced on the life of Christ. Every word that Jesus speaks is a direct quote from Scripture. That's why the film is so powerful. The Holy Spirit applies Scripture to the hearts of all that watch and listen in their own language.

To date, over one billion people have seen 'JESUS' and 57 million have indicated decisions for Christ. You can imagine that, as director of The JESUS Film Project, I have the wonderful privilege of receiving frontline reports and accounts that are amazing, even astonishing.

That's why, before writing this letter, I prayed about what I should do. Should I share these remarkable events? If so, how? I have mentally debated all the ramifications. After discussing this report with others, I have decided to simply tell you the facts, as I know them. You can then decide for yourself the merits of this most remarkable report from a 'JESUS' film team in India.

The Malto tribe lives in the north of India, in the state of Bihar. The people are resistant, even hostile, to the gospel. It's an area saturated with the worship of Satan and hundreds of false gods. And people know it is Satan, the great evil god, who oppresses them. This is why I believe, on occasion, our sovereign Lord uses extraordinary means — MIRACLES — to break down such barriers and validate His truth.

A 'JESUS' film team approached the Malto tribe. But the resistance was so stiff that they bypassed the area and went on to more receptive villages. A few days later, a 16-year-old girl died in one of the Malto villages.

It was evening, and the family had finished all the preparations for burial. Many had gathered around to pay their respects and support the family. They were about to bury her long-dead body when the girl suddenly, miraculously awoke. Like Lazarus before her, she came back to life.

In stunned disbelief the people stammered, 'Then you were not dead!' 'Yes, I WAS dead,' she told them. 'I went to the place of the dead. But God told me I must come back and tell you about the real God, the true God.'

Still astonished and greatly agitated, the villagers began to ask her, 'Then who is the true God?' She went on to tell them it was the God proclaimed by the film teams they had turned away. 'God has given me seven days to tell as many people as I can that He is real,' the girl said.

The next day, she sought out and found the film team in another village. She told them her story, and that God gave her instructions to go with them. For the next seven days, they showed the film to the now receptive Malto

44

villages. (Needless to say, word had spread everywhere about her return from the dead!) Before every crowd, she fearlessly proclaimed:

"I was dead, but God has sent me back to tell you that this film is about the true and living God. He has given me seven days to tell you. You need to believe in Him."

Then, after the seventh day, although physically she appeared fine, she collapsed and died.

Now, I can't offer you any proof that she was really dead. There was no death certificate, as we know it. I cannot explain, theologically, all the issues. However, I can tell you that even the most unsophisticated people (by Western standards) do know how to recognize death, especially in someone who has been dead several hours.

But the significant fact was the boldness demonstrated by this young girl. She had a compelling, powerful sense of mission. She sought out and traveled with a film team, willing to suffer persecution. Without fear (even though she knew she would die after the seventh day) and with unrelenting determination, she brought this message to her people.

The greatest evidence that something wondrous happened is that during those seven days, hundreds of highly resistant people who were bound by the chains of Satan, turned to the living Christ. As a result, at least six churches were established. Certainly, God was glorified!

How timely it was that, as I learned of this report, the book, Believe in Miracles But Trust in Jesus, by Dr. Adrian Rogers, had just been released. Dr. Rogers, pastor of Bellevue Baptist Church of Memphis, lists three tests to apply when you hear of miracles. I applied them to this report.

- **Check the facts carefully.**

We have. The source of the report is a ministry director with Campus Crusade for Christ, a staff member who is very responsible and reliable, who knows the area and the people, and who carefully verified the facts.

- **Check the focus. Does the miracle glorify Jesus?**
  It does. The young woman continually pointed to Christ as the one who sent her back. She testified that He alone is God.

- **Check the fruit. Are people repenting of their sin, trusting in Christ, and becoming disciples of our Lord?**
  They did. They renounced Satan, turned from their wickedness, and have formed New Life Study Groups and at least six churches.

  Praise God for His miracle! These are extraordinary days. God is at work in ways that defy human logic. And this is not the first such report we have received. Obviously, something wondrous **IS** happening."

Paul Eshleman, Director
The JESUS Film Project

THE 10/40 WINDOW

I am convinced that the prayers of intercessors are pulling down the strongholds of Hinduism, Islam, and Buddhism in what is being called "the 10/40 window." Two well-documented cases were presented here, but many other credible testimonies (not observed and documented by mission workers we know and trust) have also been reported. We should not be surprised that the millions of fervent prayers for the 10/40 window are being answered, and that God is sovereignly intervening in the affairs of men to glorify His Christ.

WORST DISASTER IN CHURCH HISTORY

Are these two reports an appetizing foretaste of what God will do on a much larger scale someday soon? Is this an omen to the church to prepare itself for millions instead of just thousands? Allow me to state this dilemma in the form of a philosophical question: What is the worst disaster that could happen to the church today?

Here is the three-part answer:

- **To NOT be prepared for the overwhelming size of the harvest.**
- **To NOT bring in our individual & collective part of the harvest.**
- **To NOT disciple this multitude.**

Brethren, unbelief is expensive in God's Kingdom. Just as Jesus confronted Paul on the road to Damascus, and the dead Malto girl, and thousands of Muslims in the Middle East, He can likewise appear to thousands, to millions, and even to billions.

If sovereign acts such as those described here are what Jesus has chosen to do in these last days, we need to ask ourselves whether we will rejoice or resist.

Which will you do? Rejoice? Or resist? ♦

QUOTES FROM CHAPTER 5

In Ezekiel 40:3 we are told that the hand of God carried Ezekiel to a very high mountain, where a man appeared to him "whose appearance was like the appearance of brass." John describes a similar vision of a man who appeared to him on the Isle of Patmos: "***his feet like unto fine brass, as if they burned in a furnace***" (Revelation 1:15).

> Here is what Ezekiel was being shown: In the very last days, the church of Jesus Christ will be more glorious, more victorious, than in its entire history. The Lord's true body isn't going to weaken and sputter. It's not going to dwindle in numbers, or decease in power or spiritual authority. No, His church will go out in a blaze of power and glory. And it will enjoy the fullest revelation of Jesus that anyone has ever known. Since the first century the church has only waded in the outpouring of the Holy Spirit, but the time is coming when we will be swimming in a flood of His glory.

Chapter 5

Old and New Testament Confirmations

Let's look at some of the Scriptures throughout the Bible that confirm a great end-time harvest. Many scholars tell us that the feast of Tabernacles is the final great end-time harvest that will close this age, and be consummated by our Lord's return. It will be the ultimate and largest harvest of all.

The history of Israel in the Old Testament revolved around three major feasts. The first of these feasts, Passover, was fulfilled by the death of Jesus. He was the Passover Lamb. The second feast, the feast of Pentecost, was also fulfilled according to the prophecy Jesus gave in Acts 1:8, where He said: ". . . you shall receive power when the Holy Spirit has come upon you."

The feast that is yet to be fulfilled is the Feast of Tabernacles (Feast of Ingathering). There is a harvest associated with each feast. Jesus was the first fruits harvest at Passover; and the harvest of souls throughout the church age is a direct result of the outpouring of the Holy Spirit at Pentecost.

God has promised to pour out His Spirit on all mankind (Joel 2:28-32). This outpouring of the Holy Spirit is likened to the early (fall) and latter (spring) rains that bring the crops in Israel to maturity for harvest (Joel 2:23; Hos. 6:2-3).

> And the threshing floors will be full of grain, and the vats will overflow with the new wine and oil. (Joel 2:24)

The ingathering will be so great that the abundance will make up for what was not gathered in previous harvests because of Satan's demonic attacks.

> Then I will make up to you for the years that the swarming locust has eaten, the creeping locust, the stripping locust, and the gnawing locust. (Joel 2:25)

UNDERSTANDING THE GLORY OF GOD

There is so much that we don't understand about what God is releasing into the world today. What's more, many of us don't understand what God has been doing throughout history. One of these seeming mysteries is in trying to understand the glory of God. Since this term, "the glory of God," will be used dozens of times in this book, it seems important to define the term now so that our understanding might be opened to what God is doing.

The prophet Isaiah describes nations and kings of the earth being drawn to the glory of God that will rest upon the church (Isa. 66:18, Rev. 21:24). The glory and the presence of God are not identical. Even though Moses would set up a "tent of meeting" in order to meet with God (in His presence), he wanted more. You would think that being in God's presence would be enough, but in one of those tent meetings Moses said to God, "Please, show me Your glory" (Ex. 33:18).

Therefore, *the glory of God* is not a physical manifestation of some kind. It's not an ecstatic feeling that overcomes you. Nor is it a kind of supernatural aura or angelic light that bursts forth. Simply put, God's glory is "a revelation of His nature and attributes!" Moses did not develop any doctrines based on these experiences; but he did develop an intimate relationship with God that is a model for us today.

God's glory is the revelation of His goodness, displayed by His mercy as He makes Himself known. The nature, character, and heart of God are revealed as He demonstrates His glory.

The Lord Himself defines His glory this way in Scripture. "Therefore, when we pray, 'Lord, show me your glory,' we're actually praying, *'Father, reveal to me who you are.'* And if the Lord does give us a revelation of His glory, it's a revelation of how He wants to be known by us.

That is why Jesus of Nazareth is the clearest expression of the glory of God ever manifested upon the earth. God's eternal nature and holiness was revealed 2,000 years ago in the man Christ Jesus. Simply stated, this One was the Lord of eternity put into human terms.

WHOLE ISLAMIC NATIONS WILL BE SAVED

This is the way Isaiah prophesied the glory of God to ancient *Zion, and to the present-day Middle East:*

1. Arise, shine; for your light has come, and the glory of the Lord has risen upon you.

2. But the Lord will rise upon you. And His glory will appear upon you.

3. And nations will come to your light, and kings to the brightness of your rising.

4. Lift up your eyes round about, and see; they all gather together, they come to you. Your sons will come from afar, and your daughters will be carried in the arms.

5. Then you will see and be radiant. And your heart will thrill and rejoice; because the abundance of the sea [of people] will be turned to you. The wealth of the nations will come to you.

6. A multitude of camels will cover you, the young camels of Midian and Ephah; all those from Sheba will come; they will bring gold and frankincense. And will bear good news of the praises of the Lord.

> 7. All the flocks of Kedar will be gathered together to
> you. The rams of Nebaioth will minister to you; They will
> go up with acceptance on My altar, And I shall glorify
> My glorious house. (Isaiah 60:1-7)

Verses 6 and 7 identify five regions of Islamic people who will be in this company of the redeemed. As fullness of the Gentiles comes to pass, Israel as a nation will also turn to the Lord (Rom. 11:25).

All people will be brought to a place of decision as the gospel of the kingdom and the glory of God is proclaimed.

> Multitudes, multitudes in the valley of decision! For the
> day of the Lord is near in the valley of decision. (Joel
> 3:14)

It will be a glorious harvest. Satan will seek to take as many to hell with him as he can, but the battle for souls decidedly belongs to the Lord! Jesus is clearly pointed out in these verses as the One who will become the Salvation of the earth in 1 Cor. 15:24-28, Ps. 110, and Ps. 2.[1]

TARES AND ESCHATOLOGY

We are about to see how the parable of the wheat and tares (as recorded in Matthew 13) describes the course of Christianity from its first century beginnings to its culmination in a great end-time harvest.

Now, advocates of all the schools of eschatology [i.e., end-time studies] use this chapter to argue for their different end-time views. In fact, the authors quoted in this chapter disagree sharply with each other on this subject [i.e., the pre, mid, & post tribulation rapture, etc]. Yet, all these authors agree that the end-time will culminate in a huge harvest. That is because all of Matthew 13 deals with the growth of *the kingdom of heaven*. Therefore, the parable of the wheat and tares is a very important proof text for us to study.

In case you don't know, "tares" probably refers to "bearded darnel," a weed that is similar to rye grass. Since both wheat and tares are in the grass family, they look similar shortly after germination. But as soon as the wheat begins to form grains, the difference becomes obvious. A more detailed definition of tares is provided in the endnotes.[2]

THE WORLD IS A FIELD

Here is a quote from Marvin J. Rosenthal[3] that expounds upon the clincher Scripture that shows us *when* the harvest will begin and *who* will bring it in.

"When the disciples asked, '*What shall be the sign of thy coming [parousia], and of the end of the world [aion]?*' (Matt. 24:3) they realized that Christ's coming would end one era and commence another (the millennial Kingdom). A biblical synonym for the end, or *the end of the age* is the phrase *the harvest* (Matt. 13:30). This phrase occurs in the Lord's parable of the wheat and the tares:

> 24. Another parable put he forth unto them saying, The kingdom of heaven is likened unto a man which sowed good seed in his field;
> 25. But, while men slept, his enemy came and sowed tares among the wheat, and went his way.
> 26. But when the blade was sprung up, and brought forth fruit, then appeared the tares also.
> 27. So the servants of the householder came and said unto him, Sir, didst not thou sow good seed in thy field? From whence then hath it tares?
> 28. He said unto them, An enemy hath done this. The servants said unto him, Wilt thou then that we go and gather them up?
> 29. But he said, Nay; lest while ye gather up the tares, ye root up also the wheat with them.
> 30. Let both grow together until the harvest: and in the time of harvest I will say to the reapers, Gather ye together first the tares, and bind them in bundles to burn them: but gather the wheat into my barn. (Matthew 13:24-30 KJV)

THE KINGDOM OF HEAVEN DEFINED

Jesus *IS* the King of the Kingdom of God, and He *IS* the Kingdom itself! The Kingdom was right in front of the people of Galilee, but they didn't see it. Jesus hid in broad daylight for 33 years.

Moses, the deliverer of Israel, hid *openly* in the house of the Pharaoh of Egypt, and no one knew it.

Since Jesus *IS* the Kingdom, and since His Spirit indwells us, God's spiritual Kingdom is hidden within us — *openly* — but very few are aware of it (Luke 17:21).

Prerequisites for entrance into the kingdom include repentance, righteousness, and childlike faith (Matt. 4:17; Matt. 5:20). Jesus said *"Truly I say to you, unless you are converted and become like children, you shall not enter the kingdom of heaven"* (Matt. 18:3).

Jesus revealed — He manifested — His spiritual Kingdom, and He called us to do likewise.

The "Kingdom of God" and "Kingdom of Heaven" are synonymous terms that were first referred to in Daniel 2:44; 4:26; 7:13,14,27. For the past 2,000 years, this Kingdom has been in its spiritual or invisible phase. During the Church age this Kingdom will contain the sum total of all Christians, from the first one to ever be saved, to the very last one to be saved. When Jesus returns to rule, heaven and earth shall *finally* be joined for eternity (Rev. 21, 22).

PARABLE OF THE LEAVEN

While we are in Matthew 13, let me point out there are those who insist that the *leaven* in verse 33 *has* to be a symbol of evil. As they point out, in all other Scriptures it is *clearly* seen as a symbol of evil (cf. Matt. 16:6, 12; 1 Cor. 5:6-9; Gal. 5:9). Let me show you that verse 33 is an exception to the rule.

> He spoke another parable to them, The kingdom of heaven is like leaven, which a woman took, and hid in three pecks of meal, until it was all leavened. (Matthew 13:33)

Notice that Jesus clearly says *the kingdom of heaven . . .* **NOT** tares . . . **NOT** the world . . . is like leaven. This, of course, is indicating the growth of the kingdom of heaven by means of the ever-expanding power of the gospel. Yet, as you well know, we Christians are much less than righteous . . . much less than perfect.

PARABLE OF THE TARES

Notice the spiritual forces at work, and the order of events, and the end result of all things in this passage.

> 37. He that soweth the good seed is the Son of man;
> 38. The field is the world; the good seed are the children of the kingdom; but the tares are the children of the wicked one;
> 39. The enemy that sowed them is the devil; the harvest is the end of the world; and the reapers are the angels.
> 40. As therefore the tares are gathered and burned in the fire; so shall it be in the end of this world.
> 41. The Son of man shall send forth his angels, and they shall gather out of His Kingdom all things that offend, and them which do iniquity;
> 42. And shall cast them into a furnace of fire: there shall be wailing and gnashing of teeth.
> 43. Then shall the righteous shine forth as the sun in the kingdom of their Father. Who hath ears to hear, let him hear. (Matthew 13 KJV)

Jesus sows the good seed, and Satan sows the tares. And the angels remove the tares and burn them. Then, at last, the angels gather the wheat harvest into the King of Heaven for all eternity.

Jesus said, "The harvest is the end of the age." The harvest is the reaping of everything that has been sown, both good and evil. Good and evil will both be coming to their full maturity at the end.

What part did Christians play in this passage? Remember our little slogan: If anything is of God, God did it. Is this passage not a clear supernatural and eschatological statement?

THE FINAL HARVEST

Verses 37 through 40 clearly shows that there are NO tares in God's Kingdom. Otherwise, if there could be, we would be saying that God couldn't police His own Kingdom.

There will be tares growing among the wheat in the Church. It seems that even the apostle Paul had ordained elders who would prove to be wolves (see Acts 20:29-30). Jesus chose Judas and included him in the inner circle.

Though these may cause great damage and confusion, they are actually working out the purposes of God. All things work for the good of those who love God. Such disruptions usually result in our becoming more dependent on the Lord and less on those who are but flesh and blood.

This is not to say we should purposely ordain traitors and include false brethren in our congregations, but it will happen, and it will work out for our good.

Rosenthal[5] goes on to explain:

> The Lord taught, in the clearest possible way, that the final harvest is the separation of the righteous and unrighteous, and that the final harvest occurs at the end of the age. That absolute identification is made: 'The harvest is the end of the age' [Greek: aion] (Mat. 13:39).

We can conclude that:
- **The kingdom of heaven is here on earth, but the world is not in the kingdom of heaven.**
- **There are tares in the world, but there are no tares in the kingdom of heaven.**
- **The kingdom of heaven will inherit planet earth when the tares are removed.**
- **Only wheat is gathered into the kingdom of heaven — past, present, and future.**
- **The harvest will be as the stars in the heavens and the sand on the seashore.**

JESUS SHOWED EZEKIEL THE LAST DAYS HARVEST

This is a reiteration of a teaching from David Wilkerson's Time Square Church Pulpit Series (January 13, 2003).

In Ezekiel 40:3 we are told that the hand of God carried Ezekiel to a very high mountain, where a man appeared to him "whose appearance was like the appearance of brass." John describes a similar vision of a man who appeared to him on the Isle of Patmos: "***his feet***

like unto fine brass, as if they burned in a furnace" (Revelation 1:15).

Of course, the man in both passages is none other than Christ himself. So it was Jesus who ushered Ezekiel to the door of God's house, where he gave the prophet this amazing vision. It was a vision of the future of God's people, revealing what the body of Christ would become as the end times draw to a close. Ezekiel writes:

> Afterward he brought me again unto the door of the house; and, behold, waters issued out from under the threshold of the house eastward: for the forefront of the house stood toward the east, and the waters came down from under from the right side of the house, at the south side of the altar. ...
>
> And when the man that had the line in his hand went forth eastward, he measured a thousand cubits, and he brought me through the waters; the waters were to the ankles. Again he measured a thousand, and brought me through the waters; the waters were to the knees. Again he measured a thousand, and brought me through; the waters were to the loins.
>
> Afterward he measured a thousand; and it was a river that I could not pass over: for the waters were risen, waters to swim in, a river that could not be passed over. And he said unto me, Son of man, hast thou seen this?
>
> And by the river upon the bank thereof, on this side and on that side, shall grow trees for meat, whose leaf shall not fade, neither shall the fruit thereof be consumed: it shall bring forth new fruit according to his months, because their waters they issued out of the sanctuary: and the fruit thereof shall be for meat, and the leaf thereof for medicine. (Ezekiel 47:1, 3-6,12 KJV)

Keep in mind those images of water in the Bible almost always represents the Spirit of God. This vision clearly reveals a mighty outpouring of the Holy Spirit in the last days. The vision was so powerful, so overwhelming in scope, Ezekiel couldn't comprehend it. He couldn't even comment on its meaning; all he could do was report what he saw. In fact, before the vision was finished the Lord stopped and asked Ezekiel, "**Hast thou seen this**?" (47:6).

God was asking Ezekiel, in essence, "Do you grasp the magnitude of what you're seeing? Are you able to comprehend the prophetic power of this vision? Do you see what these rising waters speak of, and how they indicate the way all things will end? Tell me, Ezekiel, do you see in this vision the glory of the Lord's coming? I know this revelation is awesome and mind-boggling to you. But I don't want you to miss its true meaning."

> Here is what Ezekiel was being shown: In the very last days, the church of Jesus Christ will be more glorious, more victorious, than in its entire history. The Lord's true body isn't going to weaken and sputter. It's not going to dwindle in numbers, or decease in power or spiritual authority. No, His church will go out in a blaze of power and glory. And it will enjoy the fullest revelation of Jesus that anyone has ever known. Since the first century the church has only waded in the outpouring of the Holy Spirit, but the time is coming when we will be swimming in a flood of His glory.

Is the Holy Spirit asking you the same question he put to the Old Testament prophet: do you understand that this is a great prophecy, direct from the Father's throne? Do you comprehend how it describes the church in these last days? Are you grasping the meaning of the rising river?" ◆

Chapter 6

Reviving The Fallen Away

Along with the "little flock" teaching (described in chapter 3) is the teaching of "a falling away" or the "great apostasy" that cancels any notion of a great end-time harvest. Since the Bible speaks of both, we need to sort out this seeming contradiction. Let me say up front that both have to be true, therefore there has to be an explanation, and this chapter endeavors to do that.

Here is the "falling away" proof text:

> Let no man deceive you by any means: for that day shall not come, except there come a falling away first, and that man of sin be revealed, the son of perdition. (2 Thessalonians 2:3 KJV)

I believe we are seeing the "falling away" as doctrinal error in 100% of all doctrinal groups that confess Jesus Christ as Lord and Savior today (as well as those that don't). In the 500 years since the Reformation, we have seen church splits, schisms, and terrible persecution of the brethren that should not have been a part of Christ's church.

There are some who argue that church conditions today — division, prayerlessness, lack of holiness and power — are all that we should expect in the last days church. Their argument is that Jesus also warned of a great falling away from the faith. Yes, and they are proof of it! However, because they have succumbed to unbelief, that is no reason why we should slide into such hopelessness as well.

> And this gospel of the kingdom shall be preached in the whole world for a witness to all nations, and then the end shall come. (Matt 24:14)

Jesus said, "*. . . **this gospel of the kingdom shall be preached in the whole world.***" Jesus is not referring to typical, traditional western Christianity, which has apostatized in many ways.

Jesus is not so unjust that He would offer the unsaved world a gospel spoken by powerless, sinful people.

He said, "this gospel," speaking about His message! His message comes with corresponding signs, wonders and miracles, authenticating its divine source. This is the message Jesus sent His disciples out with in the first century; and He shall send His disciples out in the last century with this same message:

> And as you go, preach, saying, "The kingdom of heaven is at hand." Heal the sick, raise the dead, cleanse the lepers, cast out demons; freely you received, freely give. (Matt 10:7-8)

It is amazing how Christians believe and, at the same time, do not believe the Bible. In the Bible we read about all the wonders and miracles God has done, yet we don't ***believe***; or should I say, we don't ***expect*** God to manifest His presence or power in our personal lives.

Our faith is often based more on our personal experience than on faith in the Word of God. Too many Christians do ***not expect conspicuous answers*** to their prayers because their personal failure repudiates their faith. These are Christians who simply do not believe what Jesus has clearly told them in the Bible, and that is apostasy.

Here is a painful fact of life — we all are guilty of at least one small area of unbelief in our lives.

DROP OUT CHRISTIANS

At the turn of the century (1900s), Christians in America started dropping out of the process that made America great. We took the Scripture that says we are to be "in the world but not of it" to an extreme. Seldom did a Christian run for any political office or vote on election days because politics, politicians, and government were considered dirty and "of the world."

That was confirmed when Roe vs. Wade, separation of church and state, and equal rights for homosexuals started coming on the scene. But all of these bad court rulings and legislation were our own fault! By default, we allowed the enemies of the church to take over our responsibilities.

But, if we believe the Bible, we will have to agree that we are supposed to rule the earth (Gen. 1: 26-28). We are to engage unrighteousness. And we are to contend for the Kingdom of God.

It is true that ***Righteousness exalteth a nation, but sin is a reproach to any people***" (Prov. 14:34). Unless the righteous reigns, righteousness will not be exalted in their nation.

There was a time when most of the schools, universities, and hospitals in America were founded and operated by Christians. Our major universities — Harvard, Yale, Princeton, and Columbia — all began as Bible schools to train pastors and missionaries.

But we dropped out of these institutions as well. We were more interested in evangelism, and thereby we dropped out of our most important mission fields — the academic and medical institutions. The loss was our own fault.

To me this was a great falling away that we are now trying to correct. But there is another area of falling away that is killing us.

THE UNIVERSAL SIN

If we were to say there is a subliminal one-world religion today that coexists with, and preempts EVERY religion, that false god or religion would have to be titled "the love of money and the power it brings."

The love of power that wealth brings is a false god that is dominant among Hindus, Moslems, Buddhists, Christians, Atheists, and New Agers — in short, EVERY religion!

As we approach the end of this age we can expect the darkness to increase and those who walk in the light to likewise grow in righteousness. Money is one of the primary things that will determine which way we go. This is why the beast is — in my opinion — an Economic power. How we handle money will be a major point of conflict at the end that will determine whom we really belong to. It is for this reason that teaching on Christian economics and ethics is going to become increasingly critical.

> We all remember the political slogan that prophesied, "It's the economy, stupid!" And we remember that many Christians voted for their pocketbook rather than the Word of God. So I ask, is it not Scriptural to conclude that God will cast down this false god . . . this false religion and its prophets?

We all know that God's judgment comes to the church first, and then the world. God eventually casts down false gods that seduce His people. So, if money and the power it brings is what we love, He will cast down our money and our power idol.

How?

In Old Testament history, God used such catastrophes as floods, hurricanes, and depressions, and that still works today. We had better repent while we still have something left to save.

> Who will cry out to society, "it's the love of money, stupid!" [1]

SPIRITUAL RACISM

> When we regard our own methodology as normative, we eventually question the faith of those who do not conform to it.
>
> — Charles Colson

Doctrinal prejudice is as much the sin of condemnation as racism, which really means ethnic (Gr: *ethnos*) or nation groups. In the true sense of the word, doctrinal groups are in fact ethnic groups.

We usually are not openly hostile to those who are different from us. We cloak our *real* feelings by *condemning them with faint praise,* saying; "Oh, they are Christians, I suppose. They may even be saved, but I can have no part of them because of . . ."

When it comes to asking all the churches in a town to join forces in a crusade to bring their town to Christ, the major objection from pastors will usually be: "Well, since I didn't initiate the crusade, I don't want to participate."

True, the crusade is not ours; it is Christ's alone!

Mathematically we all cancel each other out by the time each group has condemned every other group. No wonder we don't even know what repentance is, much less the true meaning of revival.

GUILT INVITES ONLY THE GUILTY

We compartmentalize our lives into rooms: work, play, family, sex, church, etc. We may invite God to fill many of these rooms with His righteousness, but a sign is posted on the door of some rooms that reads, "Private — Keep Out." These are our own secretive, dark little rooms we hope no one knows about — especially God.

> **Guilt invites only the guilty. Who else can you trust with your guilt but the guilty? Guilt is duty bound to tolerate the guilt of others, and is intolerant of the righteous.**

Rebellion is the result of guilt. And *"rebellion is as the sin of witchcraft, and stubbornness is as iniquity and idolatry"* (1 Sam.15: 23 KJV).

Witchcraft resorts to power or control that is not of God. That power to control can be self-assertion or Satanic intervention. Stubbornness or insubordination is arrogant, presumptuous guilt that resists repentance before God. Idolatry in this case is idolizing self; making us little gods who decide for ourselves what is good and what is evil — as Adam and Eve did. As Rick Warren said, "it is when we try to be God that we end up most like Satan, who desired the same thing."

Compartmentalizing for most Christians means that they have given God (let's be nice here and say) 90 percent of the compartments in their lives, but reserve 10 percent for self-idolizing or self-indulgence. God only gets the crumbs, the leftovers from self-indulgence in these rooms of their lives.

As you well know, God does not tolerate crumbs. Anything that competes with God in your and my life is an enemy of God. He wants all or nothing.

> 22. Seeing ye have purified your souls in obeying the truth through the Spirit unto unfeigned love of the brethren, see that ye love one another with a pure heart fervently: (1 Peter 1:22 KJV)
>
> 1. Wherefore laying aside all malice, and all guile, and hypocrisies, and envies, and all evil speaking,
> 2. As newborn babes, desire the sincere milk of the word, that ye may grow thereby:
> 3. If so be ye have tasted that the Lord is gracious. (1 Peter 2 KJV)

In this passage of Scripture, Peter commands us to fervently love the brethren with a pure heart and an unfeigned love.

The question is: do we?

Peter told us to lay aside all malice, guile, hypocrisies, and envies, and all evil speaking of the brethren.

I ask again, do we?

Brethren, this is the sincere milk of the word, and we can't handle it. How can we ever get to the meat if we can't handle the milk of the Word of God?

According to the standards set by Peter, most professing Christians will have to admit that either they never did measure up, or they have fallen away from the most basic "milk" tenants of faith in Christ, making them hypocrites.

Is that not what 1 Peter 1:22 through 2:3 tells us? Read those verses repeatedly until you are ready for the meat of the Word!

As Thomas Paine once said, "A long habit of not thinking a thing wrong gives it a superficial appearance of being right."

If this is speaking to you, please read Malachi 1:6-14 as a meditation.

A CHALLENGE

The Word of God challenges us to test everything because we are all subject to deception. We are told to *"test the spirits to see whether they are from God; because many false prophets have gone out into the world"* (1 John 4:1).

Paul exhorts us to: *"Test yourselves to see if you are in the faith; examine yourselves!"* (2 Cor. 13:5).

The test of all teaching and all doctrine is the Word itself. We are called to be like the Bereans who tested everything Paul taught by the Word of God (Acts 17:10-11).

Again, a major part of the blame for the falling away I describe here falls on the church for not preaching repentance and Lordship, as well as salvation in Jesus Christ.

ACCUSERS OF THE BRETHREN

It really hurts me to have to bring up this category of Christians who are falling away, but they are so vocal it becomes necessary.[2]

There is a popular movement going on right now that says *the apostasy* (the great falling away) has come, and the participants of this movement are deciding who has gone into apostasy and who has not. Of course, each group declares that they *have not* gone into apostasy, and they declare that everyone who disagrees with them *has* gone into apostasy.

Since every group disagrees with every other group, they all have branded each other as apostate, leaving not one group that has not been called apostate by some other group. Mathematically they have canceled each other out, leaving all as apostate and none as true.

Most assuredly, there are apostate Christian groups. And although the gates of hell will not prevail or gain the advantage against the church, this "apostasy" attitude is destructive to those deceived saints who are making these accusations. Such self-deception would be humorous if it wasn't so pitiful and so destructive to the cause of Christ.

As a result, their love is growing cold for their fellow brethren whom they now feel are apostate. And they are withdrawing their fellowship into smaller and smaller bands as they keep finding error within their own circles. Eventually, many of them will be all alone, or in withdrawn bands of two or three.

Jesus warns of this in Matthew 24:12, ***"Because of the increase of wickedness (in the world and in much of the visible church), the love of most will grow cold."*** This implies that many true believers will withdraw from active fellowship with other Christians and live in spiritual isolation for some reason, perhaps out of doctrinal differences.

They will declare those of different opinions to have fallen into error, when in fact it is they who have fallen into ***the error of separation and false accusing of the brethren***. Since it will be without repentance, they will slip even further into their paranoia and error, but all the time professing to be the purist of the pure Christians.

> Let us not give up meeting together, as some are in the habit of doing, but let us encourage one another and all the more as you see the Day approaching. (Hebrews 10:25)

The inference here is that genuine fellowship will be absolutely necessary in the final days of church history.

THE JUDASES AMONGST US

> "Did I Myself not choose you, the twelve, and yet one of you is a devil?" Now He meant Judas the son of Simon Iscariot, for he, one of the twelve, was going to betray Him. (John 6:70-71)

Francis Frangipane has a powerful insight into this passage: [3]

> In the New Testament, the Greek word translated "devil" in this text (diabolos) is rendered by its impersonal, generic definition elsewhere. The word, diabolos, simply means a "false accuser," 'slanderer' or "a malicious gossip." In fact, 1 Timothy 3:11 & 2 Timothy 3:3 both translate diabolos (Strong's concordance #1228) as "malicious gossip(s)."

In other words, what Jesus is actually saying is not, "one of you is a devil" in a biological or theological sense, but is identifying "a false accuser, a slanderer." While the disciples were almost bragging about their loyalty to Christ, Jesus corrected them, in effect saying, "Yes, I chose you, but even among you is malicious gossip, a slanderer, who will eventually betray me to my enemies."

This problem of Christians who gossip, Paul tells us, will continue right into the end of the age. Listen carefully to what Paul wrote to Timothy about the end of the age: ***"men will be lovers of self, lovers of money, boastful, arrogant, revilers, disobedient to parents, ungrateful, unholy, unloving, irreconcilable, malicious gossips...."*** (2 Tim. 3:1-3). In the midst of this list of great sins of the apostasy, the apostle includes "malicious gossips." This is exactly the same word translated as "devil" in John 6.

Brethren, we have Judases in our midst who need to repent.

REVIVING THE FALLEN AWAY

A guilty conscience justifies the areas in your life that you know do not comply with the Bible. You know you are guilty when certain Bible passages make you angry.

Although the Promise Keepers and others have been successful in bringing reconciliation between the races and doctrinal groups at their gatherings, the job is a long way from being finished. Despite the outward appearance of reconciliation between races and doctrinal groups, much of it is a superficial, polite overture that is quickly forgotten.

In countries where Christians are under heavy persecution, they cannot afford such superficiality. They are **FORCED** to join ranks in order to survive, and that might just be a blessing in disguise.

Revival is needed today because of this falling away. It has been going on for so long that we think it is an ac-

ceptable tradition. The revival will come, but it may well be by way of the woodshed.

I think that God is calling us to choose between the altar and the woodshed. If God drags us to the woodshed the rod falls, but mercy comes at the altar. I choose to do my wailing and repenting at the altar because I *want* to.

What is your choice?

Here is how Francis Frangipane[4] said it:

> We have such lofty promises awaiting fulfillment on this side of the rapture! Yet, when I survey the landscape of the church . . .
>
> I realize we have made our goals too little, too humanly attainable; we have become too worldly to perceive the possibilities of God's provisions.
>
> I, therefore, conclude that these scriptural promises (and many more like these), await us like Abraham's "impossible" potential awaited him. I don't nullify the grace of God by saying God's word cannot come to pass, but instead I embrace the Cross, I persevere in prayer, striving for this upward call of God in Christ Jesus (Phil. 3). [Emphasis added]

Picture for a moment a harvest of several hundred million — perhaps billions! I believe that the magnitude of the final stages of a worldwide harvest will require much more of the expectant church than can even be imagined at this time. During this time I expect to see society and the environment become extremely volatile. At the same time — and in direct ratio — I expect to see the church come into her glory as never before in history.

UNHEARD OF TIMES

Although the harvest will be plentiful, won't it be a tragedy if some workers — perhaps you and I — are not fully committed, and therefore, miss out on discipling due to unbelief? Our part of the harvest could be given over to another believer and they would receive our reward.

Our Father is revealing that He loves us just as we are! As we respond to His overtures of love, He changes us, for we must have His heart in order to be successful in the harvest.

If, as the saying goes, we haven't **arrived** yet, then Father God will pick us up where He finds us and escort us to our destination . . . our destiny . . . our Bridegroom, Jesus Christ.

How far are we willing to go to be conformed to the image of Christ?

All the way?

No matter the cost?

I believe Jesus is going to showcase His beloved Bride who has made herself ready for Him (Eph. 5:27; Rev. 19:7). Many Christians have perverted marriage to Christ by saying . . .

> **No Lord, I don't want you; I am married to myself. But I do want You to cleanse me and fill me with Your Holy Spirit. I do want to be on display in Your showcase so I can say, "This is what God has done for me."**

This is making ready for self, and Christ rejects such people — until they surrender to His will.

We need preachers who will cry out against the sins of the "great falling away" in their churches and open their altars to those who will repent. However, our preachers must first prostrate themselves before the altar and sanctify it with their own tears of repentance. Then they will be able to draw their congregations to their tear-soaked altar.

Will you be among the first?

Remember . . . when we ask for God's blessing (on our lives, our church, our nation), He cannot bless the status quo.

> **God's blessing is always defined as: To conform us into the image of Christ for winning the ultimate victory of Christ's Kingdom.**

And, being conformed to the image of Christ, my friend, **is** the reformation/restoration process.

> **Lord, light the fire in our hearts; help us behold Your glory in the face of Your Son, and prepare us for the days ahead. Amen. ♦**

69

THE PARABLE OF THE DUCKS

I'd like to share a parable . . . a story that illustrates the coming unity I anticipate. This parable is about a farmer who raised 12 different species of ducks in one pond; and they were separated into pens located right *in* the pond.

Heavy rains came, and over a ten-day period, the water rose higher and higher. Finally, the water in the pond rose higher than the top of the pen. Whereas the ducks had been paddling contentedly in their small, segregated pens, now they were paddling amongst each other. The refreshing, cool, clean water and the fresh, wholesome food that came with it was so great that the ducks didn't even seem to notice the absence of the restraining pens, or the presence of odd ducks. Whereas they *used* to do what ducks do *separately*; now they were doing what ducks do *jointly*.

Water can be a type of the Holy Spirit. I believe that when we allow the Holy Spirit to rise high enough in our doctrinal and ethnic pens, we won't even notice the absence of those old restraints or the presence of what we used to consider "odd ducks."

Fellow ducks, the water is rising!

Have you prayed that God will send a Holy Spirit flood to raise you above your traditional, doctrinal fence and refresh you with His complete liberty? ♦

Adapted from David Duplessis' original version.

Chapter 7

The Unity Jesus Prayed for Will Come

There will always be false unity movements in Christian circles; but the Bible says there is also the true unity. In fact, Jesus prayed — and thereby prophesied — that we may be perfected in His unity. Here is His quote:

I do not ask in behalf of these (disciples) alone, but for those also who believe in Me through their word; that they may all be ONE; even as Thou, Father, art in Me, and I in Thee, that they also may be in Us; that the world may believe that Thou didst send Me. And the glory which Thou hast given to Me I have given to them; that they may be ONE, just as We are ONE: I in them, and Thou in Me, that they may be perfected in unity, that the world may know that Thou didst send Me, and didst love them, even as Thou didst love Me. (John 17:20-23 KJV) [Emphasis added]

Was this prayer just wishful thinking on Jesus' part? Or was this prayer — and all of His prayers — a prophetic promise? Jesus said: ***The words that I say to you I do not speak of My own initiative, but the Father abiding in Me does His works*** (John 14:10 NASB). And Revelation 19:10 says, "The testimony of Jesus *is* prophecy."

And Hebrews 1:1-2 says, *"In the past God spoke to our forefathers through the prophets at many times and in various ways, but in these last days He has spoken to us by His Son"* (NIV). This verse says that Jesus was a prophet.

Paul confirmed this (in 2 Cor. 1:20) when he said: *"No matter how many promises God has made, they are "Yes" in Christ. And so through him the "Amen" is spoken by us to the glory of God"* (NIV).

> It should be self-evident that if Jesus is who He said He is, very God, then all of His prayers are a prophetic promise!

Not one time did Jesus ever pray amiss. Every time Jesus prayed, He revealed the *perfect* will of His Father. To hear from Jesus was — and is — to hear from God. To say it another way, the words of Jesus were actually the "Word" of God — the second Person in the Trinity (John 5:19).

> When God speaks, He always reveals what He is going to do — not what He wants us to do for Him (John 1:1-3).
>
> When Jesus prayed, "that they may be in us," He was saying that all Christians can be ONE in the Trinity even as the Trinity is ONE in us.
>
> When we allow the Spirit of Christ IN US to flow with the Holy Spirit and the Spirit of God IN US, then we will begin to understand how our eternal human spirit can be in unity with the Omnipresent Spirit of God.
>
> We must come to understand that the Spiritual unity Jesus prayed for can only be between God and man, never between man and man. We must get past the notion that unity in the Spirit means: all Christians being in unity with each other.
>
> Unity movements that attempt to unite Christians "in the faith of man", or "in the spirit of man (small 's')", are always false unity movements because they are of the flesh.

When more of Christendom understands this Spiritual truth, an ever-increasing number of Christians will come into Spiritual unity with Christ.

If our only thought, purpose, and intent is to know Jesus' voice, have faith in Him, and do His will, we will be in perfect unity with Him. We will be in tune with Him as a piano is in tune to a tuning fork. Pianos tuned to the same tuning fork will also be tuned to one another. Yet, these pianos will play many different tunes. After all, unity — not uniformity — is God's perfect will.

Allow me to simplify this statement.

When we know His voice (according to John 10:27) . . .

> And know His will for our lives
>
> And are totally obedient to His will
>
> And glorify Him in our every thought and deed (as Jesus does unto His Father)

Then we are in perfect unity with Jesus.

The Song of Solomon says such a romance with the Groom is more than possible, it is the very heart of God, and God's love is perfect!

Since Jesus prayed for unity, there can be no question as to **whether** unity will come. The remaining question is: **when** will this happen?

Why not right now? Will you confess RIGHT NOW that Jesus' prayer was indeed a prophecy that will be fulfilled, and that you want to be in unity with Him?

THE BABEL UNITY PRINCIPLE

It is possible for a group of people, such as with the ancient city of Babel, to become **ONE** people without God's help. But, among the disciples of Jesus, becoming **ONE** is impossible without God's Spirit.

> Here is a simple but profound spiritual law. If anything is of God, it is because God is doing it — through us! His Holy Spirit is the only power capable of bringing the unity Jesus prayed for.

God stopped Satan's counterfeit unity at the tower of Babel and made His genuine unity available to us on the day of Pentecost; the day when God's Holy Spirit came to dwell in every believer.

Now let's carry that statement to its logical conclusion.

The Holy Spirit resides in every Christian and He speaks every language that ever existed (1 Cor. 13:1). Conversely, that also means that every believer speaks the language of the Holy Spirit. After all, Jesus said, *"My sheep know My voice* **(Greek:** *phone)."* (John 10:27; 2 Cor. 3:14-18; John 8:47).

> **If every believer knows the voice of the Spirit of the Lord (and is obedient to His voice) then God's Holy Spirit can speak the same message to every believer in the world simultaneously; and each believer would respond to this message with immediate obedience. This demonstrates the ONE language of the Holy Spirit although it is EVERY human language at the same time. Now we can see how each believer can be in unity with God's Spirit and, therein, be in unity with all believers.**

Compare this to what the Lord said about the city of Babel, *"Behold, they are one people, and they all have the same language . . . and now nothing which they purpose to do will be impossible for them"* (Gen. 11:6).

> **I believe that nothing will be impossible for the universal body of Christ when we HEAR His universal language, and OBEY Him universally.**

That is what defines unity with Christ — hearing and obeying.

The potential for unprecedented power and authority to be released by this unity may be a major key to bringing an end-time harvest of hundreds of millions of souls.

Unfortunately, the Anti-Christ system seems to understand this principle of unity better right now than the church does. Let me give an example.

Summarizing the book of Revelation in 50 words or less: It is a common belief that the Anti-Christ will soon reign as a one-world dictator for a brief period over the whole earth. Then Christ will overthrow this despot and reign as King of the world for a millennium — then forever.

If we believe that Christ will return, we must accept the fact that, according to this teaching, the Anti-Christ will rule planet earth first. And, what will make the Anti-Christ needed by, and acceptable to, the world? He will promise to remove the apocalyptic turmoil and strife coming upon the earth, and he will deliver on his promise, just as Hitler did before World War II.[1]

Brethren, we might as well quit fretting over the coming "one-world" government! God is simply going to use this Beast to prepare the world for Christ's "one-world" Kingdom, because:

> God has put it in their hearts to execute His purpose by having a common purpose, and by giving their kingdom to the beast, until the words of God should be fulfilled. (Revelation 17:17)

Why does . . . *how* does the Anti-Christ win in this race, even temporarily, for one-world domination?

It is my opinion that the "one-worlders" have **a common purpose.** They have more **unity** and more **oneness** than the Church presently does; and they have had it for a long time. These one-worlders are actually many diverse groups that disagree with each other on many issues, but **they are in perfect unity in one area.** They all are united as *one* powerful force against Christ and the Kingdom of God because they are of their father — Satan (John 8:44). They all have **a common purpose**: to speak the same hateful Anti-Christ language and to tolerate anything *but* Christianity!

UNITY MUST COME BEFORE THE GREAT HARVEST

Some pastors would chastise us over our concern for unity when we *should* be directing **all** of our attention to saving souls. This raises the question: What should the priority of the church be, saving souls **for** Christ, or seeking unity **in** Christ?

The counter question is: Which did Jesus **command** us to do? **Did Jesus pray for unity, for souls, or for both? Can the church ignore the one and expect full success in the other?** Jesus said:

All authority has been given to Me in heaven and on earth. Go therefore and make disciples of all the nations, baptizing them in the name of the Father and the Son and the Holy Spirit. (Matthew 28:18-19)

A new commandment I give to you, that you love one another, even as I have loved you, that you also love one another. By this all men will know that you are my disciples, if you have love for one another. (John 13:34-35)

Notice that Jesus didn't base oneness on doctrine, but on love. All men would know for sure that we are disciples of Christ IF we love one another as Jesus prayed. Since we don't, evangelism is thwarted! And the great harvest we all pray and long for is delayed!

In these two verses (in Matthew and John) the phrase, "A new commandment I give to you," and "Go therefore . . ." are both clear commandments to the church. Again, when Jesus speaks, He always reveals what **He** is going to do. Therefore, "making disciples of all the nations," and "that we love one another," are prophetic promises that we are to confess and proclaim as God's Word.

Jesus' instruction that the church teach all nations "to the end of the age," "*all* things that I have commanded you," is strangely ignored. This self-explanatory message declares that Jesus expected the end-time church to believe, preach, and do, the same works He required of the first century church.

Those who have spiritual ears to hear will allow God, by faith, to accomplish His will through them; and faith is obedience demonstrated by works. *Go* therefore, love one another, and make disciples.

Who would dare ignore even one commandment, one prophetic promise from Jesus, while justifying themselves by putting an overemphasis on another request that the Lord made? We need balance!

Who was the Lord speaking of in John 13 when He said, "A new commandment I give to you"? (See vs. 34, 35 above.) Was He speaking only of those people in your denomination or doctrinal group, or was He speaking of **every** Christian — the **whole** church — **the worldwide body of Christ**?

Every congregation requires unity within their walls, and that is good, but that is a very nearsighted view of the whole church — as Jesus saw it (in John 13:34-35 and John 17:20-23 above).

UNITY BRINGS POWER AND AUTHORITY

The police department in any city, but especially a mega-city, demonstrates my point. When a police officer stands at an intersection on a busy street and raises his hand to a lane of traffic, that means "Stop," and every car stops. When the police officer says, "Go," every car goes. He has the authority to direct the traffic because the city that *he represents* — the city that *sent him* to that intersection — has the power to back him. When the police officer said, "Go," the whole city was in unity and agreement with him — the city said, "Go." When the police officer raises his hand toward a lane of traffic, the whole city raised its hand — symbolically. And that symbol is the badge prominently displayed over the heart of the police officer. One man spoke with persuasive *authority* because the immense *power* of millions of people gave him that authority.

Spiritual power and authority works the same way. We believe that bigger is better. The bigger a prayer group is, the more power our prayers will have. An example of this power is demonstrated in the importance we put on The National Day of Prayer. One person leads the nation in prayer, and millions agree with the one, saying the amen. Wouldn't it be wonderful and appropriate if some prominent Christian leader were to organize a "**WORLD** Day of Prayer?"

THE POWER OF AGREEING
WITH FATHER GOD

18. Truly I say to you, whatever you shall bind on earth shall be bound in heaven; and whatever you loose on earth shall be loosed in heaven.

19. Again I say to you, that if two of you agree on earth about anything that they may ask, it shall be done for them by My Father who is in heaven. (Matthew 18)

We may not have thought of it this way before, but unity brings power, and power brings authority to bind and loose.

Keep in mind that the work of God can only be carried on by the power of God.

The church is a spiritual organism fighting spiritual battles. Only spiritual power can make these biblical truths function as God ordained.

> Any kingdom divided against itself is laid waste; and any city or house divided against itself shall not stand. (Matthew 12: 25)

PURPOSE OF THE UNITY
JESUS PRAYED FOR

When we don't understand the *purpose* of unity, we are apt to abuse it. For example: God created sex for a *purpose*. But if a person doesn't understand what that purpose is, they will abuse it. If we know anything, we know that sex is greatly abused in our nation (i.e., abortion, homosexuality, adultery, etc.), and unity is also abused.

An analogy of this would be to think of Christian denominations (or doctrinal groups) as battalions in God's armed forces. This great host of battalions (under One Commander) *should be* coordinated in their single-minded task of defeating the enemy — the forces of darkness — *100 percent of the time*. However, these battalions spend far too much time battering each other (i.e., accusers of the saints, clubbing each other with the Bible, etc). Unfortunately, getting sidetracked like this only leaves time for a *part-time* war against the forces of darkness. And an army (like a kingdom or house) divided against itself is laid waste and shall not stand.

To make matters even worse, most of us only work part-time at being obedient and Christ centered. No wonder we are losing! It is time to take stock — and that's not to be confused with stealing sheep.

> And James and John, the two sons of Zebedee, come up to Him, saying to Him . . . grant that we may sit in

Your glory, one on Your right, and one on Your left.
(Mark 10:35,37)

It would seem that many battalions want to win the war *by* them-selves, *for* themselves, and crowd out all the others — as James and John wanted to do. Too often, it looks as if each group wants *all* the converts, *all* the glory, *all* the crowns, *all* for themselves. We must ask ourselves, are we in God's army, or are we in the private army of some denomination or preacher?

> **This is not a political campaign, nor is it a competitive sport. There is no championship to win for our team! But there is the Judgment Seat of Christ, and those who would be first shall be last. Everything we hold dear is at stake here.**

I believe that without unity we will continue to be as powerless as we are now. And being so powerless, we will continue to lack the spiritual authority needed to bring in a great harvest. Therefore, the call for a ministry of reconciliation and accountability is needed to manifest this authority.

Brethren, God does hold us accountable. So, who among us will be obedient and Christ centered; and who will be competitive and ministry centered?

> **Those that are obedient, and those with a ministry of reconciliation will pray for, plead for, and pursue unity until the battle is won. At that time, we will have the power and the authority to bring in a great harvest for our beloved Warrior King, Jesus. That is the purpose of unity.**

A nationwide men's movement, the Promise Keepers, is an inter-denominational, interracial and interethnic group that places a strong emphasis on evangelism. I refer to the strong attributes found in this movement, not to the potential weaknesses some fear are present in this organization.

The Promise Keepers emphasize reconciliation more than unity, but reconciliation is an important first step toward the unity Jesus prayed for. Brothers of differing races are being reconciled to each other and to God. Men are being reconciled to their wives, and are taking their place as spiritual leaders in their homes. Godly men are learning that they can worship God together without first asking the man beside him what doctrinal group he identifies with.

True unity will not come through the efforts of any person or movement seeking to bring *visible* unity. It must be a *spiritual* unity. These visible unity movements (such as the Ecumenical movement) always prove to be a serious blunder because they are works of the flesh that diminish anything supernatural. Clearly, the unity that Jesus intended in His high priestly prayer (in John 17) was for spiritual unity — a supernatural manifestation that only the Holy Spirit can accomplish.

> Oh Lord, Oh Commander of the armies of God, we bind all that hinders Your great end-time harvest (Matt. 18:18,19); and we loose all that will cause this harvest to be all that You have prophesied. In Jesus name, amen.

BEHOLDING THE GLORY OF THE LORD

I believe that the Holy Spirit is bringing a unity that will weather every storm — one not dependent on us (God's creation) but dependent on God's Spirit.

> It takes the power of God to make God known. It takes the power of God to make mankind love God. It takes God in us to love God, and it takes God in us to know God. And it takes God to fulfill Bible prophecy. It just takes God "period." We can do nothing — except be informed, prepared, and obedient.

In the Lord's own prayer for the unity of His church He stated, *"The glory which Thou hast given Me I have given to them; that they may be one just as we are one"* (John 17:23).

According to this verse, the church currently has the necessary means to be one, because Jesus said He has already given us the necessary "glory" to be one. Unfortunately, it is a lack of desire and determination on our part to be one.

Those of us who actually enter the unity of the Spirit will not even be aware of it. Our attention will not be on the church and her great accomplishments, but on Jesus — the Lord of the church.

HIS SHEEP KNOW HIS VOICE

Jesus said, *"My sheep know My voice* (Greek: *phone*).*"* And in Romans 8:14 it says: *"Those who are led by the Spirit of God are sons of God."* If every believer knows the voice of the Spirit of the Lord, and is obedient to His voice (i.e., is <u>led</u> by His Spirit), each believer can be in unity with God's Spirit and, therein, be in unity with all believers.

I believe that nothing will be impossible for the universal body of Christ when we **HEAR HIS VOICE,** and **OBEY** Him. The potential for unprecedented power and authority to be released by this unity may well be a major key to bringing an end-time harvest of hundreds of millions of souls — worldwide.

We cannot truly desire revival if we reject unity, because both are mandates of God! Therefore, we are compelled by the love of Christ to work with equal zeal for both the unity and the saving of souls that Jesus so earnestly prayed for. To leave one undone is to leave the other undone — and be in error!

If we believe the Bible we must confess that every promise God made is available and obtainable to every generation — by faith. Furthermore, if anything is of God, it is because God is doing it through us! The gift of salvation was *not* obtainable until Jesus died and rose again in order to purchase our salvation.

Becoming "one in the Spirit" with Christ was *not* obtainable until Jesus asked the Father to give this unity to the church. And, as we will see later, "unity of the faith" was *not* obtainable until Jesus sent His Holy Spirit to (among other things) manifest God's faith in and through us (1 Cor. 12:7,9).

Jesus made all of these gifts (salvation, unity of the spirit and of the faith) available to every Christian in every generation — by faith.

Lack of vision, lack of unity in the Spirit, and lack of faith has stymied the church's conclusion for almost 2,000 years. But I believe these hindrances are being

81

removed at an accelerated rate of reformation and restoration in these last-days. As our generation grows in unity and faith in Christ, we will see Him glorified by a great end-time harvest.

I believe that the next great move of God will not be Southern Baptist or Pentecostal — or of any other group. The "next" will be a synergism that will transcend all the previous moves of God. I doubt that this move of God that is now building to its highest point will ever be given a name. It will simply be called something like "the glory," and will continue unabated until Jesus comes!

Brethren, if this message is true, it is also urgent.

Who can ignore or oppose the unity that Jesus prayed for and not pay the price for their willful disobedience? We need to find out what God is doing today and join Him. ♦

Section Two

Spiritual Power

God has equipped us with the indwelling of the Holy Spirit, and with authority in Jesus' name, so that we might do the things Jesus did, and even greater.

When the Law of Moses is read, they have their minds covered over with a covering that is removed only for those who turn t o the Lord. The Lord and the Spirit are one and the same, and the Lord's Spirit sets us free. So our faces are not covered. They show the bright glory of the Lord, as the Lord's Spirit makes us more and more like our gracious Lord. (2 Corinthians 3:15-18) [The Promise]

A Reading For Section Two

There is never a time during which Jesus is not speaking. Never. There is never a place in which Jesus is not present. Never. There is never a room so dark . . . a lounge so sensual . . . an office so sophisticated . . . that the ever present, ever pursuing, relentless tender Friend is not there, tapping gently on the doors of our hearts—waiting to be invited in. Few hear His voice. Fewer still open the door.

— Max Lucado

Chapter 8

Does God Speak To Us Today?

Much of our lifestyle; much of what we hold dear to our hearts is cultural and traditional — things we never question. But God may be calling us to choose between our old traditions (old wine) and His way (new wine).

"I am Italian." "I'm Native American." "I am a Methodist." "I'm Baptist." "I am a Democrat." "I'm a conservative." "I am a Texan." "I'm a mid-westerner." We say these things with pride and confidence, and there is nothing wrong with that, until God tells us to choose between our old traditions and His way. Christ does not conform to our culture. We must conform to Him and the culture of His Kingdom.

Our belief that God does or does not speak to us today is — more often than not — a comfortable tradition that we grew up with and never questioned. Such views were birthed out of our *experience* (or lack of it), matured into our *tradition*, and instituted as our *doctrine*, thereby becoming our *lifestyle*.

We Evangelicals — and Pentecostals[1] are Evangelical — like to think that the Scriptures must make a clear statement about an issue before we can take a dogmatic, doctrinal stand on it. Here is an analogy to help explain:

> **Conventional wisdom has always functioned on belief rather than fact. Belief will always win out in an argu-**

ment, as it requires no proof, and it is immune to disproof. Although science clearly demonstrated that the earth is round, the belief that it is flat held sway for centuries, and those who threatened to upset the status quo were often jailed and tortured.

Nowhere is the dichotomy between belief and truth more evident than in medicine — and in theology. Hungarian obstetrician Ignaz Semmelweis' insistence 150 years ago that physicians wash their hands before assisting women in labor to avoid the spread of "childbirth fever" was met with scorn and derision. Years later the medical establishment initially banned Jonas Salk's polio vaccine.

AVAILABLE BUT UNKNOWN

When Louis Pasteur (1822-1895) developed antiseptic surgery, many surgeons were deeply offended by Pasteur's so-called proof that they were doing something wrong. These doctors were not stupid, and they were doing all they believed there was to do. It was just that Pasteur found a new medical procedure that was also an ancient truth begging to be put into practice.

The truth is . . . one will not practice truth until one first believes truth.

Of course, God foreordained the invention of antiseptic surgery eons before He formed the earth. So this was nothing new and controversial to God, just to the doctors of Pasteur's generation.

However, since surgeons had practiced for centuries without antiseptics, experience (or tradition) dictated to them that the use of antiseptics was medical quackery. They might have said to themselves, "We don't use antiseptics because we have never used antiseptics, and if it isn't broken, don't fix it."

Likewise, this analogy applies to a large number of Christians today. Many devout Christians have carried forth the Great Commission quite successfully — thank you — by using Scripture alone. Therefore, their experience and tradition dictate to them that the notion of God speaking to His people today is religious quackery.

Actually, these Christians are not deliberately practicing error. They just aren't aware of — or don't believe — all of the truth that God has made available to them (Mark 13:11).

Those nineteenth-century surgeons felt they had high-minded reasons why they should rejected Pasteur's research, but their reasons were not scientific. They just *sounded* scientific.

Likewise, these well-meaning Christians have reasons that *sound* scriptural as to why they believe that God doesn't speak outside of the Bible today. Actually their reasons, like those surgeons of Pasteur's day, come from tradition and experience, and not from the Bible. Eventually, Pasteur's newly discovered truth won out over a long-held medical tradition — and so will God's voice.

THE CESSATIONIST VIEW

The view that I am presenting here states that "the Holy Spirit era" (or church age) started on the day of Pentecost and will continue without change until the Second Coming of Jesus. In the upcoming chapter titled, *Peter's Definition of the Last Days*, I will prove to you conclusively that we are in the Holy Spirit era.

The cessationist view states that God became silent and all miracles ceased when the last apostle died, and that we are now in "the Bible era" (so to speak). This view says: "Scripture alone speaks to us today."

If you believe that God speaks to His own today (John 10:27) then you probably are not a cessationist. A person who is not a cessationist is usually referred to as a continuationist, or non-cessationist.

I am sure that there are fine Christians on both sides of this issue. However, I feel that many have accepted the "cessationist" view simply because the "Holy Spirit era" teaching has not been presented in the way it is presented here. And, if you already believe as I do, the following presentation will arm you with a scriptural basis for your faith.

John W. Kennedy presents the cessationist view eloquently in his excellent book on church history *"The Torch of the Testimony."*[2] This is his entire statement:

> The Church and the Scriptures developed together, and the church ultimately recognized in the truth of the

written revelation her complete foundation. The Bible [*I think he means the New Testament*] is the expression of the divine Word, at one time spoken directly from the lips of Christ, and then through the apostles. The New Testament embodies the continuance of the apostolic ministry, the revelation of Christ that was completed with the committal to Paul of the mystery of the church (Col. 1:24-27). From this, it follows that the ministry of apostleship and prophecy as embodied in particular people was but a temporary expedient. It was vitally necessary during the transition period when the written Word was being formulated and was gaining acceptance among believers, but when the written Word was completed, the particular ministry of the apostle and the prophet became redundant, just as the observation of the Old Testament sacrifices had to give way to their fulfillment in Christ. The principle came into operation, *"But when that which is perfect is come, that which is in part shall be done away"* (1 Cor. 13:10). The function of the apostle and the prophet still exist, but embodied in the written Word, not in any man.

Although John Kennedy *inferred* that miracles and prophecy disappeared along with the apostles and prophets, he didn't say it specifically, as most cessationists do. However, Dr. Charles Caldwell Ryrie, Th. D., Ph. D., does in his Bible commentary. Here is his commentary on 1 Corinthians 13:11.

After the church began, there was *a period of immaturity*, during which spectacular gifts were needed for growth and authentication (Heb. 2:3-4). With the completion of the New Testament and the growing maturity of the church, the need for such gifts disappeared.

When Dr. Ryrie speaks of *a period of immaturity*, he is referring to the high water mark, the glory days of the church. To refer to this period as "immature" is to insinuate that the apostles and the authors of the New Testament were immature. Dr. Ryrie catches himself in a contradiction. By this logic, he should be able to pen for us a much more mature Scripture and doctrine than the writers of the New Testament gave us.

> I ask a rhetorical question: Could the mature New Testament come out of an immature church?

In a coming chapter, *Surprising Bible Manuscript History*, we will dig deeper into this intriguing subject of *"the completion of the New Testament"* Dr. Ryrie spoke of.

This chapter has stated the cessationist view by quoting two notable authors who champion this view. Many books have been written promoting this view, but enough has been presented here to give a fair understanding of the cessationist view.

An equally academic, and equally gracious (but opposing) discourse on what I call the *continuationist view* can be found in the next chapter. ♦

Imagine for a moment . . .

That God might manifest His presence in your life in a powerful, unusual — even supernatural — way. Suppose He were to stand at your side, waiting to infuse your spirit with a fullness beyond your most cherished dreams or imagination. And what if He invited you to join Him in the most exciting, provocative, creative adventure of your life, promising you that He was ready, willing, and able to carry you into an experience so lofty, so eternally memorable, that you would never be the same?

Dr. Ronnie W. Floyd, Pastor
First Baptist Church,
Springdale, Arkansas

Dr. Ronnie W. Floyd, *The Power of Prayer and Fasting: 10 Secrets of Spiritual Strength*, (Nashville: Broadman & Holman Publishers, 1997) pp. xiii, pp. 97.

Chapter 9

When the Perfect Comes . . .

The cessationist view states that God became silent and all miracles ceased when the last Apostle died.

Some have said: **"The miracles, signs, and wonders of the book of Acts were temporary. They served to authenticate the apostles and prophets until the New Testament could be written. Now we have the completed Word of God, which erases the need for supernatural happenings."**

The punch line from the cessationists' favorite proof text says: ***"When the perfect comes, the partial will be done away."*** Here is their proof text:

> 8. Love never fails; but if there are gifts of prophecy, they will be done away; if there are tongues, they will cease; if there is knowledge, it will be done away.
>
> 9. For we know in part, and we prophesy in part;
>
> 10. But when the perfect comes, the partial will be done away.
>
> 11. When I was a child, I used to speak as a child, think as a child, reason as a child; when I became a man, I did away with childish things.
>
> 12. For now we see in a mirror dimly, but then face to face; now I know in part, but then I shall know fully just as I also have been fully known. (1 Corinthians 13)

The Greek word used for "dimly" or "darkly" is ***en ainigmati*** and means "in an enigma." The dictionary defines "enigma" as: "a perplexing or baffling matter, usually an ambiguous statement or riddle; to speak in a riddle."

Glass mirrors were probably introduced in Paul's time. However, the surfaces of most first century mirrors were usually made of a polished metal — a mixture of tin and copper. At best, those ancient metal and glass mirrors were unequal to our modern glass mirrors and, more often than not, were tarnished and dim.

Paul implies that he is speaking of a great truth that is hard to see, or perplexing; and that it takes spiritual eyes to "see" this insight by inspiration of the Holy Spirit.

There are several Greek words for the English word "glass," but in this Scripture, it clearly means a looking glass . . . a mirror. Both the Strong's and Young's concordance were compiled for use with the King James Version of the Bible. Here is how they define "glass."

- *Esoptron*: looking glass (1 Cor. 13:12; James 1:23)
- *Hualos*: anything transparent (Rev. 21:16, 21)
- *Hualinos*: made of glass (Rev. 4:6; 15:2)

FACE TO FACE WITH JESUS

For now we are looking in a mirror that gives only a dim (blurred) reflection [of reality as in a riddle or enigma], but then [when perfection comes] we shall see in reality and face to face! Now I know in part (imperfectly); but then I shall know and understand fully and clearly, even in the same manner as I have been fully and clearly known and understood [by God]. (1 Corinthians 13:12 The Amplified Bible)

The expression "face to face" has to be in reference to the return of Christ. Obviously, we can only meet a person face to face, and that person can only be Jesus (Rev. 1:7). In the Old Testament, the expression "face to face" meant to see God personally. For example, Jacob saw God face to face as he wrestled with the angel of the Lord (the pre-incarnate Christ) (Gen. 32:30). Also, after the angel of the Lord had visited Gideon in the winepress, Gideon exclaimed, "I have seen the angel of the Lord face to face (Judg. 6:22).

As a final example, Exodus 33:11 says that, ***"The Lord would speak to Moses face to face, as a man speaks with his friend."***

When Paul uses the expression *"face to face,"* he is referring to the *time* when we shall see Jesus face to face. That *time* can only refer to His return, when every eye will see Him (Rev. 1:7).

Obviously, we cannot meet face to face with the Bible, or some nebulous idea or event. We can only meet a person face to face, and that person can only be Jesus — when every eye will see Him — at the Second Coming!

In the natural, we would see our own reflection when we look into a mirror, but spiritually we are to reflect Jesus because God is conforming us to His image. Yet, all we *can* see is a *poor* reflection of Jesus through our Adamic eyes, until we see Jesus face to face — beyond the veil of flesh. We can't even see ourselves clearly in that spiritual mirror because we are wretched sinners who need God's mercy, grace, and forgiveness every day.

WE SHALL KNOW HIM FULLY

Then we shall know Him *fully*, just as He has *fully* known us! This statement also can only refer to the Lord's return. Paul is not saying that when the Lord returns, believers will be omniscient like the Lord. Rather, we will know Jesus accurately without any misinformation, or lack of information, or misconceptions because we will be mature — we will have our glorified, eternal bodies.

Being face to face with Jesus will be sufficient to provide edification far beyond our present comprehension. In this new environment, we will know everything clearly, completely, and emphatically.

JUST WHAT IS "THE PERFECT"?

The Greek word used in verse 10 for "perfect" is *teleios*, and means . . . *ended, complete, absolute, or mature*. Some argue that Paul's reference to "the perfect" speaks of a conception of something in its most excellent form, and not to anything specific. However, there are those who argue that it means the Bible. Yet, most commentaries will also admit that "when the perfect comes" refers to the Second Coming of Christ. A valid question is: which of these options can best be defined as "the perfect," 1) something excellent, 2) the Bible, or 3) Jesus?

First we will consider Jesus (the Living Word) and the Bible (the written Word) to see which of these two comes the closest to being the "perfect" in verse 10.

> In the beginning was the one who is called the Word. The Word was with God and was truly God. From the very beginning the Word was with God. (John 1:1 The Promise)

> The Word became a human being and lived here with us. (John 1:14a The Promise)

> And His name is called The Word of God. (Revelation 19:13b NASB)

> And there are also many other things which Jesus did, which if they were written in detail, I suppose that even the world itself would not contain the books which were written. (John 21:25 NASB)

> Many other signs therefore Jesus also performed in the presence of the disciples, which are not written in this book; but these have been written that you may believe that Jesus is the Christ, the Son of God; and that believing you may have life in His name. (John 20:30-31 NASB)

A summary of these verses might be: Jesus — the *Living Word* — is complete (John 1:1). Therefore, Jesus is greater than the Bible — the summarized, written Word about Him (John 21: 25). Although the Bible is God's revealed Word to us, and is without error, we are waiting for Jesus — the Living Word — to be revealed at His Second Coming.

> **The revelation of Jesus Christ begins by seeing Him *first* as *The Living Word of God!***

PERFECT, BUT TEMPORARY?

Canonization of New Testament books (the determination of which books were authentic and should be included in Scripture) was not done until the year A.D. 367. If, by this time in church history, Paul's teachings on the gifts of the Spirit had become obsolete, why were they included? Why were they canonized? Here is how Charles Carrin [1] explains this seeming contradiction:

> **If it be true that First Corinthians 12 and 14 became imperfect when the Bible was completed, then the long-awaited "perfect" book was not perfect at all. Canonization had only destroyed its perfection. Who can sincerely believe this? The idea is absurd. It defies logic. Paul himself terminated such an argument when he wrote Timothy: "All Scripture is given by inspiration of God and is profitable for doctrine, for reproof, for correction, for instruction in righteousness, that the man of God may be complete, thoroughly equipped for every good work." (2 Tim. 3:16-17.)**

If 2 Timothy is Scripture, then Paul has told us that chapters 12 and 14 in 1 Corinthians are also Scripture. If that is so, then both are given to us so that ***the man of God may be complete, thoroughly equipped for every good work.***

"THE PERFECT" IS SOMETHING EXCELLENT

Now we will consider the possibility that "the perfect" is a conception of something in its most excellent form. As you may know, Greek nouns are assigned a gender — either feminine, masculine, or neuter. When referring to a noun in the feminine gender, one uses the pronoun "she"; when referring to a word in the masculine gender, one uses the pronoun "he"; and, when referring to a noun in the neuter gender, the pronoun is "it."

The word "perfect," as used in verse 10, is used in the neuter gender. That means it cannot refer to a person, but it can refer to a group of things, which can include a person.

A ship (or boat, or vessel) [2] is an example of a noun that can be in the neuter gender that can include its cargo, its equipment, and its crew, as well as the ship itself. And the Second Coming [3] is — in a manner of speaking — our ship that is ***coming in.*** And on board is Captain Jesus, His crew, and His fulfillment of all Messianic prophecy.

95

I believe that "the perfect" is **BOTH** Jesus **AND** the fulfillment of all messianic prophecy that will transpire at the Second Coming.

The next chapter, titled ***"The Partial Will Be Done Away,"*** will thoroughly explore this subject.

MY OWN AMPLIFIED VERSION

We just read 1 Corinthians 13:8-12 from the New American Standard Version Bible. Now we are about to read my own amplified reiteration of the same Scripture that clarifies what we have just learned.

Before we get started, notice that 1 Corinthians 12, verses 1, 4, and 31 imply that all nine "gifts" are "of the Spirit" collectively, even though not all of them are individually called "gifts." Therefore, I took the liberty of referring to all of them collectively as "gifts" of the Holy Spirit in order to keep things simple.

Now, here is my version . . .

> 8. Love — an eternal virtue of God — never fails or comes to an end (1 John 4:8), As for [the gift of] prophecy, it will be fulfilled and pass away (1 Cor. 12:10), as for [the gift of] unacquired] tongues, they will cease (1 Cor. 12:10), As for [the gift of] knowledge, [4] it will pass away (1 Cor. 12:8), 4 All of these spiritual gifts will be superseded by the physical presence of JESUS.

> 9. For our present knowledge [of Jesus, the Living Word] is fragmentary, incomplete, and imperfect, and [the gift of] prophecy is fragmentary, incomplete, and imperfect.

> 10. But, at the Second Coming, when JESUS comes to bring all messianic prophecy in the Bible to completion and to rule His Kingdom, the incomplete and imperfect gifts of the Spirit will disappear; Spiritual gifts will become something we have outgrown and discarded, LIKE CHILDHOOD TOYS WHEN WE REACH ADULTHOOD (1 Cor. 12; Eph. 4:11, 14-15).

> 11. Because, when I was a child, I talked like a child, I thought and reasoned like a child. Now that I have be-

come a man, I am done with childish ways and have put them aside.

12. For now we are looking in a mirror (through our natural eyes) that gives only a dim or blurred reflection (of the glory of the Lord) as in a riddle or enigma (2 Cor. 3:18). But, AT THE SECOND COMING OF JESUS, when Jesus (the Perfection) comes, we shall see Him face to face — in physical form! Now I know JESUS in part, or imperfectly because I am still IN MY NATURAL BODY; but then, IN MY GLORIFIED BODY, I shall know and understand JESUS fully and clearly, even in the same manner as I have been fully and dearly known and understood by JESUS (1 John 3:2).

[My own amplified reiteration of
1 Corinthians 13:8-12]

In condensed form, 1 Corinthians 13:8-12 is saying that at the Second Coming of Christ the partial, incomplete spiritual gifts (1 Cor. 12) and the five incomplete ministries (Eph. 4:11) will no longer be needed because Jesus is the perfect consummation of all of them, and we will be like Him.

Meanwhile, until the Second Coming, everything is still in place that Paul described in 1 Corinthians 12, 13, and 14. This is called the continuationist or non-cessationist view.

After hearing an explanation that is hard to remember, you will enjoy hearing Jim Cymbala's response to this issue:

If we have a completed revelation in written form, are we seeing at least as much advance for God's Kingdom, as many people coming to Christ, as many victories over Satan as those poor fellows who had to get along with just the Old Testament? If not, why not? Are we missing something valuable that they felt was essential?[5]

JUST ASK: IS IT SCRIPTURAL?

Perhaps our faith boils down to the simplest of issues. For instance, do you believe the Bible, or do you prefer the traditions of the elders? If God gives you a better understanding of a Scripture, are you free to bring the required change into your life, or are you in bondage?

Again, Jim Cymbala speaks from his considerable experience.

> Unfortunately, I have learned firsthand that many Christians who pound the Bible the hardest and most strongly defend the verbal inspiration of Scripture are the most unbelieving and cynical about God ever doing a new thing in His church. They seem so intent on preserving tradition that any spontaneity is spurned as "emotionalism." My question is: If Jesus is the same today as He was in the Bible we defend, why shouldn't we believe Him to do great things among us and through us, so we can touch people's lives in powerful ways as did the first-century apostles? Peter was no perfect saint, as evidenced by his denial of Christ; many churches today would hardly allow such a failure to stand in their pulpits. But God chose him on the Day of Pentecost and used him mightily — and God can do the same with us if we look to Him with childlike faith in our hearts.[6]

Allow me to have a little fun with my own denomination, Southern Baptist, to illustrate a point. Just because one Christian group may have come into a scriptural truth before another group did, that should not make this truth private property, and therefore untouchable or unacceptable to other groups. No doctrinal group has exclusive rights to any part of the Bible. We can assume that *all* Bible truth is available to *all* believers.

For example, wouldn't it be ridiculous to assume that if some group were to start baptizing by submersion they (thereby) would lose their old identity and become Southern Baptists.

Nonsense! They would simply become Scriptural! [We Southern Baptists would think so anyway.] The question should be "Is it scriptural," not "Is it Southern Baptist?"

Some argue that the parts of the book of Revelation that make perfectly good sense in plain English should be taken literally. If that argument is true for the book of Revelation, then why is it not also true for 1 Corinthians 12,13, and 14?

The bottom line is: All Christians are compelled to grow and be faithful to the Word of God. ♦

Chapter 10

The Partial Will Be Done Away

As long as we are living in these mortal bodies, our knowledge and understanding of supernatural things will be unclear, tarnished, and partial, until we come face to face with Jesus! Then, at that time we will understand all things. "For we know in part, and we prophesy in part; But when the perfect comes, the partial will be done away." (1 Corinthians 12:9-10)

In the simplest of terms, the *partial* is what we have now, and the *perfect* is what we will have at the Second Coming. A better understanding might be that it is <u>we</u> who are partial — until *we* are complete in Him.

Between our partial knowledge and our lack of knowledge, let's face it, all of us are in partial error. The trouble with partial error, partial knowledge, or no knowledge is that we don't know what it is we don't know! It is the nature of fallible, sinful, incomplete beings to stumble.

The Bible is the inerrant, immutable, universal Word of God, but our understanding of the Bible is not inerrant or immutable. Therefore, we cannot preach the whole counsel of God because we do not know the whole counsel of God.

> **The New Testament is also perfect, but it is a partial, incomplete record of the events in the lives of Jesus and the apostles. (John 20:30-31; 21:25)**

Realizing these things should be enough to humble us.

THE TWELVE DISCIPLES DID NOT UNDERSTAND

Not until the Second Coming will Jesus complete all messianic prophecy and bring absolute perfection into His Kingdom. Therefore, our present knowledge and understanding of spiritual things is ***partial, limited, and unclear***. Allow me to expound . . .

The Jews believed that ALL of the blessings of the Kingdom of God would arrive in one coming of the Messiah. That is why the followers of Jesus could understand the concept of the Kingdom of God coming in the person of Jesus. But the disciples did not understand the form of the Kingdom that Jesus brought until ***after*** they watched His gruesome death.

Specifically, the disciples could not embrace the idea that Jesus did not break the Roman yoke from Israel's neck, remove the presence of sin, wipe away every tear, destroy poverty, and throw death and Satan into hell.

But when they experienced the power of His resurrected life, then they were able to understand and embrace this new Kingdom. It was only then that they realized that the Kingdom Of God, as prophesied in the Old Testament, was to enter into this world through two comings of the Messiah, and not just one (1 Peter 2:9-10).

We need to recognize that conditioning and cultural assumptions are very stubborn and are not replaced in our minds by a once-for-all decision.

> **The disciples of Jesus could not grasp a two-part fulfillment and held firmly to a one-part fulfillment. They needed to be told regularly that Christ had to suffer and die. They certainly heard the message regarding the Messiah's suffering and death and perhaps, at last began to grasp it.**

Even so, the change of their worldviews regarding the Messiah's work was a slow and painful process. This two-part coming is what Jesus' disciples stumbled over.

Perhaps we also stumble over our own worldview. After all...WE LIVE IN THE REALM OF THE PARTIAL AND THE INCOMPLETE.

More than 200 years ago, William Law bluntly declared that the church of his day was **"in the same apostasy that characterized the Jewish nation . . . The Jews refused Him who was the substance and fulfilling of all that was taught in their Law and Prophets. The Christian church is in a fallen state for the same rejection of the Holy Spirit."**

He said further that just as the Jews refused Jesus and quoted Scripture to prove their point, **"So church leaders today reject the demonstration and power of the Holy Spirit in the name of sound doctrine."**[1]

We know that the Old and New Testament is the infallible Word of God, inspired by the Holy Spirit. And although fallible men penned them, the Scriptures remain infallible. That is probably why Paul taught that all prophetic and revelatory utterances (and writings?) are to be judged (1 Cor. 14:29) and tested (1 Thess. 5:19-22).

Even though there were many Christian writings in the first century, only a handful of them were canonized (judged and tested, and declared to be perfect and of God) by a progression of elders in the second, third, and fourth centuries.

It is possible — but rare — for a Christian to be in tune with the Holy Spirit to such a large degree that they can perform a complete and perfect work. To expect consistent perfection and completion from humans is to have stumbled.

Again, here is a simple spiritual law that should be self-evident to be true. If anything is good, and perfect, and glorifies God — God did it!

WE ARE ONLY PARTIALLY COMPLETED

All Evangelicals, whether charismatic or Baptist, agree that Jesus' primary mission at His first coming was "to give his life as a ransom for many" (Matt. 20:28). But although atonement is His chief and central work, it was not the only work accomplished by Christ's first coming.

Jesus sent His Holy Spirit to us (on the day of Pentecost) so that we could have power to minister as He did (John 7:39; 14:26; 1 John 2:27; Acts 1:5, 8). His first coming also included bringing a piece of eternity into time through the proclamation and demonstration of the Kingdom of God.

> You are not [consciously] falling behind or lacking in any special spiritual (gift) endowment or Christian grace [the reception of which is due to the power of divine grace operating in your souls by the Holy Spirit], while you wait and watch [consistently living in hope] for the coming of our Lord Jesus Christ and [His] being made visible to all. (1 Corinthians 1:7 Amplified Bible)

In this verse, Paul connects spiritual gifts with the return of the Lord Jesus Christ. In fact, Paul is saying that Christians will not be lacking in any of the spiritual gifts (until when?) until that glorious day of the Second Coming of Christ. The gifts that Paul speaks of are given free of charge . . . free of obligation . . . at the discretion of the Giver — the Holy Spirit.

Things are not simple in this age, because we lie between the already and the not yet. But knowing in part is better than not knowing at all! Isn't it wonderful to know that we are children of God! And even though it has not appeared as yet what we shall be, we know that when He appears, we shall be like Him, because we shall see Him just as He is (1 John 3:2).

God desires to take us *as we are* and lead us to where we need to be — conformed to the image of Christ. Where we are is always less than perfect. We are only *partially* completed. Therefore, we need to quit lying to each other, the world, and ourselves and admit that our doctrine, our understanding of the Bible, and probably 95 percent of what we do is *less than perfect.*

That would include prophecy and the prophetic ministry, and healings and miracles. This would also include the most overlooked imperfection of all — our teaching!

A person may receive a healing from one disease, only to become sick again later. Even Lazarus died a second time. And although Peter was miraculously delivered from prison, while Stephen was stoned to death.

Agabus prophesied correctly concerning Paul being bound hand and foot, but he did not properly understand that it was actually God's will for Paul to be bound.

> **Agabus believed that the vision showed what would happen IF Paul went to Jerusalem. Paul understood the vision as showing what was to happen to him WHEN he went to Jerusalem.**

For that reason, Paul saw Agabus's vision as confirmation that God was sending him. And the binding was in God's plans and will for Paul (Acts 21).

This raises another interesting question. Since Agabus (and all those present) missed God, did that make Agabus a false prophet? I think not.

INCOMPLETE BUT STILL VICTORIOUS

Yes, we are incomplete! Our salvation is incomplete! The gifts of the Spirit are incomplete! And even the Bible is incomplete! Oh how we yearn for the Second Coming of our redeeming Lord and King! In the meantime, we have a Great Commission to fulfill, and we were given the power to accomplish it.

That power is the person of the Holy Spirit that is resident *IN* us, who desires to manifest His great power *THROUGH* us. He alone can bring this victory into our lives individually, and the church corporately. He alone can instruct us in the infallible written Word. He alone can teach us the voice of the blessed One who promised us that His sheep know His voice (Greek: *phone*).

> **Our tools and programs can only be of the flesh. Collectively and individually, we are the walking, talking temples that the Holy Spirit of God uses to accomplish His work through.**

PRACTICING WHAT WE PRAISE

It isn't mandatory that we *receive* . . . but why would any Christian *reject* . . . a blessing from his loving heavenly Father? Any gift from the Holy Spirit is *more* than acceptable, it is *more* than desirable! Therefore, I am sure that *most* Christians would not *knowingly* reject God's best.

> It's clear that even though we are to study and believe the Bible, the Christian religion is mainly experiential — not just mental agreement. Jesus wants fellowship. He said: "My sheep know My voice." We are to subjectively experience His presence — the presence of His Holy Spirit in us — and, objectively, experience the manifestation of His presence through us.
>
> We can study and observe this, we can understand this, and we can believe in this intimate fellowship. BUT, if we do not experience Jesus we are missing the major aspect of the Christian faith. Christianity is an experience, a fellowship, a relationship, not just scholarship or a philosophical belief system.

On the day of Pentecost the 120 believers in the upper room had a sense of expectancy, but they didn't know *what* to expect. They simply were obedient to "tarry" and pray in unity until they "received the promised Holy Spirit." We also are to have a sense of expectancy and pray in unity in order to come into the next move of God.

CONCLUSION

At this time we are "the partial," but perfection will come for us at the Second Coming. Until that time — if Jesus is our Lord and Savior — we are forgiven and have eternal life with Him.

Our victory will be in direct ratio to our obedience to His perfect will for our lives.[2]

How obedient will we be? ♦

Chapter 11

Do You Believe The Bible?

Get ready for an introduction to what is probably the oldest, most important (but least known) Bible manuscript discovery within the last 2,000 years! Then you'll be well on your way to recognizing the excitement it has generated in me, and hopefully it will in you, too.

When John Maxwell[1] held a seminar at our church, he peppered his presentation with this little phrase, "Do you believe the Bible?" He then proceeded to show many of us that we didn't believe the Bible nearly as much as we thought we did.

It took a little time for us to realize that we were alternately funny and pathetic. We laughed and we cried, but when we left that service we were changed people . . . people who hopefully had a stronger belief in the Bible.

Now, let's see if you believe the Bible as much as you think you do.

One of the most challenging verses in the bible is found in Mark 16:17. This verse says: ***These signs will accompany those who believe . . . .*** " The trouble is, just about every Bible commentary tells us Mark did not write that verse in his Gospel. The scholars who write these commentaries tell us that some unknown person, some presumptuous person, some unauthorized person, wrote the last twelve verses that purportedly quote Jesus, including verse 17.

What a powerful statement! Isn't it just too bad that Mark didn't actually say, ***"These signs will accompany those who believe . . .,"*** or did he?

You're in for a **BIG** surprise . . . .

First we need to document the conventional view presented by these scholars before getting to our surprise. Two of the most ancient Bible manuscripts, the Codex Sinaiticus and Codex Vaticanus, do not contain the last twelve verses that appear in the King James Version of Mark's Gospel.[2d] Here is what the Nelson Study Bible's footnotes say about those verses in Mark:

> The authenticity of these last twelve verses has been disputed. Those who doubt Mark's authorship of this passage point to two fourth-century manuscripts that omit these verses. Others believe that they should be included because even those two manuscripts leave space for all or some of these verses, indicating that their copyists knew of their existence. The difficulty is in knowing whether the space is for this longer version of Mark's ending or for one of the alternate endings found in the manuscripts. Practically all other manuscripts contain vv. 9-20, and this passage is endorsed by such early church fathers as Justin Martyr (A.D. 155), Tatian (A.D. 170), and Irenaeus (A.D. 180). It does not seem likely that Mark would end his story on a note of fear (v. 8).

Here is what the Ryrie Study Bible commentary says about Mark 16:9-20:

> These verses do not appear in two of the most trustworthy manuscripts of the N.T., though they are part of many other manuscripts and versions. If they are not a part of the genuine text of Mark, the abrupt ending at verse 8 is probably because the original closing verses were lost. The doubtful genuineness of verses 9-20 makes it unwise to build a doctrine or base an experience on them (especially vv. 16-18).

Yet, the Nelson Study Bible makes this historically accurate statement about verses 17 and 18.

> These signs were evident in the early church. Casting out demons demonstrated victory over Satan (Acts 16:18). Speaking with new tongues began at Pentecost (Acts 2:4-11). Healing the sick occurred in several instances, including Acts 28:8. Taking up serpents occurred in Paul's encounter with a poisonous snake, which did not produce ill effects (Acts 28:1-6). The New Testament does not record Christians drinking anything deadly without harm."

Well, this scholarly speculation is about to end.

CODEX WASHINGTONENSIS

The trouble is, these scholars are not aware of another ancient Codex[2d] (or manuscript) that completely blows away all of their skepticism and speculation.[2f] Allow me to introduce you to the great manuscript discovery I alluded to earlier — Codex Washingtonensis, or Codex W for short. [2b] But first let me explain to you (if you are a non-scholar) why this discovery is so tremendously important to everything you and I believe.

CODEX W IS AN ORIGINAL! In fact, it is the ONLY original First Century Gospel Manuscripts ever found, and therefore the greatest gospel manuscript discovery ever made. All other translations are taken from copies of other copies of originals.

This Codex is a bound collection of four separate manuscripts that were written (in whole or in part) in the actual handwriting of the four Gospel authors. We can see the signatures and seals of Matthew, Mark, Luke, and John written both in Greek and Aramaic! Just seeing their signatures is an awesome experience![2e]

This Codex is just loaded with marvelously informative Aramaic notes and dates. For that reason this discovery just begs for Dead Sea scroll scholars to study these enlightening Aramaic notes.

In short, this is an incredible find that authenticates what these four holy men set forth for us to read and believe.

As of this writing I am one of the few non-scholars aware of these facts, and I have a passion to share this good news with you.

A SHORT HISTORY LESSON ABOUT CODEX W

After this incredible manuscript of the four Gospels was discovered, several prominent Greek scholars studied it. But it wasn't until 1981[2a] that a scholar who had the right combination of credentials read this manuscript and made discoveries the other Scholars overlooked. This scholar is Dr. Lee W. Woodard who has a background of forty plus years in Biblical, Paleographical, Historical, and linguistic studies. He recorded his research findings in a fascinating 184-page book containing many facsimiles of pages from this ancient codex.[2]

This Codex was found in 1906 during an excavation of some sandy ruins in Medinet Dimay, a walled and fortified city in Egypt.[2c] Codex W was bound[2h] with a wood cover, then sealed in a case and buried in the sand under a church. It is not known when Codex W was buried, but probably sometime in the second century during one of the several periods of persecutions by the Roman government.

If you want to know more about this incredible find you will want to read my extensive and informative endnotes.[2]

MARK WROTE ALL THE ENDINGS

Now for the big surprise we have been working up to!

Mark himself wrote those endings to his gospel over a period of three years, between 69 A.D. and 72 A.D. His official seal and the date are by each ending, and he signed his name at the bottom for all to see. Therefore, these endings are as valid, as inspired, and canonical as the rest of the gospel of Mark.[2g]

R. C. H. Lenski's commentary on Mark contains a lengthy discussion dealing with the theories made by the commentators above. Briefly, his answers to the above theories are in order:

- Mark wrote under the inspiration of the Holy Ghost. He quit when the anointing lifted. The Bible says all Scripture is given by inspiration of God.

- Tradition says that Mark lived a number of years beyond the writing of his Gospel. If the last page was lost shortly after he wrote it, he could have supplied it again.

- This makes God (who knows all things, and therefore knew when Mark would die) so inept that he didn't start anointing Mark early enough to that he would have time to finish the work before he died.

If I could enter a fourth answer to Lenski's three, it would emphasize that the disputed passage is a purported quote from Jesus Himself. It is absolutely outlandish to suggest that any scribe would be so audacious and presumptuous as to put words in His mouth. Now we have a quote from Jesus himself that confirms Paul and Luke's account of these spiritual gifts as they described them in Acts and in 1 Corinthians.

The King James Version translates Mark 16:14-20 correctly (as seen in Codex W), but I will use "Throckmorton's Synopsis of the Four Gospels" in order to show the longer ending unique to Codex W.

14. Afterward he appeared to the eleven themselves as they sat at table; and he upbraided them for their unbelief and hardness of heart, because they had not believed those who saw him after he had risen.

15. And he said to them, "Go into all the world and preach the gospel to the whole creation.

16. He who believes and is baptized will be saved; but he who does not believe will be condemned.

17. And these signs will accompany those who believe; in my name they will cast out demons; they will speak in new tongues; they will pick up serpents, and if they drink any deadly thing, it will not hurt them;

18. they will lay their hands on the sick, and they will recover."

19. So then the Lord Jesus, after he had spoken to them, was taken up into heaven, and sat down at the right hand of God,

20. And they went forth and preached everywhere, while the Lord worked with them and confirmed the message by the signs that attended it. Amen.

Here is Mark's longer ending that extends from verse 20 in Codex W, as seen in Throckmorton's translation.

21. And they replied saying, "This age of lawlessness and unbelief is under Satan, who by means of unclean spirits does not allow men to comprehend the true power of God; therefore reveal now thy righteousness." Thus they spoke to Christ; and Christ answered them: "The limit of the years of the authority of Satan is fulfilled; but other afflictions draw near, even for those sinners on whose behalf I was delivered up to death, in order that they might return to the truth and sin no more; that they might inherit the spiritual and incorruptible glory of righteousness which is in heaven."

Mark must have felt led to include this ending in 72 A.D. after seeing the extreme wickedness manifested in the horrible siege of Jerusalem and destruction of the Great Temple, etc., in 70 A.D. He felt that what he was including (as to the expansion of Jesus' words) was fully in accord with the earlier revelation from Jesus, following the Resurrection.

It should be pointed out that the contents of Codex W are essentially the same as the good copies mentioned above. What makes this discovery different and exciting is the fact that:

- **Codex W is the only first century original, and**
- **Matthew, Mark, Luke, and John did indeed write the gospel attributed to them, and**
- **Mark did indeed write all those endings himself, therefore**
- **Codex W is the most reliable of all gospel manuscripts.**

WHAT DOES THIS MEAN TO US?

Now that we know Mark actually wrote all the endings to his gospel, we can dismiss the opinion of all those well-meaning scholars who said someone else wrote them. And for that reason we will now have to take this passage seriously. Let's read it again.

> And these signs will accompany those who believe; in my name they will cast out demons; they will speak in new tongues; they will pick up serpents, and if they drink any deadly thing, it will not hurt them; they will lay their hands on the sick, and they will recover. (Mark 16:17-18)

This is no "bow your head and repeat after me" prayer. The early apostles proclaimed God's word "*in demonstration of the Spirit and of power*," that the faith of those who listened would "*not rest on the wisdom of men, but on the power of God*" (1 Cor 2:4-5). Notice how much that passage sounds like this undisputed quote from Jesus.

> And as you go, preach, saying, "The kingdom of heaven is at hand.'" Heal the sick, raise the dead, cleanse the lepers, cast out demons; freely you received, freely give. (Matthew 10:7-8)

Dear friend, how many of these gifts have ever followed you?

I don't think he meant that **ALL** of these signs would follow **EVERY** believer. Most probably he meant that one or more of these signs (at the absolute minimum) would accompany a believer at least once in their lifetime.

For instance, a viper bit Paul while he was gathering firewood. He didn't deliberately handle the viper and tempt God, as is the practice of some. And, according to legend, John the Revelator's persecutors forced him to take a cup of poison. He didn't deliberately drink anything deadly, but he was not harmed by it.

People tend to get hung up on these more exceptional "signs" and as a result, overlook the "signs" that we see following hundreds of believers in the book of Acts and in 1 Corinthians 12.

These "signs" follow true believers because the Holy Spirit indwells them. So, these Spiritual "signs" or "gifts" are a virtue of the

Holy Spirit to use at His digression. Since the Holy Spirit indwells us, He can manifest His gifts through us as He wills. We have no control over the Holy Spirit or His "signs" or "gifts," but we must allow, and not resist, the Holy Spirit to work through us.

Verses 17 & 18 are really saying that God is well able to protect us from all harm and danger. The mission field can often be a perilous place. Come to think of it, **EVERY PLACE** is a perilous place these days. All Christians have to believe that God will provide the means and the protection that must go with our calling, or the strength to die a martyr's death that glorifies Him. We see examples of both in the Bible.

Further down we will look at another scriptural way to understand this passage.

> **The point is: God really did deliver Paul and John with these rare and exceptional "sign" gifts. And Jesus Himself spoke these words — these are red-letter words — so therefore they are a commandment and prophecy to us.**

Some will argue that Jesus was speaking only to the eleven apostles in this passage. But verses 15 and 16 make it clear that Jesus was talking to *"he who has believed and has been baptized"* as a result of the evangelization of the eleven.

Since water baptism does not save, Jesus was undoubtedly talking about baptism in the Holy Spirit. If you have believed and were baptized, that verse includes you. Have any of these signs accompanied you since you have believed?

A final thought: Even without Codex W there is more than enough evidence presented here to prove that verses 17 through 20 were, and are, valid. This brings us back to our nagging question: Do you believe the Bible?

PARTIAL AND INCOMPLETE

Again, here is a simple spiritual law that should be self-evident to be truth. If anything is good, perfect, and glorifies God — then God did it!

Such non-apostles as Stephen, Philip, and Ananias, and such congregations as the ones in Galatia, Corinth, Philippi, and Jewish Christian congregations; all experienced and practiced the ministry of the Kingdom. Their Kingdom message included more than the proclamation of the forgiveness of sins. They also proclaimed and practiced the healing of sickness and the driving out of demons. Many passages in the Bible tell us about ordinary Christians who cast out demons, spoke in new tongues, and laid hands on the sick.

We, like the disciples, stumble if we do not do likewise, even if we misuse and abuse and prove ourselves to be the imperfect, stumbling, bumbling saints that we are. Jesus brought His Kingdom into the messiness of the world, knowing that his Holy Word would be misused and abused, as would the precious gifts of His Spirit.

But, back to the question: Do you believe the Bible?

Let's put it to the test. We will examine (or re-examine) three subjects that some modern Christians have attached a faith-shattering stigma to. As you read about these subjects, ask yourself, "Is this in the Bible?" And, "Do I believe the Bible concerning these stigmas?"

THE SNAKE STIGMA

Now let's read this part of verses 17 and 18 again:

> These signs will follow those who believe. . . . they will take up serpents . . . . (Mark 16 NKJV)

This passage, "They will take up serpents," has caused two controversies. At the suggestion of handling snakes, some (who say they believe in the infallibility of the Bible) have rejected the passage altogether. Another doctrinal group takes this passage as a literal commandment to handle rattle snakes in church. As a result, some have suffered snakebites and died. Needless to say, neither position is valid.

While the scholars (who don't know about Codex W yet) argue whether verses 17 and 18 were penned by Mark and whether they were inspired or not, we can go to other Bible verses (as the Nelson commentary points out) to confirm the same message.

Now, before making a careful study of verse 18, let's read it one more time. It says, "They will take up serpents . . ." The Greek verb, *airo*, "take up," means, "to seize, bear away, cast out," in the sense of removing violently. Keep in mind that Paul did not pick up that snake on Patmos Island. The snake attached itself to Paul and he violently cast it off into the campfire (see Acts 28:1-6).

John the Baptist used the same word, ***ario***, in introducing Jesus. *"Behold! The Lamb of God who takes away the sin of the world!"* (John 1:29). Jesus never touches sin; He casts out . . . He takes away sin . . . violently.

The verse that says, *"They will take up serpents,"* is a parallel to *"I give you authority to trample on serpents . . ."* (Luke 10:19). Jesus spoke these two parables to teach Christians how to "trample" and "snatch away" demonic power using the authority of Jesus' name (see Mark 9:38).

Is this a solidly scriptural teaching?

Do you believe the Bible?

THE TONGUES STIGMA

The day of Pentecost in Acts 2 marked the glorious beginning of the Church (see Matt. 16:18). Then, in Acts 10 and 11, we see another major event that is sometimes called "the Gentile Pentecost."

In both events we see a group of people gathered together to hear from God. And in both events, the Holy Spirit fell upon all that were present, and they spoke in tongues.

> 44. While Peter was still speaking these words, the Holy Spirit fell upon all those who were listening to the message.
> 45. And all the circumcised believers who had come with Peter were amazed, because the gift of the Holy Spirit had been poured out upon the Gentiles also.
> 46. For they were hearing them speaking with tongues and exalting God. (Acts 10)

In Acts 2, the Jews ran out into the street and in Acts 10, the Gentiles stayed in the room. In Acts 2, the Jews spoke in the languages of the crowd on the street, and in Acts 10 we are not told what language they spoke.

Now, let me show you in Acts 19:2 where Paul asked some disciples in Corinth, "Did you receive the Holy Spirit when you believed?"

If the gift of the Spirit and tongues are given at the time of believing, why did Paul ask them a redundant question?

However, that aside, *"when Paul had laid his hands upon them the Holy Spirit came on them, and they began speaking with tongues and prophesying"* (Acts 19:6). Again, we don't know what languages they spoke, and we do not know what they prophesied. Furthermore, there is no mention of interpretation of tongues.

Those who argue that tongues are for *the exclusive purpose* of evangelizing run into a real problem. Here is why Acts 2 makes a weak argument for them. Acts 2:11 says, *"We hear them in our own tongues speaking of the mighty deeds of God."* Speaking of *"the mighty deeds of God"* is witnessing, and not necessarily evangelizing. It was Peter who evangelized when he began to preach his famous message recorded in Acts 2:14-36. In all the other instances recorded in Acts, everyone present was already saved, and no one preached after tongues were spoken, and no one heard of the mighty deeds of God in tongues. Tongues are for a sign.

Here is another problem. Paul said in 1 Cor. 13:1, ". . . I speak with the tongues of men and of angels . . . ."

What is angel language? If Paul had only said he spoke in the language of angels, we could point out that the word "angels" could (and often did) mean "men." But since he mentioned *both* men *and* angels in the *same* sentence, it would be ridiculous to conclude that Paul actually said, "I speak in the language of men and men."

If tongues are for evangelism only, then does that mean we are to evangelize angels?

> 14. For if I pray in a tongue, my spirit prays, but my mind is unfruitful.
> 15. What is the outcome then? I shall pray with the spirit and I shall pray with the mind also; I shall sing with the spirit and I shall sing with the mind also. (1 Corinthians 14)

If you will read 1 Corinthians 14:14-21, it will be clear to you that praying and singing in tongues helps us give praise to God and to allow the Holy Spirit to intercede for us, because in some difficult situations we don't know how to pray (Rom. 8:26-27).

The point is: 1 Corinthians 14 makes it clear that the use of tongues is not always for the purpose of evangelizing!

Those who make this "evangelism" argument are trying their very best to discourage the use of tongues. They pay lip service to tongues because they can't deny that tongues are Scriptural. They assure us that there is a proper place for tongues, but they never seem to find that place. And if they did, many churches would ask them to leave. It is an enigma . . . a stigma.

Surely it is time to admit that tongues are valid for today, and rather than deny or ignore tongues any longer, we must now hear God's call to incorporate this Spiritual gift into our churches. I am sure that incorporating tongues into the traditions and style of worship of all the different doctrinal groups will result in a lot of diversity, but that is only to be expected.

THE ISAIAH 28:11-12 SIGN

There is another peculiar objection to tongues. The proof text this argument uses is found in 1 Corinthians 14:21 where Paul quotes Isaiah 28:11-12 (which is very similar to a passage in Deut. 28 and Jer. 25).

> In the law it is written, "By MEN OF STRANGE TONGUES AND BY THE LIPS OF STRANGERS I WILL SPEAK TO THIS PEOPLE, AND EVEN SO THEY WILL NOT LISTEN TO ME," says the Lord. (1 Corinthians 14:21)

The Ryrie commentary on this verse says: "Tongues were given as a sign to provoke the Jews to consider the truth of the Christian message." That is an excellent explanation, but not all explanations are so valid.

For instance, there is the teaching that tongues were for a sign, or prophecy, to Jews only; and that tongues ceased to exist in A.D. 70 when this Isaiah 28:11-12 prophecy was fulfilled and Judea ceased to be a nation. Since Mark dated his last entry in his Gospel in the year A.D. 72, that really discredits the A.D. 70 theory. Besides, it should be pointed out that in Acts 10 it was the Gentile Romans who spoke in tongues, not the Jews. And if anyone gave an interpretation of those tongues, as 1 Cor. 14:27-28 requires, it is not mentioned.

At any rate, this teaching goes far beyond the context of what Paul was saying about tongues being a sign gift. And to this day most Jews still are not listening to what God is telling them about their Messiah.

Before we get too harsh with these dear brethren we need to ask ourselves, "Do *I* believe the Bible?" As John Maxwell points out, we Christians are just sure we do, and are shocked to discover that there are some Bible verses we wish were **NOT** in there. What verses do you and I stumble over?

Since it is a fact that these verses are often left out of the discussion on tongues, one has to ask, "Why?"

THE EXORCISM STIGMA

And as you go, preach, saying, the kingdom of heaven is at hand. Heal the sick, raise the dead, cleanse the lepers, cast out demons; freely you received, freely give. (Matthew 10:7,8)

You believe that God is one. You do well; the demons also believe, and shudder. (James 2:18)

When the seventy-two followers returned, they were excited and said, Lord, even the demons obeyed when we spoke in your name! Jesus told them . . . I have given you power to. . . defeat the power of your enemy Satan. Nothing can harm you. (Luke 10:17, 19 The Promise)

13. Some of the Jewish exorcists, who went from place to place, attempted to name over those who had the evil spirits the name of the Lord Jesus, saying, "I adjure you by Jesus whom Paul preaches."
14. And seven sons of one Sceva, a Jewish chief priest, were doing this.
15. And the evil spirit answered and said to them, "I recognize Jesus, and I know about Paul, but who are you?"
16. And the man, in whom was the evil spirit, leaped on them and overpowered them, so that they fled out of that house naked and wounded. (Acts 19)

Notice that the evil spirit manifested itself and spoke to these seven foolish brothers (Acts 19). And notice that the seventy-two cast out demons in Jesus name (Luke 10).

What difference was there between the seven and the seventy-two? As believers, the seventy-two had the authority to invoke the power in Jesus' name to defeat the power of Satan and cast out demons without suffering harm. The seven got beat up for using Jesus' name as sort of a magical charm. Exorcism is dangerous unless the exorcist is anointed by the Holy Spirit and is genuinely dealing with real demonic powers.

Although exorcism is solidly scriptural, few practice it today because we are too sophisticated to believe in the boogieman anymore. Besides, we prefer psychology to exorcism. Yet, there is no Scripture that in any way hints the demonic world became silent and harmless.

DEMONIC CESSATIONISM

This may be an oxymoron question, but did the demons leave planet earth (close shop, or diminish their activity) when the last apostle died? Here is what Paul said about the spiritual forces of wickedness and how we can stand firm against them:

> Put on the full armor of God, that you may be able to stand firm against the schemes of the devil. For our struggle is not against flesh and blood, but against the rulers, against the powers, against the world forces of this darkness, against the spiritual forces of wickedness in the heavenly. (Ephesians 6:11-12)

We all have heard numerous sermons and Sunday school lessons on what it means to **"put on the full armor of God, that you may be able to stand against the schemes of the devil."**

In the Spirit world, nothing has changed since before the Garden of Eden; but there will be a big change when Jesus comes again. Yet, some cessationists believe that the demons — as well as God — do not manifest themselves (i.e., speak or intervene) in the affairs of sophisticated, modern man. In short, some Christians do not believe in the supernatural. Yet, whatever the Spirit world was in the Garden of Eden, it still is. And whatever Satan's B.C. agenda was, it still is in the

A.D. And since demons are still in our midst, we still need power to overcome them.

It seems to me that we would not have authority to defeat the power of demons in Jesus' name today, and we would not need the full armor of God — **IF** — the cessationist view were valid. But the demons are still with us, are they not? Therefore, we still need an offensive weapon against them.

Or, are we now at their mercy?

God forbid!

THE RESTORATION MESSAGE

Jesus Christ has not changed. God has not replaced Christ's gospel of the kingdom of heaven with impotent religion; both Christ and the Holy Spirit are with us, *"even to the end of the age"* (Matt 28:20). We should expect ever-increasing power to companion the church, and the gospel of heaven to be proclaimed with miracles worldwide, *"and then the end shall come"* (Matt 24:14).

The last days message shall be manifested in Christ's followers with all the power and authority that was embodied in Jesus Himself (John 14; Eph 4). No longer will Christians be identified merely as people going to heaven, but as people actually coming from heaven with the power and character of heaven, to herald the king of heaven and His return to earth.

> **Dear brethren, the first century text is still the last century text (Heb. 1:1-2). Nothing has been added to, or taken away (Rev. 22:18-19). Let us walk in this divine truth. And may we truly believe the Bible. ◊**

QUOTES FROM CHAPTER 12

Somehow it gets overlooked that "the fruit of the Spirit" is in fact "the fruit of the Holy Ghost"; and that this "fruit" is as much a "gift" (a manifestation) of the Holy Spirit as "the gifts of the Spirit" are.

True Christians — true prophets, preachers, and Sunday school teachers — miss God once in awhile! Sometimes they make mistakes, and even sin! But they are true because they repent, they confess their faults before the brethren, and they go on manifesting the fruit of the Holy Spirit. The "true" manifest the fruit of the Spirit. The "false" do not — period.

Chapter 12

Not False... Just Fallible

The idea that God expects perfection from us is unscriptural. God always provides for us what He expects from us (see Gen. 22:8-14). He is not expecting instant maturity, but He does expect us to grow into maturity. God wants us to eventually walk in all of His fullness, but this will only come as we are rooted and grounded in His love.

No one questions whether or not we are allowed to stone a person for breaking a Mosaic law today — we know we can't. Yet, we effectively stone Christians today with disfellowship and defamation for actions and teaching that we pronounce to be false and unbiblical. Jesus said, *"He who is without sin among you, let him be the first to throw a stone [at the law breaker]"* (John 8:7). Of course, we must preach and practice sound doctrine to the best of our ability — however limited. After all, when we think we are fighting heresy, *sometimes* we are actually resisting the Holy Spirit.

> **For Paul, it took a Damascus road experience to show him the difference between fighting heresy and resisting the Holy Spirit.**
>
> **Brethren, it is not our job to be heresy hunters or to disfellowship Christians (by our own definition) because we consider them to be in error. Soon enough we all will stand before the Judgment seat and answer for our own heresy and error.**

Jesus said we are to love, accept, and prefer one another, even as God loves His Son and He loves us.

How desperately we need each other! How desperately we need our Lord and Savior!

THE REAL EXTREMIST

What hindrances will come against the next great harvest of souls?

Some of the major hindrances are things we consider to be an integral part of acceptable, contemporary Christianity in the Western Hemisphere. Words such as "tradition" or "mind-set" come to mind. When it seems that everybody does "it," whatever "it" is, then "it" is considered the norm, something the majority is comfortable with.

Surely no Christian would knowingly hinder God from initiating a new and great move — like He has many times in the past.

In every great revival there were those who carried the newly discovered truth of that movement to extremes. Others, because of the extremes, rejected these newly discovered truths altogether. *Both groups missed God.* Those who carry truth to extremes are *usually* corrected (over the years) and learn valuable lessons from their mistakes.

The sad thing is those who are the most fearful of error are often the most difficult to lead into the light, and usually spend their lives in a dry, dreary place.

There is an inherent danger in our attempts to make walking with God safer than He has made it. If we become overly focused on the extremes and mistakes of a small minority in order to establish safety for others, we will formulate teachings that cause people to become eccentric or off-centered.

Those who consistently sit under teachings designed to correct extremes will eventually become extreme themselves — extremely cautious and fearful of mistakes. This perspective is exactly opposite to the faith required to walk with God.

There will always be mistakes. Even the greatest leaders in the early church made mistakes, including those who walked with Jesus during His earthly ministry. As long as God works through fallen men, we will witness mistakes and errors. If we lose sight of this and become reactionary in our teachings, we make the biggest mistake of all by creating stumbling blocks that hinder us from God's provision.

WE ALSO NEED THE GIFTS OF THE SPIRIT

While we must not overreact to mistakes, we cannot ignore them either. We must learn from them and grow into maturity. Nevertheless, we need to be careful that the fear of mistakes does not cause us to propagate teachings that appear to be balanced, yet are contrary to what the Bible teaches. For instance the myth that says: "We don't need the gifts of the Spirit, just the fruit."[1]

Although this concept sounds wonderfully balanced, it is biblically inaccurate. We will not see our society changed without all of the gifts of the Spirit operative in the church.

It is supreme arrogance to imply that we do not need God's spiritual gifts. If we limit any of the gifts or ministries, we are rejecting that particular aspect of Christ.

The dove is not only a symbol of the Holy Spirit; it is a symbol of the balance found in the fruit and gifts of the Holy Spirit. The dove has nine flight feathers in each wing and is perfectly balanced for flight. In that same pattern, there are the nine gifts of the Spirit and nine fruit of the Spirit. As the dove needs an equal number of feathers in each wing for flight, so the church needs the full quota of the Spirit's gifts and fruit for successful ministry. These are God's provision for unhindered flight.

We need everything God has provided for us. If we are going to be ***all*** that we are called to be, we must open our hearts to ***all*** of Him.

123

This teaching was probably born in reaction to a few people who were interested in having the power of God to the exclusion of His character. Although seeking God's power without also pursuing His character is an error; we should not attempt to correct it by misstating the significance of spiritual gifts. By attempting to correct one error, we may create another that is even more destructive.

Related to the first myth is the idea that we should only seek God, not spiritual gifts. While this makes for a pithy sermon title, it is also a biblically inaccurate concept. Of course, we need to seek God. However, we should hunger for spiritual gifts as well. We are actually rejecting God himself when we reject His spiritual gifts — a spiritual manifestation of God Himself in our midst.

> **While we may judge those who hunger for God's power and authority as being extreme and unbalanced, God may be more pleased with them than with those who appear humanly righteous, but who are saying "No thank you" to His provision. Rejecting anything that is of God is extreme and unbalanced, is it not?**

Another myth states that asking for spiritual gifts opens us to demonic deception. Some leaders assert that a person who is seeking the Lord for a vision, dream, or revelation can inadvertently receive a *demonic* revelation. This teaching has effectively stopped multitudes from asking God for spiritual gifts.

Although many may not be able to imagine this being taught from pulpits, it has been an accepted teaching in some circles for years. Not only is there no scriptural basis for this concept, it is a direct contradiction to Jesus' teaching in the Gospels.

> 5. Suppose one of you shall have a friend, and shall go to him at midnight, and say to him, "Friend, lend me three loaves;
>
> 6. For a friend of mine has come to me from a journey, and I have nothing to set before him,"
>
> 7. And from inside he shall answer and say, "Do not bother me; the door has already been shut and my children and I are in bed; I cannot get up and give you anything."

8. I tell you, even though he will not get up and give him anything because he is his friend, yet because of his persistence he will get up and give him as much as he needs.

9. And I say to you, ask, and it shall be given to you; seek, and you shall find; knock, and it shall be opened to you.

10. For everyone who asks, receives; and he who seeks, finds; and to him who knocks, it shall be opened.

11. Now suppose one of you fathers is asked by his son for a fish; he will not give him a snake instead of a fish, will he?

12. Or if he is asked for an egg, he will not give him a scorpion, will he?

13. If ye then, being evil, know how to give good gifts to your children: how much more shall your heavenly Father give the Holy Spirit to them that ask Him? (Luke 11:5-13)

31. But covet earnestly the best gifts: and yet show I into you a more excellent way. (1 Corinthians 12 KJV)

Even though the Corinthians exercise of spiritual gifts had already created a chaotic situation, Paul nevertheless urges the Corinthians to "earnestly covet" spiritual gifts! The same Greek word translated *earnestly covet* could also be rendered as *zealously lust after*.

Why would God implore us to hunger for, and even "lust after" spiritual gifts, and then allow us to receive something demonic instead?

The answer is that He is the perfect Father and would never do such a thing! We are encouraged to seek, from Him, the supernatural ability to minister to those His Son died for.

A major problem in the church today is unbelief in the supernatural. In other words, *human reason* has replaced *spiritual gifts* in some Christian circles. We need to be freed from our humanistic thinking and teachings, so we can be yoked with the Lord in fruitful ministry.

BALAAM AND SELF DECEPTION

Rather than insert Numbers 22:1-23 here, I will assume that you are familiar with Balaam. The life of Balaam provides amazing insight into the terrible dangers of deception accompanying idolatry. His life also trumpets a stern warning of how even someone who is gifted prophetically can become deceived in their guidance from God.

This takes us back to the fruit of the Spirit. Balaam was not operating in the fruit of the Spirit . . . or right motives. Therefore, he set himself up for error when seeking to operate in the gifts of the Spirit. When we are not operating in the fruit of the Spirit, we have no business trying to minister in any capacity, whether we believe in the gifts of the Spirit or not.

> Self-deception comes when we do not operate in the fruit of the Spirit. The truth is that God never works with our "flesh," or old nature — that's how depraved it is. That is why we never stop needing the power of the Holy Spirit during our entire pilgrimage here on earth. We never reach a place where we can live victoriously apart from His daily grace in our lives. Only the Spirit can produce His fruit — in and through us — that makes us the people God wants us to be. And God has to show us regularly how needy we are.

> Somehow it gets overlooked that "the fruit of the Spirit" is in fact "the fruit of the Holy Ghost"; and that this "fruit" is as much a "gift" (a manifestation) of the Holy Spirit as "the gifts of the Spirit" are.

KNOWING THE FALSE BY THEIR FRUIT

> Beware of the false prophets, who come to you in sheep's clothing, but inwardly are ravenous wolves. You will know them by their fruits. Grapes are not gathered from thorn bushes, nor figs from thistles, are they? (Matthew 7:15 NASB)

Today, we might say it is Scriptural to judge a person by their fruit-ability rather than by their fallibility. Does the person in question manifest holiness, meekness, humility, and commitment to Christ in their everyday life? The true do! The false don't! Period! That is the message of 1 Corinthians 13 in a nutshell.

Galatians 5:16-26 through 6:1-5 and 1 Corinthians 13 is important to our subject, and I encourage you to read these passages in their entirety before continuing. However, here are some brief excerpts from these passages

> But the fruit of the Spirit is love, joy, peace, patience, kindness, goodness, faithfulness, gentleness, and self-control; against such things there is no law. (Galatians 5:22-23)

> Love is patient, love is kind, and is not jealous; love does not brag and is not arrogant, does not act unbecomingly: it does not seek its own, is not provoked, does not take into account a wrong suffered. (1 Corinthians 13:4-5)

> But now abide faith, hope, and love, these three; but the greatest of these is love. (1 Corinthians 13:13)

Agape love is the summation of — and the greatest of — the fruit of the Spirit. The major theme of this chapter is that love (one of the nine fruits of the Spirit) is greater than all of the nine gifts of the Spirit (1 Cor. 12) because love is eternal and a virtue of God; whereas the gifts and offices (Eph. 4:11) are incomplete and temporary.

The gifts of the Spirit are **"a noisy gong or a clanging cymbal"** unless the fruit of the Spirit is being manifested simultaneously (1 Cor. 13:1). Furthermore, the gifts of the Spirit are needed only until we see Jesus face to face, whether at death or at His Second Coming. In the meantime, we can spot the false by their fruit.

IDENTIFYING THE REAL FALSE BRETHREN

Modern Pharisees perceive those who have deviated from their interpretation of doctrines as enemies, false teachers, and false prophets.

However, the apostle Paul's interpretation of who the real false brethren are is quite different from what is now popularly accepted.

Paul warned against *"false brethren who had sneaked in to spy out our liberty, which we have in Christ Jesus, in order to bring us into bondage"* (Gal. 2:4).

> **Those who use fear and intimidation to control others and force them to conform to their beliefs should more often be categorized as false teachers than those they so vehemently attack.**

We don't have to be as fragmentary, incomplete, and imperfect as we are. If we are as sincere and committed as we say we are about desiring a great new move of God, we will do whatever God requires of us to accomplish it. That will include repentance for everything we are doing to obstruct His will.

We are not disciplined enough in prayer and fasting, in giving time for our insights to mature, in allowing mature and gifted believers to judge these insights, and in being dead to self.

We may never become sinless, but we can become more repentant, more humble, and more obedient. The accuracy and quality of the spiritual insights that God's Spirit gives us will improve as more understanding, maturity, and anointing comes.

DESPISE NOT PROPHESYINGS

Despise not prophesyings. Prove all things; hold fast that which is good. (1 Thessalonians 5:20)

To *"despise not prophesyings"* is a direct command. But the words that follow, "Hold fast that which is good," clearly imply that there will be some "prophesyings" that will not be good, and should therefore not be held fast.

That is why Paul taught that all prophetic and revelatory utterances are to be judged and tested (1 Cor. 14:29, 1 Thess. 5:19-22). We are not to despise the gift, or its operations; we are to recognize and accept the imperfect vessels through which God chooses to administer His spiritual gifts — born-again Christians!

Every moral decision, every supposed manifestation of the Spirit, every sermon by a preacher — no matter how clever or charismatic

— is to be judged by God's Word. That is what should shape our theology and practice, rather than religious traditions or secular philosophy.

THE FORGOTTEN STANDARD

Jim Cymbala, pastor of the Brooklyn Tabernacle, said this about tradition in his book, *Fresh Faith*.[2]

> I am repeatedly amazed as I travel across the country and meet Christians who do not use the Bible as their guide and goal in pursuing spiritual things. Instead, people merely follow the particular spiritual culture into which they are born, never carefully comparing it to the biblical model. In fact, many devote themselves to perpetuating their way of doing things as if they had found it in Scripture itself. Their faith is stale because they are relying on something other than the living God who reveals Himself to us through the Bible.
>
> To give an analogy: I was born in a Brooklyn hospital to a Polish mother and a Ukrainian father. I did not ask to have Eastern European parents; I did not ask to be white. That was simply the accident of my birth. To make a big thing about my color or ethnic background is senseless; it just happened to be the way I providentially came into this world. When people get all puffed up about these things, it is really an extension of their own ego. If they had been born a different color or raised in a different country, they would be boasting about that instead.
>
> The same is true about the circumstances of our spiritual birth. The church or denomination where we started out just happened to be where we found ourselves at the time of receiving God's salvation. And as in our natural birth, our initial surroundings gave far-reaching shape to our understanding of things. Our first church atmosphere, with its pastors and teachers, automatically set the definitions for many key words such as prayer, worship, church, evangelism, God's power, faith, even the word Christian itself.

We didn't first learn those concepts so much from the Scripture as from what we saw around us at church. We unconsciously absorbed a Presbyterian or Baptist or Nazarene or Pentecostal understanding of those important words.

Today those impressions still leap to the forefront of our minds every time we hear the words — whether they are what God intended or not. Thus, instead of coming to the Scriptures like a child, saying, 'God, teach me,' we go looking for ammunition to back up what we've already embraced. Too often, our main goal is to perpetuate the traditions handed down from our elders. We're not really that open to change and growth.

The little church where my parents took me as a boy had some very good qualities to it — but it was also an all-white, mostly Eastern European group in the middle of Bedford-Stuyvesant, one of the best-known black neighborhoods in America! And the church members clearly wanted the church to stay the way it was. They did not seem at all interested in welcoming people who were 'different.'

Even though I learned many truths from the Bible there, should I now spend my life trying to replicate that tradition just because it's the place where I started out learning about Jesus? When I stand before God, I will not be asked, 'Were you a good Evangelical?' nor 'Were you a good Charismatic?' In fact, God doesn't recognize our divisions. His calling is for us to be Christ like rather than a good member of some man-made denomination.

What will really matter is whether we honestly search God's Word and let it shape our spiritual thinking and values. This is one of the great battles in the Christian life: to approach the Bible without presuppositions, letting it shape us instead of vice versa.

I love what the great John Wesley, catalyst of the Methodist awakening, said in the 1700s: 'Would to God that all party names, and unscriptural phrases and forms which have divided the Christian world, were forgot . . . I should rejoice . . . if the very name [Methodist] might never be mentioned more, but be buried in eternal oblivion.'[2a] A century later, the equally great Charles Spurgeon, prince of Baptist preachers, said from the pulpit, 'I say of the Baptist name, let it perish, but let Christ's name last forever. I look forward with pleasure to the day when there will not be a Baptist living.'[2b]

This kind of talk may burst a few bubbles, but here is the truth: Neither your personal background nor mine is the norm! What the Bible teaches is what we should pursue. Whenever any of us encounter something new or different, we should not ask, "Am I used to that when I go to church?" but rather "Do I find this in the Bible?"[3]

DISCERNING FALSE TEACHERS

Let not many of you become teachers, my brethren, knowing that as such we shall incur a stricter judgment. For we all stumble in many ways. If anyone does not stumble in what he says, he is a perfect man, able to bridle the whole body as well. (James 3:1-2)

But false prophets also arose among the people, just as there will also be false teachers among you, who will secretly introduce destructive heresies, even denying the Master who bought them, bringing swift destruction upon themselves. (2 Peter 2:1)

Several Scriptures, such as 2 Peter 2:1, indicate that the major characteristic of a false prophet is that they promotes false teachings, or false doctrines.

Peter places false forthtelling on an equal par with false foretelling. "Foretelling" means to describe future events, and "forthtelling" is the exposing of sins, and giving instruction and encouragement (1 Cor. 14:31). Therefore, false prophets can fall under the same category as false pastors, evangelists, teachers, and apostles. Here are five symptoms:

1. They are out of God's will for their lives.
2. They teach contrary to that taught by Jesus and His Apostles.
3. They are self-centered, not Christ- centered.
4. They are self-seeking, self-promoting, and self-preserving.
5. They do not manifest the fruit of the Spirit . . . a prerequisite to ministry . . . the message of 1 Corinthians 13.

Actually, I only consider someone a false teacher when they teach doctrine that violates or contradicts the basic doctrines of the faith, such as the Cross, which is necessary for salvation.

So long as there is humility and fruit of the Spirit in a teacher, his false teachings do not necessarily make him a false teacher. After all, we all are guilty of that to some degree.

As I often point out, we all are in error about something. But there are false teachers that we must be aware of and shun. False teachers cause a falling away.

Perhaps you have been embarrassed by what you would describe as "the foolishness of the Pentecostal, the Charismatics, and the full gospel churches." But they all have known the power of God! And it is easy to understand why many would shy away from the gifts of the Spirit and the prophetic movement. But this too, is one of the tests that separate the true believers from those who just know creeds or doctrines.

WHAT ARE WE TO DO

God has called the foolish things of the world to confound the wise. *Only* the humble will flow in what God is doing, and He will *only* give His grace to them.

Denying that there are true prophets today will not change God's mind about His prophets, or the prophet's mind about his or her calling.

> True Christians — true prophets, preachers, and Sunday school teachers — miss God once in awhile! Sometimes they make mistakes, and even sin! But they are true because they repent, they confess their faults before the brethren, and they go on manifesting the fruit of the Holy Spirit. The "true" manifest the fruit of the Spirit. The "false" do not — period.

> Brethren, even if a man is caught in any trespass, you who are spiritual, restore such a one in a spirit of gentleness; looking to yourselves, lest you too be tempted. (Galatians 6:1)

Some fallible humans are called of God to be pastors. Others are equally called to be prophets, evangelists, etc. Can we fallible Christians forgive and restore our fallible pastor who repented after God showed him that he had been teaching a false doctrine for twenty years? This question arises . . .

Are we to shoot our wounded prophets, preachers, and Sunday school teachers? Brethren, we all have sinned and fall short of the glory of God! We all are in error and deserve death. If we are to shoot the wounded, are we saying that we should shoot ourselves? ♦

THE LAW OF FIRST EXPOSURE

Dr. Neighbor teaches (in his book: ***The Seven Last Words of the Church: We've Never Done it That Way Before***) that our enslavement to tradition can cause us to miss out on the present leading of the Holy Spirit.

An alternate and related expression of "enslavement to tradition" is "the law of first exposure." Larry Gilbert, President of Church Grown Institute in Lynchburg, Virginia, defines the law of first exposure this way: "The first exposure a person has to a principle or teaching is the one which dominates his beliefs about that principle or teaching regardless of what he is taught or how much he is taught thereafter."

In the end, we conserve only what we love. We will love only what we understand. We will understand only what we are taught."

— Unknown

An old joke I heard years ago says: some people's minds are like concrete, thoroughly mixed up and permanently set.

Despite these discouraging words, my own testimony is; God had miraculously changed my mind several times — radically — and He will probably do it again. If God can bring that much radical change into my life, He can change anyone. There is hope for us all.

Chapter 13

Peter's Definition of "The Last Days"

There is one single Scripture that tells us very literally *the time* when God would pour out His Holy Spirit, and *the time* when signs and wonders will all culminate.

I am referring to that glorious and historic day of Pentecost when Peter preached his classic sermon recorded in Acts 2:17-21. Early that morning in Jerusalem, 120 Spirit-filled believers came pouring out of the upper room and into the street —seemingly drunk. Peter proclaimed: "This is what was spoken of through the prophet Joel" (from Joel 2:28-32):

> 17. "And it shall be in the last days," God says, "that I will pour forth of My Spirit upon all mankind; and your sons and your daughters shall prophesy, and your young men shall see visions, and your old men shall dream dreams;
>
> 18. "Even upon My bondslaves, both men and women, I will in those days pour forth of My Spirit and they shall prophesy.
>
> 19. "And I will grant wonders in the sky above, and signs on the earth beneath, blood, and fire, and vapor of smoke.

20. "The sun shall be turned into darkness, and the moon into blood, before the great and glorious day of the Lord shall come.

21. "And it shall be, that everyone who calls on the name of the Lord shall be saved."[1] (Acts 2)

We Evangelicals believe that we are living in **the last days**! But do we know when the last days started, and when they will end? Peter told us precisely **when** in his Pentecost sermon.

THE FIRST DAY OF THE LAST DAYS

Peter said: on **the first day** they would receive the indwelling of the Holy Spirit, with the evidence of spiritual gifts such as the visions and prophesy that Joel mentioned.

That *first* day, Peter said, was **the day of Pentecost**! As the Amplified Bible says, that was **"[the beginning of] what was spoken by the prophet Joel."** Then, in verse 19 and 20 Peter told us when **the last day** of the last days would be. That **last** day, Peter said, will be **the day of the Second Coming of Christ**. Otherwise, why didn't Peter just quote verses 17 and 18[2] and stop? To reiterate . . .

> Peter said that the first day of "the last days" started on the day of Pentecost, and the last day of "the last days" will take place on the day of the Second Advent of Christ. And on every day between the first and last day of "the last days," anyone who calls on the name of the Lord shall be saved. And — lest we forget — prophetic messages, visions, and dreams could potentially be poured out by God's Spirit during this whole 2,000-year period!

Again, Peter said: "The gifts of the Holy Spirit (outlined in 1 Corinthians 12) are to be poured out in **the last days**, and the last days **started** on the day of Pentecost, and will **end** on the day of the Second Coming. The Bible *clearly* says that the fulfillment of this prophecy of Joel's **started**, even as Peter was speaking it, on the day of Pentecost. Peter based his whole argument on that premise.[3]

We need to understand that Peter wasn't just preaching to those present on that day 2,000 years ago, but to us as well — according to Acts 2:38-39. He was an anointed oracle of God, a prophet, speaking the fulfillment and the revelation of a prophecy made by Joel 835 years earlier.

> And Peter said to them, "Repent, and let each of you be baptized in the name of Jesus Christ for the forgiveness of your sins; and you shall receive the gift of the Holy Spirit. For the promise is for you and your children, and for all who are far off, as many as the Lord our God shall call to Himself." (Acts 2:38-39)

THE APPARENT CONTRADICTION

Two things bothered me for a while. First, the crowd of foreigners watching this exuberant scene wondered if the upper room occupants were drunk (Acts 2:15). It struck me as a curious contrast with many sober-side pulpits of today that the first Christian sermon should begin with a stout denial by Peter that he and his 120 friends were drunk. But, since their intoxicating experience is scriptural, I got over being bothered.

Second, it bothered me that there is an apparent contradiction in this passage. Using the King James Version this time . . . Peter said, "***This is that*** which was spoken of by the prophet Joel." When Peter used the word "this" he obviously was referring to (and pointing at?) the 120 that were speaking in languages ***unknown*** to them (verse 6). However, the crowd of foreigners from several nations that gathered around (to see what the commotion was all about) heard the 120 speaking in their native language.

So, the "***this***" was the "other" tongues, and the "***that***" was Joel's prophecy (1 Cor. 13:1). Yet, Joel's prophecy does not mention tongues. And, worse yet, the 120 were not manifesting the prophecy, visions, or dreams that ***are*** listed in Joel's prophecy. Is this inconsistent or a contradiction?

Consider all the unlikely things happening here. Even though Isaiah 28:11-12 may be the exception . . . this was the first time in history that tongues were mentioned or manifested, yet Peter seemed to *suddenly* understand what was happening.

How could that be?

I believe the key phrase is in verse 17, "I will pour out my Spirit upon all flesh." By divine revelation the Holy Spirit caused Peter to understand what Jesus had said (in John 16:7 and Acts 1:6-8): *. . . the comforter will . . . come unto you . . . I will send him to you . . . on the day of Pentecost . . .*

HOW COULD PETER HAVE KNOWN?

We can all agree that the Holy Spirit inspired Peter, and by divine revelation he suddenly *knew — this is that —* spoken of by the Prophet Joel. Perhaps Peter experienced the word of knowledge[4] here (1 Cor. 12:8; Acts 2, verses 17 and 18 happened that morning — figuratively speaking). Then verses 19 and 20 (which sound like Matthew 24:29, 30)[5] tell of an event sometime in our future; but verse 21 (see Romans 10:13) is for *ALL* of the church age. Therefore, *in context*, Peter is saying that **all** of this passage is for the whole church age (the last days) from that day to this.

TIME TO RESTORE THIS TEACHING

Brethren, we are in the *same* "last days" that Peter was in. He saw them start, and our generation will (as taught by most Evangelicals) see the "last days" end. Isn't that exciting? Therefore, if we believe Peter, we can and should expect to see Christians prophesying, and having prophetic dreams and visions *today!* As further proof, Jesus commanded the apostles to:

> Go . . . and make disciples of all the nations . . . teaching them to observe all that I commanded you . . . . (Matthew 28:19, 20)

> **Here is what Jesus is saying to us in this verse: In every generation the whole church is to do everything that Jesus commanded the apostles to do.**

There is no biblical reason to exclude prophecy, prophetic dreams, or visions (or any other spiritual gift) from the "everything I have commanded you" in the Great Commission any more than we would exclude witnessing or prayer.

And, if that were not enough, Paul tells the whole church that:

> 9. Whatever you have learned or received or heard from me, or seen in me — put it into practice. (Philippians 4)

Part of that "whatever" is found in 1 Corinthians 12, 13, and 14.

Since Paul was writing to the parishioners at Philippi, common Christians like you and me, it cannot be argued that only apostles could practice the Pauline precedent.

Now is the time to restore this teaching and expect these experiences, because God has never changed!

> 3. How shall we escape if we neglect so great a salvation? After it was at the first spoken through the Lord, it was confirmed to us by those who heard,
> 4. God also bearing witness with them, both by signs and wonders and by various miracles and by the gifts of the Holy Spirit according to His own will. (Hebrews 2:3-4)

It is vital in this hour that God would give us a heart for *signs and wonders*. Hebrews 2:3-4 says God testifies to our great salvation by *signs, wonders, miracles and gifts of the Holy Spirit*. He gives us these signs to create a hunger in our hearts for Him. We need to go on with God, and He often uses the supernatural to rekindle our spiritual passion.[6]

LATTER RAINS

Listen carefully to what Robert Coleman (in his book, *The Coming World Revival*)[7] credits Billy Graham with saying on the "latter rains" and Joel 2:28.[8]

> Billy Graham in his last message at the Lausanne Congress in 1974 expressed succinctly both the realism and the hope we have in awaiting the climatic movement and the total fulfillment of what was done on the Cross.

139

Then, reflecting upon the future, Billy Graham added:

> I believe there are two strains in prophetic Scripture. One leads us to understand that as we approach the latter days and the Second Coming of Christ, things will become worse and worse. Joel speaks of 'multitudes, multitudes in the valley of decision.' He is speaking of judgment.
>
> But I believe as we approach the latter days and the coming of the Lord, it could be a time also of great revival. We cannot forget the possibility and the promise of revival, the refreshing of the latter days of the outpouring of the Spirit promised in Joel 2:28 and repeated in Acts 2:17. That will happen right up to the advent of the Lord Jesus Christ.
>
> Evil will grow worse, but God will be mightily at work at the same time. I am praying that we will see in the next months and years the 'latter rains,' a rain of blessings, showers falling from heaven upon all the continents before the coming of the Lord.
>
> — Billy Graham

IT'S JUST SCRIPTURAL

Some people will get nervous when Peter talks to us about prophecy and visions. It sounds so Pentecostal . . . so Charismatic. Yet, these doctrinal groups also practice water baptism by submersion, and the Lord's Supper the same way Southern Baptists do. That does not make them Baptists. But it does make them solidly scriptural.

That is how we are to look at prophecy and visions. They are scriptural. And they are as much for us today as water baptism and the Lord's Supper. ***"For the gifts and the calling of God are irrevocable"*** (Rom. 11:29 NKJV).

The question is not **IF** the spiritual gifts are Scriptural and revocable, but **SINCE** they are Scriptural and irrevocable, how are they to be defined and practiced today?

Perhaps they are now diminished and less frequent than their first century counterpart. Perhaps they are not. The Bible is silent on this issue. But, whether diminished or not, they are still valid for today.

That is a separate issue that needs to be studied by Evangelicals. However, we won't pursue it here.

Baptists do not have to adopt the traditions or theology of the Pentecostals and Charismatics, and vice-versa. One tradition is as good, bad, or indifferent as any other. This being true, we Baptists [Evangelicals] are free to allow the Holy Spirit to manifest His gifts in us — according to our own Baptist [Evangelical] style and traditions.

The bottom line is: All Christians are compelled to be (1) faithful to the Word of God, (2) obedient to the leading of the Holy Spirit, and (3) acceptant of these gifts experientially, even as the Holy Spirit chooses to manifest Himself through us. ♦

Kenneth Uptegrove

QUOTES FROM CHAPTER 14

The theme of this book can be summed up in this one statement: The purpose of all Christian ministries and the ministry of the Holy Spirit is to reveal and magnify Jesus Christ — that, and that alone. And the most wonderful miracle gift of all is still simple salvation. But God has given us many tools — as described in this book — to fulfill this great commission.

142

Chapter 14

Observing All The Lord Has Commanded

In Ephesians chapter four, the apostle Paul gives a clear outline for teaching disciples in every age, including ours, to observe all that the Lord has commanded. Paul assures us in verse seven that grace was given to each believer because of the ascension of Jesus. Specifically, this grace was Christ's gift that came in the form of five kinds of ministry.

Here is our Scripture reading.

> 7. . . .To each one of us grace was given according to the measure of Christ's gift.
>
> 11. And He (Jesus) gave some as apostles, and some as prophets, and some as evangelists, and some as pastors and teachers,
>
> 12. for the equipping of the saints for the work of service, to the building up of the body of Christ;
>
> 13. Until we all attain to the unity of the faith, and of the knowledge of the Son of God, to a mature man, to the measure of the stature which belongs to the fullness of Christ.

14. As a result, we are no longer to be children . . .
(Ephesians 4:7, 11-14)

Ephesians 4:11-13 reveals another unfulfilled prophecy. This passage tells us:

- **What** Jesus put in place — the five ministries
- **Why** He put it in place — equipping the saints
- **When** it will cease — the Second Coming

Jesus set the five ministries in place for the purpose of equipping the saints until the Second Coming. That makes this verse a prophecy and a commandment. Therefore, until this prophecy is fulfilled, these five ministries are still valid, are scriptural, and are still intended to function in the church today, just as it was in the first century church.

PURPOSE OF THE FIVE MINISTRIES

If *Christ's gift* — He being the consummate gift — is to *equip the saints* (vs. 12), is it not self evident that His gifts equip them through the work of these five ministries? And what is the purpose of the work of these five ministries if it is not for *the building up of the body of Christ* — the Church?

How long did Jesus give His apostles, prophets, evangelists, pastors, and teachers to equip the saints? Ephesians 4:13 tells us how long:

Until we all attain to these four goals:
1. **The unity of the faith**
2. **The knowledge of the Son of God**
3. **A mature man**
4. **The measure of the stature which belongs to the fullness of Christ**

How can we casually read this verse and not observe that the modern church has not aspired to even one of these four goals of the church? Since this sentence (in verses 11-13) is seventy-eight words long, we can assume that Paul thought it was of extreme importance and a mandate from Jesus Christ, our Lord. *"As a result, we are no longer to be children,"* but we are — obviously! Read verse 14 again. Two thousand years later and we are **WHAT**? Children!

In **the first goal**, the phrase "unity of the faith" (in Eph. 4:13) is usually interpreted to mean "all Christians will eventually be in the same doctrinal group." Sadly, to some Christians it is an unspoken assumption that this doctrinal group is obviously *their* doctrinal group; otherwise known as pure, presumptuous pride.

No matter what "unity of the faith" (Eph. 4:13) actually is, it would be difficult to argue that any significant measure of unity of the faith was ever achieved at any time in church history. I have devoted most of a chapter in this book to defining this term.

The second goal (Eph. 4:13) is "the knowledge of the Son of God." Not even once in the entirety of church history has this kind of knowledge existed in the body of Christ. The reason being is that this experience is reserved for the time of the Second Coming. At that time we will know Jesus as He is . . . **WHEN** we meet Him face to face (1 Cor. 13:12). This, again, tells us when these Ephesians 4:11 ministries will pass away.

"Knowledge of the Son of God," and **the third goal**, the state of being "a mature man," is an eschatological state.[1] Eschatology, again, is the study of the age immediately prior to the Second Coming.

This phrase, "a mature man," sounds like "When I became a man" in 1 Corinthians 13:11, which was discussed at length in the chapter: *When The Perfect Comes*.

The fourth goal is "the measure of the stature of the fullness of Christ." It is obvious that all in the church have not reached the same level of maturity as is evident in Christ. Therefore, "the end" is described in terms of ultimate spiritual growth of the believer into the absolute perfection that is found in Christ. The metaphor of a mature person is used to portray the resurrected body of believers (cf. 1 Cor. 13:10-12).[2]

> Plainly spoken, these four goals make it clear to us that these five-fold ministries will be in place until the Second Coming.

SPEAKING THE TRUTH IN LOVE

Jesus alone could perform all the five ministries needed for equipping the church because He was the consummate Apostle, Prophet, Evangelist, Pastor, and Teacher. When He ascended, He gave aspects of His ministry to many different persons.

Together, the intent of these five equipping ministries was to accomplish His purpose of causing disciples to grow up "in ALL aspects into Him."

If all of this is scriptural, then the church will never become all that Jesus required of it until all of these ministries function together. And, if we limit any of these gifts or ministries, we are limiting or rejecting that aspect of Christ.

Is it not this aspect of "Jesus in us" that will do the works that He did, and even greater, when He walked the earth? (John 14:12). If this is so, then it is logical to conclude that the Great Commission cannot be fulfilled until all of the equipping ministries are working together in obedience to Ephesians 4:11-16.

In other words, Jesus will not return physically until the church comes closer to reaching the spiritual maturity called for in these verses.

It was not God who diminished supernatural power and authority; it was religious men who substituted their authority for God's. The early church began in a place of light and regressed into the darkness of the Dark Ages due to *"the trickery of men, by craftiness in deceitful scheming."*

The last day church — starting with Martin Luther — is coming out of this darkness and progressing toward increasing light. It is my observation that this light — the light of the world — will increase until the fullness of day comes with the full revelation of Jesus (Matt. 5:14).

ALL FIVE MINISTRIES CEASED

The rules of logic say: If even one of these ministries were "temporary," then *all five* had to be temporary because all five are in context — in one sentence. Every translation that I am aware of lists all five of these ministries in one sentence. Conversely, if even one is valid, they all have to be valid.

If this rule does not apply here, it can't apply anywhere in Scripture and the Word of God would be in chaos.[3]

For instance, consider the fruit of the Spirit listed in Galatians 5:19-26. What can we leave out in this Scripture? Read it! You're in for a surprise.

> **Historically speaking, all five — not just two — of these Ephesians 4:11 ministries did, in fact, go out of use some time after canonization of the New Testament in A.D. 367, as indicated by the Didache.**

More about the Didache, an ancient apocrypha writing, will be shown in chapter 17.

In their place came priests, monks, friars, bishops, and — eventually — popes. In terribly persecuted non-Catholic Christian groups some ministry people were called barbs, Lollards, preachers, etc. Of course, many Christians over the centuries still functioned in the original five ministries whether or not they were recognized as pastors and prophets and so on.

In the Book of Acts we see the church elders ordaining (laying on hands and confirming) certain people as apostles and prophets. Therefore, the difference between the ministries in Ephesians 4:11 and the gifts in 1 Corinthians 12 is ordination. Pastors and evangelists are ordained, but those who occasionally manifest gifts of the Spirit are not.

Surprisingly, these ministries are being restored in the reverse order they went out. With Martin Luther (1520s), the pastor was finally restored after 1,200 years. With the Wesley brothers (1739), the evangelist was restored. With the Charismatics (1960s), the teacher was restored. I think we are seeing a reformation/restoration process that started with Martin Luther and will continue unabated until the Second Coming.

John Wesley was condemned by many church leaders of his time for the "unspeakable presumption" of referring to himself as an evangelist. Now some church leaders are saying the same thing about anyone who would be so presumptuous as to refer to him or herself as being a prophet. The restoration of every ministry to the church has come with a greater opposition from the church than it did from the world.

ARE PASTORS SCRIPTURAL?

The last few books of the New Testament seem to be unexplainably quiet about the Spiritual gifts (the ending in Mark being the exception). Interestingly, the Scriptures are also distressingly silent about all of the fivefold ministries (Eph. 4:11). For instance, the word "pastor" is used only once in the New Testament, and is actually the Greek word for "shepherd." So, in truth, the "pastor" is **NEVER** found in the original Greek. No matter how hard we try to justify using the word "pastor" we have — at best — a weak argument.

List the names of apostles, prophets, evangelists, pastors (shepherds), and teachers found in the New Testament and see how many of each you have. Specifically, how many pastors did you count?

And, most humiliating of all, 1 Corinthians 12, 13, and 14 never even mention pastors or evangelists, but go on at length about the other ministries.

Perhaps we can conclude that pastors never were numerous or important and had ceased to exist by that time.

Of course that is not so. One could make such an argument from silence, but as you know . . .

> **We cannot use what the Scriptures don't say as proof for some obscure doctrine.**

For example, the Bible does not tell us that Peter had children (although it does say he had a mother-in-law), but we're not justified in concluding from the Bible's silence on this point that Peter was childless. That is what is meant by an argument from silence.

Pastors (and all the other ministries and spiritual gifts) are therefore *assumed* to be present when the New Testament was being written.

RESTORATION OF THE EPHESIANS 4:11 MINISTRIES

Before jumping into this controversial subject, I would like to make this disclaimer: Although you may (or may not) have some trouble accepting the following discourse on Ephesians 4, I ask you to bear with me. As was said in the preface of this book, this discourse is but a mild prelude to the discussions and decisions that will soon confront us all in the not-too-distant-future.

Now is the time to rid ourselves of unbiblical understandings of the church based upon preference or past traditions. It is our duty to return to the mission of the New Testament church as stated by Jesus and recorded in Acts 1:8.

At the time of this writing we may not know how to define — with any finality — the issues touched on here; but I am confident that we will recognize God's apostles and prophets when the Holy Spirit reveals them to us in His own good time.

Please hear my heart. I am not trying to establish doctrine here, I'm trying to propose some ideas for your consideration, and I plead for openness to what the Holy Spirit may be doing in the church today. Most assuredly, this is the time for "reaching forward to what lies ahead."

We can never fulfill the Great Commission until we go *beyond* making converts. Our job is to transform converts into disciples who are taught to *observe all the Lord has commanded us*. Or, as Paul said: Jesus *"gave some as apostles, and some as prophets, and some as evangelists, and some as pastors and teachers, for the equipping of the saints for the work of service, to the building up of the body of Christ; until we all attain to the unity of the faith . . . ."*

Since we want to observe, *"All the Lord has commanded us,"* we are compelled to examine the coming ministry of the end-time apostle and prophet. We want to know what they will, or will not, be like.

Evidently, the ministry that began the church age will be the one to close it. I refer you to Revelation 18:20 where John said: *"Rejoice over her, O heaven, and you saints and apostles and prophets, because God has pronounced judgment for you against her"* (Rev 16:6; 18:24).

In context with the rest of chapters 4 through 18, does this verse belong in the time of the Second Coming, or in the first century?

Doesn't it make just as much sense to take verse 20 literally and in context as it does to separate the people from the event?

Those who project this event into the time of the Second Coming are correct. Where else could we put this judgment event? The trouble is, there are those who relegate the people (mentioned in verse 20) into the *first* century without a thought as to why they did it.

The reason can be explained with one word: tradition. When exegetical proof should be presented to support their belief they will, instead, give a plausible answer based upon their cessationist views. Since — according to this teaching — the apostolic and prophetic ministries ceased in the first century, these people (in Rev. 18:20) must be relegated to that century.

However, we settled the subject of "cessationism" in earlier chapters so we don't need to rehash that subject again. Except to say that it is impossible to be a *partial* cessationist, just as it is impossible for a woman to be *partially* pregnant. Either she is or she isn't.

Either all five of the Ephesians 4:11 ministries are valid, or Paul was in error. God does not allow us to edit the Bible, does He? (See Rev. 22:18-19.)

PURPOSE OF THE POWER GIFTS

Before we finish the subject of cessationism verses continuationism, this cautionary disclaimer needs to be made. We should not get the notion that because all these gifts are valid and for today, that miraculous manifestations of the Holy Spirit will happen every time we have a church service. They may or may not, but that is up to the Holy Spirit.

The four Gospels show us that it was not an everyday occurrence for Jesus, or the Apostles, or any other first century Christian to raise the dead, heal the sick, or deliver a prophecy to the church, or to a nation.

My observation is that the manifestations of the power gifts are the exception rather than the rule when the church meets. But that might change as the time of the Second Coming approaches.

Some refer to the more miraculous gifts, such as instant healings and the ministry of the apostle and prophet, as "the power gifts." I want to warn of the danger of centering our teaching and ministry on these wonderful gifts.

The theme of this book can be summed up in this one statement: The purpose of all Christian ministries and the ministry of the Holy Spirit is to reveal and magnify Jesus Christ — that, and that alone. And the most wonderful miracle gift of all is still simple salvation. But God has given us many tools — as described in this book — to fulfill this great commission.

APOSTLES OF A GREATER AND LESSER STATURE

There were "twelve Apostles of the Lamb" who had unique and special authority to lay the foundation of the Church, and whose writings are endorsed by the Holy Spirit to have the authority of canon Scripture. However, for the sake of clarity — since the New Testament reveals the names of twenty-three apostles — we should distinguish the "twelve Apostles of the Lamb" with a capital "A" and use the lower-case "a" for the others who held the apostolic office.

I do not believe that there will ever be any more capital "A" Apostles with that stature and authority. However, since Ephesians 4:13 demonstrates that God's ordination will remain on the office of apostle until the Second Coming, we can expect God to raise up some endtime, small "a" apostles. They, of course, will be of a lesser stature — like the apostles Barnabas and Apollos.

For most Christians it is a shock just to hear that there were more than 12 apostles. And to hear their names is really shocking. Apostle Barnabas! Apostle Apollos! Apostle James! Apostle Andronicus! Apostle Junia! Apostle Silvanus! Apostle Timotheus! Apostle Epaphroditus! See endnote 4 and get acquainted with these little known apostles of God.

UNNAMED OLD TESTAMENT PROPHETS

By a ratio of at least 100 to 1, there are a lot more unnamed prophets in the Old Testament than named. What's more, none of their prophecies are recorded. Have you ever wondered why? I believe they were on a par with the unnamed New Testament prophets whose prophecies also were not recorded.

Consider King Saul. The Bible says he prophesied right after he became the king. Yet none of this famous king's prophecies were ever recorded. It makes you wonder, why not? If they were false and fleshly, I think the Bible would have said so.

I suspect there is as much diversity in the prophetic ministry as there is among evangelists and pastors. Again, on a scale of one to ten, some pastors and evangelists are ones and some are tens, and everything in between. So, why would that not also be true of apostles and prophets?

As for Saul's prophecies, perhaps he was not actually a prophet. In 1 Samuel 10, where we are told about Saul's prophecies, the author does not tell us, he asks us: Is Saul a prophet?

Perhaps his prophecies can be compared to 1 Corinthians 12, 13, and 14 where the "gift of prophecy" is differentiated from the "prophetic ministry." Because Saul prophesied, that did not make him a prophet, and that would have to be true today as well.

I think that Samuel just wanted us to know that Saul was truly called and anointed when Samuel made him king, and his wonderful experience was manifested evidence of his calling (1 Sam. 10:5-12; 1 Kings 18:4-40).

PROPHETS OF A GREATER
AND LESSER STATURE

The only New Testament prophets, who might be capital "P" Prophets, were also the capital "A" Apostles who wrote Bible prophecies that are still unfulfilled to this day. This puts them on par with the Old Testament patriarchs who foretold future events.

Although nine prophets are mentioned by name in the New Testament, the only one we know anything about is Agabus. And he only had foreknowledge of relatively minor events that happened in his immediate future. Worse yet, he did not fully understand the vision God showed him concerning Paul being bound if he went to Jerusalem (Acts 11:28; 21; 10). [5]

Therefore, our only standard for a New Testament and modern day prophet is poor Agabus.

Therefore, the Deuteronomy 18:20-22 standard used to judge Old Testament prophets can only be applied to Apostles who penned yet unfulfilled New Testament prophecies.

If that is so, then the modern apostle and prophet (evangelist, pastor, and teacher) can miss God, have a prophecy fail, and still not be a false prophet.

As was stated in the chapter, *Not False — Just Fallible*, all Christians . . . *all* ministries are to be judged by their fruit . . . the fruit of the Spirit. Are they repentant when they miss God? Do they minister in the fruit of the Spirit? If they do, then they are true. If they don't, they are false.

Although the Bible tells us very little about New Testament prophets, evangelists, pastors and teachers, it should be self-evident that there was a lot more of them than we have imagined. It is amazing how we have come to define these ministries since Martin Luther initiated the return of the pastor, based on the sketchy description we have of this office in the Bible.

The possibility of there being a real, live apostle and prophet today is shocking to most of Christendom. However, if this ministry really is valid for today, what are the signs of a true apostle and prophet? How will we know them?

BUILDING ON THE FOUNDATION

19 . . . You . . . are of God's household,

20. having been built upon the foundation of the apostles and prophets, Christ Jesus Himself being the cornerstone,

21. in whom the whole building, being fitted together is growing into a holy temple in the Lord;

22. in whom you all are being built together into a dwelling of God in the Spirit. (Ephesians 2:19-22)

Paul speaks of Christ as the sole foundation of the church in 1 Corinthians 3:11, but in Ephesians 2:20, he then turns around and says God's household is built upon the foundation of the apostles and (New Testament) prophets.

Now! Which is the foundation? Christ? Alternatively, the apostles and prophets? As the old saying goes: Never mind what Paul said, what did he mean? Let's turn to Peter for a clue:

> You also, as living stones, are being built up as a spiritual house for a holy priesthood, to offer up spiritual sacrifices acceptable to God through Jesus Christ. (1 Peter 2:5)

It is widely accepted that this "whole building being fitted together" is possibly the "living stones," or "a spiritual house" that Peter described.

This is speculation on my part, but I suspect that Paul meant that a major function of apostles and prophets is to place "the living stones" in their rightful place in "a spiritual house, a holy temple."

The living stones are Christians, and Jesus is both the foundation and cornerstone. If apostles and prophets find these building stones incorrectly placed, they clear away what is essentially rubble and start over. They do this by bringing order in the arrangement of the stones upon the foundation — a restoration/reformation work.

Don't we see a lot of this in the book of Acts and the Epistles? Isn't this needed in churches today?

This so-called rubble would be people with flawed architectural ideas that result in a church being built off plumb line. If the first course of stones laid on the foundation is out of kilter, the whole building will be off, and will get further off as we build higher.

Some suggested examples of things that displace or dislodge Christian ministries are these: (1) Pharisaic traditions that are accepted without question as Canon, and (2) excessive church government, resulting in shortsighted, out-of-balance teachings.

All of these are primarily the work of non-visionary leaders who replaced the visionary founders of their doctrinal group.

One such visionary founder was Martin Luther. His message was the ancient and classic prophetic message: ***repent/reform and return/restore the Apostolic teachings.*** That is why Luther was called a reformationist/restorationist. Oh, how desperately we need some courageous restorationist/reformationists today!

We have no lack of preachers or prophecy, but we are pitiably short of prophetic preachers. There is now little scope left to foretell for we have the Book and the unveiling of the Lord's mind in it. But we need men to forthtell. The prophets are never expected, never announced, never introduced — they just arrive. They are sent, sealed, and sensational. John the Baptist did no miracle — that is, no rivers of derelict humanity swept down on him for his healing touch. But he raised a spiritually dead nation! Preachers make pulpits famous; prophets make prisons famous.

— Leonard Ravenhill

VISIONARIES, ORACLES, AND CHIEF ELDERS

Solomon said, *"where there is no vision, the people perish . . . .* Other translations say the people are *unrestrained"* (Prov. 29:18; see Ps. 74:9; 1 Sam. 3:1). Apostles and prophets are visionaries who bring life, but little order. Managers and administrators bring order, but not much life. Both are essential, but divine order necessitates managers under the direction of the visionary apostles and prophets.

Obviously, being an apostle or prophet requires more than vision. After all, we have always had visionaries.

If my theological speculation is accurate, the function of the modern apostles and prophets is to bring the saints together as a functioning local expression of the body of Christ. A correct foundation anticipates and promotes the multiple, *diverse* anointing of the Ephesians 4:11 equipping ministries and the Romans 12:6-8 serving ministries. Then each member can attain the place of service they have been called to in Christ.

Diversity is a characteristic of God, and is best demonstrated in His ordained marriage of a man and a woman — two becoming **ONE**. This same diversity is also seen in the five abrasively different ministries working together to prepare the **ONE** bride of Christ.

Now, if you will allow me to speculate just a little further, did you notice that the apostle and prophet both seemed to do the same thing: arrange stones? What is the division of service here?

155

I believe that the prophet is frequently more gifted as an oracle of God than the apostle is. An oracle is simply one who repeats verbatim what God tells them.

It stands to reason that the oracle/prophet informs the head elder apostle of what the Holy Spirit is indicating. The apostle then confirms the prophet's message — as the Holy Spirit prompts — and sets in place what is indicated, or he rejects the prophet's message and corrects him (1 Cor. 14:29). The chapter entitled; *Not False — Just Fallible* applies here.

THE SIGNS OF A TRUE APOSTLE

But how about signs, wonders, and miracles, and all that other supernatural stuff? What else is in the apostle's and prophet's credentials?

> The signs of a true apostle were performed among you with all perseverance, by signs and wonders and miracles. (2 Corinthians 12:12)

This passage occurs in the midst of Paul's defense of his apostolic office and ministry. In most of chapter 12, Paul is more inclined to boast of his weaknesses than in the great revelations he has received, because it is in his weaknesses that the power and grace of God is truly seen.

Some teachers use this passage as proof that miracle working is the evidence of apostleship. They would have us believe that miracle working was restricted to apostles only, or it would not prove that Paul was an apostle.

Other teachers have pointed out the problems with this view. For instance, if doing miracles had been the common experience of ordinary Christians, it would be foolish for Paul to cite miracles as proof of his apostleship.

We have to remember that Paul was addressing a group of Christians who accepted the apostolic ministry — no questions asked. Since there are those who are looking for ways *not* to recognize this ministry today, the following defense is necessary.

The term "signs" is not used in the same sense in the first part of the verse as it is in the second part. The first usage is to signs in a general sense. The second use refers specifically to miracles and wonders.

The "signs of the apostle" are probably the following: (1) the changed lives that resulted from Paul's preaching: (2) the transformed Christ-like life of the one who preaches the apostolic message; (3) his suffering, hardship, and persecution; (4) spiritual power in conflict with evil; (5) jealous care for the welfare of the churches; (6) true knowledge of Jesus and His gospel plan; (7) self-support; (8) not taking material advantage of churches; (9) being caught up into heaven; (10) contentment and faith to endure a thorn in the flesh; (11) gaining strength out of weakness; (12) a spiritual father who reproduces his ministry in others; and (13) being a witness of the Lord's resurrection.[6]

All of these apostolic signs were worked *"with all perseverance."* Finally, Paul's implied contrast is not with other Christians, but with false apostles who were disputing Paul's authority (2 Cor. 11:13-15, 33).

While the *"signs and wonders and miracles"* may be part of the *"signs of the apostle,"* in Paul's view it is not the predominant one. Therefore, this verse cannot be used to prove miracle working is unique to the apostles, or that it is something that distinguishes them from other Christians. However, this passage *may* imply that the apostles work miracles more consistently than others.

> **Clearly, the likelihood of finding any man on the scene today fulfilling all these thirteen criteria is small. However, there is no way to verify that all of the original apostles could live up to Paul's credentials.**

But, since the Scriptures tell us the names of 23 apostles, our generation is left with the task of defining this present day apostolic ministry. These "a" apostles certainly did not live up to these thirteen signs. But — again — they are not to be defined as "Apostles of the Lamb." Instead, we have the task of defining (and ordaining?) small "a" apostles, such as Barnabas and Apollos — when the time is right.

Also, it should be pointed out again that not all pastors and evangelists are equal, so why should we expect apostles and prophets to be equal.

If we were to demand that every evangelist be a Billy Graham, and every pastor a Bill Bright, we would be in a world of hurt, wouldn't we?

The question remains: How will we recognize these present-day apostles and prophets when God places them in our midst? Although the two authors[7] of "Empowered Evangelical" have treated this subject, I prefer to only present a case for the validity of these ministries for today. After that, I wish to support research, prayer, and discussion among evangelicals concerning this subject.

MISTAKES WILL BE MADE

Whatever mistakes are made in the process of reinstating the apostolic and prophetic office, they will not be as detrimental to God's end-time purposes as the mistake of rejecting what God has instituted. As long as God works through fallen men, we will witness mistakes and errors. Even the capital "A" Apostles made mistakes! If we lose sight of this and become reactionary in our teachings, we make the biggest mistake of all by creating stumbling blocks that hinder us from God's provision.

While we must not overreact to mistakes, we cannot ignore them either. We must learn from them and grow into maturity. Nevertheless, we need to be careful that the fear of mistakes does not cause us to propagate teachings that appear to be balanced, yet are contrary to what the Bible teaches.

Those Christians who resist the reformation and restoration movement going on in these last days will be motivated to find ways to use the titles without allowing the function. Since they can't invalidate the prophetic and apostolic ministries, they will try to diminish them and strip them of everything supernatural.

A good way to diminish them is to *"prove"* that an apostle is like the president of our denomination, and the prophet is like our present day evangelist. Even so, God will eventually end this controversy.

PROPHETS MAKE PEOPLE UNCOMFORTABLE!

What does a modern prophet do? What is his function in the Church and Kingdom of Jesus Christ? Some say they foretell. Others say they forthtell. I say, neither and both. In a word, prophets are oracles.

The prophets' primary calling and heart is to compel Christians to center on Christ, hearing His voice and being obedient to Him. The telling of future events is a secondary calling that — no matter how infrequent — is equally scriptural and valid. Notice that several Old Testament prophets only recorded one to six prophecies in their lifetime.

Prophets repeat verbatim what God tells them to tell us. Like Old Testament prophets, they may write the message down and then read it many places, or send it to be read. Then they were very apt to give a history lesson, as Stephen the evangelist did the day he was stoned to death, or as the apostles Peter and Paul did before the Sanhedrin (Acts 6-8).

Today a good way to get Christians mad at you is to tell them the truth about their own history as Stephen did. They will set out to silence you.

Israel silenced the heart's cry of many prophets under a pile of rocks. Stephen mentioned this in his history lesson, and Israel silenced him as well. Today the prophet's forthtelling is silenced by character assassination. He is very apt to lose financial support and his welcome.

Again, "foretelling" means to describe future events, and "forthtelling" is the exposing of sins, and giving instruction and encouragement (1 Cor. 14:31).

All of the Old Testament prophets exposed sin while, at the same time, they foretold the future. Therefore, we can safely assume that the first century prophets also exposed sin, even though we can't quote chapter and verse from the New Testament. We can come close enough by quoting Peter and Paul when they exposed the sins of the Sanhedrin. Who will deny that they were both apostles and prophets?

Although we usually think of Stephen as being an evangelist, on the day he was stoned he functioned primarily as a forthtelling prophet. Yes, the message was also evangelistic, but no less so than in Jeremiah's expose in Jeremiah 3, 4, and 27.

THE RENEWAL OF OLD WINE SKINS

This reformation/restoration message calls for expectation, not planning.

If we have a better concept of what God is about to do through the saints, our level of expectancy and faith will rise. We will know more accurately how to pray, how to teach, and how to conform to the image of Christ.

The old wineskins will not be able to contain the new wine that is about to come, so the call is out for the renewal of our old wineskins.

The literal wineskins in Christ's day, as metaphors for our spiritual lives, needed to be renewed. The wineskins were soaked in water for several days, which for us symbolizes the Word of God (Eph. 5:26). Then they were rubbed with oil, which symbolizes the Holy Spirit. If we will allow Him, the Lord will soften us with the Word and His Spirit until we can again receive new wine.

Interestingly enough, the word for "new wine" in this passage is different than the word for "new wineskin." The word "new" in "new wine" is **neos**, which means **numerically** new, but not **qualitatively** new. We receive new doses or outpourings of the Holy Spirit, but it is the same spiritual drink, the same wine. It may be packaged differently, the Holy Spirit may pour it differently, but it is the same wine.

The new wineskin is derived from a different word for "new." The word is **kainos**, which means qualitatively new, different. The wine of the Spirit doesn't change, but we, the wineskins, must. We must allow the Holy Spirit to work newness into us, changing us from glory to glory. We cannot expect to stay the same, never changing size, shape, or texture, and expect to be able to receive the new thing that God is doing. *Neos wine must go into kainos skins.*

We must be willing to change. We don't have the right to say to God, "Send revival, pour out Your Spirit, send the river, but do it my way and conform to my shape and expectations." This is the mistake made by the religious people of Christ's day. They were in fact, the reason for His teaching on the wineskin.[8]

PROPHETIC EXERCISE

God's Lordship in the hearts of men and churches and in the world must be *spoken into being* much as Ezekiel was able to prophesy over the dry bones.

Today's prophetic ministry will grow out of the ministry of intercessory prayer and worship. This teaches us that we must confess with our mouths that (1) unity of the Spirit, (2) unity of the faith, and (3) making disciples of all the nations — as prophesied by Jesus — will become a reality in His church.

Prophecy — forthtelling and foretelling — is simply repeating what God has told us (1) back to Him in prayer, and (2) to the saints in exhortations from the pulpit, and (3) to ourselves in the words of our praise and worship songs.

Oracles are Christians who repeat verbatim, who say aloud, who prophesy, in the presence of people what God has told them in their inner man.

That being true: To believe prophecies found in Scripture is to say them, and to say them is to prophesy — repeating God's Word verbatim.

Do you believe the Bible? Have you ever quoted prophecy from it? If you have, you prophesied! "For the testimony of Jesus is the spirit of prophecy" (Rev. 19:10).

Let's practice what we preach — right now — and read Ephesians 3:20-21 out loud, and declare it to be an on-going prophecy to all generations.

Now to Him who is able to do exceedingly abundantly beyond all that we ask or think, according to the power that works within us, to Him be the glory in the church and in Christ Jesus to all generations forever and ever. Amen. ◆

QUOTES FROM CHAPTER 15

Dr. Bright says the coming revival is going to be *a sovereign move of God* — a confirmation to the message of this book. Here is that quote.

> My mind was swirling with the realization that God Himself will move His people to fast. I began to see that this revival will actually be a sovereign move of God. That He is not through with America. That He still has plans for our beloved country. My heart nearly burst with thanksgiving and praise to the Lord. As my eyes filled with tears, I knew I had to do all that I could to relay this message to the Christian world.

In their book *Experiencing God*, Henry Blackaby and Claude King, perhaps in response to Amos 3:7, said:

> When God gets ready to do something, He reveals to a person or His people what He is going to do . . . When God spoke, they knew it was God. They knew what God was saying. They knew what they were to do in response.[2]

Chapter 15

Being on the Cutting Edge
of
What God is Doing Today

God's gateway to supernatural power can become ours when we come to our heavenly Father with contrite hearts and obedient spirits in fasting and prayer.

This is how Dr. Ronnie Floyd, my pastor, ended the preface to his book: ***The Power of Prayer and Fasting***.

I have waited until this chapter to discuss the first and most important ingredient for end-time preparation of the great harvest. God's gateway to reaching everything this book advocates is through "contrite hearts and obedient spirits in fasting and prayer."

Since you have read this far, you probably are largely in agreement with its message. But here is where the rubber meets the road. Bill Bright and Ronnie Floyd are two prominent spiritual leaders in our land who each have completed several forty-day fasts, and who believe that God is sending a great harvest! Their respective books are a major message of vast importance to God's people everywhere.

They both combine brilliant biblical insights and profound experiences with prayer and fasting to offer powerful, life-changing principles to every reader. These two men are on the cutting edge of what God is doing today.

Bill Bright, the director of Campus Crusade for Christ, wrote a book that I consider mandatory reading: ***The Coming Revival: America's Call to Fast, Pray, and "Seek God's Face."***[1]

A MANDATORY READING ASSIGNMENT

For several weeks before he began his fast, Bill Bright had sought information from medical doctors and Christian leaders on to prepare. He found only two people who had fasted forty days. One was his national director and beloved friend, Dr. Joon Gon Kim in Korea. The other was Dr. Julio Cesar Ruibal in Colombia, an internationally-known evangelist with post-graduate studies in health.

When he couldn't find any material on how to conduct such an extended fast, he sought the Lord's wisdom because he didn't know what to do. He prayed, "Lord, I know You've called me to fast for forty days, but I can't find the help I need. I don't want to do anything foolish. I don't want to destroy my body. It is your temple. Please help me."

We can pray, witness, read the Word of God diligently, attend church, be active for Christ, and aggressively do things to honor the Lord — all of which are commendable. But the major key to meeting the conditions of 2 Chronicles 7:14, is fasting. Certainly, we cannot fast and pray for a prolonged period without humbling ourselves and turning from our wicked ways.

He said that after three weeks of fasting, he received the assurance from God that He would visit America in transforming, revival power. Because this implied that God spoke to him, he went on to explain. "There are those who say God does not speak to you except from His written Word. Of course, the Word is the primary means by which He speaks. But He also talks to us by His Spirit within us (John 14:26; 16:13). His divine impressions are always consistent with His holy, inspired Word."

> Dr. Bright went on to say, "Now, in answer to my question about how to persuade millions to fast, I felt the Holy Spirit saying to me that this was His responsibility, not mine; that He will draw people to repent, fast, and

pray. And something even more amazing: that He will lead two million to fast forty days; that He will give them the desire and ability to do it."

In another place Dr. Bright said that this revival is going to be *a sovereign move of God* — a confirmation to the message of this book. Here is that quote.

> My mind was swirling with the realization that God Himself will move His people to fast. I began to see that this revival will actually be a sovereign move of God. That He is not through with America. That He still has plans for our beloved country. My heart nearly burst with thanksgiving and praise to the Lord. As my eyes filled with tears, I knew I had to do all that I could to relay this message to the Christian world.

In their book ***Experiencing God***, Henry Blackaby and Claude King, perhaps in response to Amos 3:7, said:

> When God gets ready to do something, He reveals to a person or His people what He is going to do . . . When God spoke, they knew it was God. They knew what God was saying. They knew what they were to do in response.[2]

Dr. Bright felt strongly impressed to write letters to several hundred of the most influential Christians in the country, inviting them to Orlando, Florida, as guests of Campus Crusade to fast and pray. It was to be a time for seeking God's direction on how His servants can be channels of revival for our nation and for the world.

> Dr. Bright is absolutely convinced that if believers truly love God, trust His promises, and obey His commands, He will fight our battles for us, and once again we will be a nation under the rule of God.

These prominent authors with diverse backgrounds wrote approving blurbs in Bill Bright's book, ***The Coming Revival***:

Dr. Adrian Rogers
Pat Robertson
Kay Arthur
Ralph D. Winter

GOD IS BRINGING A TRUE AWAKENING

Dr. Ronnie Floyd's book, ***The Power of Prayer and Fasting***[3] is a truly inspired word to the church. Dr. Floyd has been my pastor since 1991 at First Baptist Church of Springdale, Arkansas — a 13,000 member Southern Baptist Church. Back when I was writing this book, he asked for permission to use the phrase, "The next great move of God," whenever it seemed appropriate. I am pleased to report that one of the many times he used this phrase was in a sub-heading in his book being quoted from here.

Dr. Floyd asks, "What will be the tangible results in the lives of those who trust and fear God?" Then he goes on to quote from Joel 2.

> 28. And afterward, I will pour out my Spirit on all people. Your sons and daughters will prophesy, your old men will dream dreams, your young men will see visions.
>
> 29. Even on my servants, both men and women, I will pour out my Spirit in those days.
>
> 30. I will show wonders in the heavens and on the earth, blood and fire and billows of smoke.
>
> 31. The sun will be turned to darkness and the moon to blood before the coming of the great and dreadful day of the LORD.
>
> 32. And everyone who calls on the name of the LORD will be saved; for on Mount Zion and in Jerusalem there will be deliverance, as the LORD has said, among the survivors whom the LORD calls.

THE NEXT GREAT MOVE OF GOD

Dr. Floyd, as does Bill Bright, believes that the next great move of God will be a sovereign act of God in which He will compel His people to return to Him with their whole heart.

When God's people repent in humility and desperation, and when we return to Him with our whole hearts, God will bring a true awakening just prior to the Second Coming of our Lord. God says He will do mighty, miraculous works. He will demonstrate His power with supernatural things in our midst, but only if we return to him with our whole hearts. There is no other way. The exam is not multiple choice. And the fulfillment of this passage from Joel will not occur until moments before the return of Jesus Christ.

How close is this day?

A large part of the answer lies in our own hearts and minds: How serious are we about returning to God with our whole hearts, humbly asking His will for our lives? But, let's see how Dr. Floyd addresses this question.

When the awakening does come, we will see God do things we have never observed before. He will unleash a power unknown to us, or anyone who came before us in human history. We will experience a touch from God that will shake us individually, shake this country, and shake this world.

It will move the gospel of Christ across the globe faster than a signal from CNN and at greater speeds than the latest NASA rocketry. It's past time to strip off the garments of the skeptic. It's time to remove the mentality of the critic. It's time to eliminate the perverse thinking of the jealous. It's time to shed the skins of the proud and the arrogant.

God is moving in a great way, and it's important that we realize He will move with or without us. But because He is our loving Father, He wants us to make the right choice — to go His way, to do His bidding, to be His children. Our God does not need us; we need Him. So it follows that if we are going to come to **Him**, we must get on **His** ground, operate on **His** terms, and let God do what God wants to do.

THE STAGE IS BEING SET

Another question Dr. Floyd address is, just how important is it for us Christians to come to the Lord?

> If God does not step into our personal lives and enter our churches with miracle-working, supernatural power, we will never capture the world's attention.
>
> Why should we? Without His power working through us, we won't be any different than those who don't know the Savior. That's why we need radical men and women of God who will not bend, who will refuse to bow, who will not crumble under minor pressure.
>
> We need those who will not succumb to an ungodly world system, who want the fullness of God in their lives, and who long for a supernatural filling of the Spirit and God's anointing upon them more than anything else in this world, no matter what the cost.

One of the greatest moves of God this nation has ever seen took place in 1858. Out of a thirty million population over one million people acknowledged Jesus as their Savior. If we had a revival of similar proportions today, in one year alone we should see 8.5 million people come to faith in Jesus Christ.

This great move of God happened because hundreds of pastors across America agreed to preach on the subject of Holy Spirit revival on the first Sunday of 1858. Then on the first Thursday of that year, thousands of God's people across the nation took up the challenge, obeyed, and experienced a day of humiliation, prayer, and fasting for revival in their time.

These Christians were willing to pay the price. Dr. Floyd gives his own testimony of how God called on him to pay the price. Ask yourself this question:

WILL YOU PAY THE PRICE?

> I cry before God for that kind of revival for us. As I fast and pray, God keeps telling me, "Ronnie, pay the price. Do what it takes. Get off your high horse of ego-centered living, and live for Me alone. Get out there on

the edge, Son. Don't worry what anyone else says about you. You might feel you're alone sometimes, but I'm with you — closer even than a brother is. Stay with me in humility, fasting, and fervent prayer. Know that I am God and that I will heal your land. But I will not do it until you and others come to me humbly, with contrite spirits, and with your whole hearts. Your job is to tell my people what I've spoken for generations. If you are faithful in telling them what I said — and if they truly love me — they'll do it. If they don't, they won't. You just keep on being my man. Revival will come to your heart and to your people."

Right now, God is on the brink of ushering in a great spiritual awakening across this land through this mighty gateway to His supernatural power. When it comes in power, this awakening will be the manifest presence of God in the lives of His people. It will cut through the clutter, it will demand we get our spiritual houses in order, and it will happen only when we keep our hearts and eyes focused on Jesus. Here is how Dr. Floyd describes this coming move of God.

This awakening will be nothing more or less than a fresh, new awareness of the importance of obedience to God. It will transcend all man-made barriers. It will come only when God's people humble themselves and pray, stand with God in His holy presence, and see sins for what they are: conscious, willful alienation from almighty God. The immediacy of the hour calls us to act now — not later. Revival will not come from the next election — as important as it is to exercise our right to vote. It will not come from playing church or maintaining the status quo.

That is a guaranteed formula for failure. Revival, and the spiritual future of our nation, will be determined by the people of God who will get down on their knees, pray, fast, and believe that God is bigger than their circumstances, bigger than any election, bigger than the Democrats, bigger than the Republicans, and much bigger than we are.

These prominent authors with diverse backgrounds wrote approving blurbs in Dr. Ronnie Floyd's book, ***The Power of Prayer and Fasting:***

Dr. Bill Bright
Dr. Adrian Rogers
H. B. London Jr.
Dr. Steve Farrar,

CONCLUDING REMARKS

Such prominent spiritual leaders as Dr. Bill Bright and Dr. Ronnie Floyd are delivering the message on what else is needed among the kingdom of believers today. Two organizations, the Promise Keepers and the National Day of Prayer Task Force, and their leadership are also delivering the message. They are calling all Christians to a solemn time of repentance, prayer, and fasting, and to unity in the Spirit, across all doctrinal and racial and ethnic barriers. With them, I believe that God is preparing to bring a great harvest — perhaps hundreds of millions worldwide.

The message they convey and the conviction in their voices testify that they have indeed heard God. They may not fit the typical model of a Southern Baptist, but they do not fit the typical Charismatic or Pentecostal model either. They are simply men of God who know His voice and what they advocate is simply scriptural (John 10:27).

This is not to be construed in any way to be a slam against our Charismatic and Pentecostal brethren. They too are simply men and women of God who know His voice and believe the Bible.

Yet, someone might want to hurl a challenge at these brethren to this effect . . . "If combining the Spiritual gifts with the Great Commission were all that was needed, why haven't the Charismatics and Pentecostals brought the world to Christ?

The truth is, in other countries, they have brought more than twice as many converts to Christ than all of their non-charismatic brethren combined — which should show us something.

On the other hand, this same group has been into certain truths for so long now that these truths have become just another tradition — old wineskins. The next great move of God will not be a replay of the Charismatic or Pentecostal movement. Nor will it be a replay of any other past movement. God is always doing a new thing. I believe the next move will be bigger and purer than any other past move.

Here is a bold statement of faith that we should consider:

> **The next move of God is not going to just be built around another doctrine. The next great move of God is simply going to be God moving. The Lord is going to suddenly come into His temple, and the whole world is going to know it. When His glory fills His temple — the church — no flesh will be able to minister, but will flee.**
>
> **— Rick Joyner**

This verse should be the testimony and example of every gathering of saints.

> After they prayed, the place where they were meeting was shaken. And they were all filled with the Holy Spirit and spoke the word of God boldly. (Acts 4:31 NIV)

Here is how Jim Cymbala sums it all up. He said:

> **"Whether we call ourselves classical Evangelicals, traditionalists, fundamentalists, Pentecostals, or Charismatics, we all have to face our lack of real power and call out for a fresh infilling of the Spirit. We need the fresh wind of God to awaken us from our lethargy. We must not hide any longer behind some theological argument. The days are too dark and dangerous."** [4]

Some of our traditions may be different, but our love for Christ and the Word of God is the same. Can we accept that? Are you . . . am I . . . on the cutting edge of what God is doing today? ♦

171

QUOTES FROM CHAPTER 16

When did God cease talking to His people? Logic and history would conclude that God fell silent sometime after 1456 when the printing press was invented and the Reformation started. The Bible says . . . never!

Chapter 16

Surprising Bible Manuscript History

A big part of the cessationist view is based on the belief that the Bible replaced the gifts of the Spirit, and the ministry of the apostle and prophet. But Bible manuscript history conclusively proves the exact opposite.

We know that the books of the New Testament were written in the first century. But when were all the books of the New Testament *compiled under one cover*? When was this compilation actually *called and accepted* as the New Testament? And when was all (or part) of this New Testament *available to* the common man?

In short, exactly when did this supposed transition take place? Does history support this cessationist argument? History gives us an answer that may surprise you.

Here is part of the cessationist view that was quoted in chapter eight: [1]

> The ministry of apostleship and prophecy as embodied in particular people was but a temporary expedient.
>
> It was vitally necessary during the transition period when the written Word was being formulated and was gaining acceptance among believers, but the written Word completed, the particular ministry of the apostle and the prophet became redundant, just as the observation of the Old Testament sacrifices had to give way to their fulfillment in Christ.

173

Surely, the **old** wouldn't exit until the **new** was established. We need to ask . . . when was the new established, and when did the old exit the scene? *The Origin of the Bible* — a book listed in the bibliography — answers such questions.

BIBLE MANUSCRIPT HISTORY

When Paul wrote a letter to "the church at Corinth" (or any other city) his letter was passed around from church to church in that city to be read aloud. All of these congregations in Corinth were collectively called "the church of Corinth." The average first century Christian was fortunate if, in his lifetime, he was to hear even three such letters when they were read to a congregation. It was even more rare for anyone to have the privilege of reading three letters. Of course, copies of these manuscripts would eventually be stored (along with Old Testament scrolls) in church archives.

The Gospels and the letters of Paul were circulated as working documents among churches, but only the Old Testament books were formerly recognized as Scripture in the first century.

Nobody owned a New Testament, much less a whole Bible in the first or second century because **there weren't any!** However, an almost complete collection of all twenty-seven books that now make up the New Testament were in use for the first time in Rome by about A.D. 180 — but this was only one set. The first church council to list these twenty-seven books was the Council of Carthage in A.D. 397.

Early in the third century (around A.D. 210), Tertullian, an outstanding Christian writer, popularized the title, the "New Testament". The acceptance of this new title placed the New Testament Scripture on a level of inspiration and authority with the Old Testament for the first time.

> **The Gospels and the Pauline Epistles did not gain importance equal to the books of the Old Testament until the third century. Until then, the church could not accept even the possibility of there being a second or a New Testament.**
>
> **This is comparable to us anguishing over the possibility of there being a third Testament written after the Second**

Coming of Christ. We instantly reject the idea as un-thinkable, don't we? So did they.

CANONIZATION OF THE BIBLE

The word *canon* means "rule" or "measuring rod," and in relation to the Bible, it refers to the collection of books that passed a test of authenticity and authority. It also means that those books are our rule of life.

Several books were canonical even before they were tested. That's like saying that some students are obviously intelligent before they take any tests. The test only proves or measures what is already intrinsically there. In the same way, neither the church nor councils made any book canonical or authentic. Either the book was authentic when it was written or it was not. The church or its councils recognized and verified certain books as the Word of God, and in time — over the second, third, and fourth centuries — those so recognized were collected together in what we now call the Bible. [Ref. *A Survey of Bible Doctrine*, by Dr. Charles C. Ryrie.]

BIBLES EXTREMELY EXPENSIVE

Until the invention of printing with movable type in A.D. 1456, the text of the Bible could be transmitted only by laboriously copying it letter-by-letter and word-by-word. In fact, it took up to a year for a scribe to hand copy just one new book. Therefore, it took the equivalent of a year's wages of the average man to buy a book the size of a Bible.

Today, if we were to pay someone eight dollars an hour, and this person worked for fifty weeks making a copy of the Bible for us, the cost would be $18,000 — before taxes. Not only was there a huge price tag on a new book, but very few people could read and write in those days. As a result, for over a thousand years there were very few individuals or congregations who could afford (or read) a Bible.

Even if they could, the Roman church outlawed the ownership of Bible up to the time of the Reformation. A priest could read a passage from a Bible on Sunday mornings, but it usually was not in a language the congregation knew. Several Godly men were persecuted for translating the Bible in the language of the people.

LET'S GET REAL

Now, let's look at that cessationist statement again. **" . . . but the written Word completed, the particular ministry of the apostle and the prophet became redundant . . . ."**

We know when the Bible was completed, but when was the Bible compiled? When was it recognized as being a "New" Testament? When was it named or titled "The New Testament?" How many clergy and lay people had access to the written Word in their language at a price they could afford?

> Based on these more realistic questions, when did God cease talking to His people? Logic and history would conclude that God fell silent sometime after 1456 when the printing press was invented and the Reformation started. The Bible says . . . never!

WHAT IS GOD TELLING US?

The writing of Bible text by first century Christians ceased with their death — that is true. And these texts were canonical even before some men decided they were — that is true. However, the Scriptures they left attest to us that everything Jesus instituted is still very much in place today.

Does God still speak to us today? Yes, ever since Adam's day! Now we must ask, "what does He tell us?" In 1 Corinthians 12 Paul said God's Holy Spirit manifests Himself in us, His words of wisdom and words of knowledge; and He tells us who He is about to heal, etc. In Ephesians 4:11, Jesus said He established certain ministries (see 1 Cor. 12; Rom. 12:6-8).

> These ministries and gifts may be ignored . . . they may be misunderstood and misused, but they are still valid and in place for today.

Brethren, *this* generation needs to witness "sign gifts" *far more* than the first century people did — and we will. All we have to do is say, **"Yes Lord!"** ◆

Chapter 17

The Reformation's Greatest Weapon

There are those who teach that, "Scripture alone" is the source of absolute truth, and that it is the only voice of God that we have today. These people contend that God has spoken in a clear manner through the Scriptures, and that only Scripture can interpret Scripture (with no Scripture to support their view). Yet there is something like 25,000 Protestant denominations, and most of them espouse *solo scriptura,* which means "Scripture alone."

This would force some people to a logical deduction that concludes: God has spoken 25,000 clear but different messages.

God forbid!

The great motto of the Reformation, ***solo scriptura***, was initially penned in reaction to the indiscriminate instituting of Christian doctrines by the popes, many of whom were actually in conflict with the Scriptures. The justification for this was the Papal claim that the residing Pope's authority exceeded that of the Scriptures.

This practice by church leaders led to the greatest spiritual darkness — the Dark Ages — that the world has ever known, and this motto, ***solo scriptura,*** could be cited as the primary force to break that darkness and begin the release of every true spiritual advance since. But one can go too far with a great motto, especially after it has served its purpose in history. Today this motto must be challenged as a philosophical system called rationalism. Here is why:

> **It takes reasoning power to determine when, where, and how Scripture has, in fact, interpreted Scripture. So, "Scripture alone" boils down to "reason alone."**

> **With our human reasoning power we compare Scripture to Scripture to see what we think it says. And our reasoning power boils down to the sum total of our experience, which is a muddled mindset. In short, many conservative Evangelicals trust more in rationalism than in a relationship with Jesus.**

RATIONALISM & BIBLIOLATRY

The post-enlightenment culture has gained an understanding of the natural world primarily through the use of reason and intellect: The world, we believe, is accurately mediated to us through our intellects and our reason, rather than intuition and emotion.

> **The priority that westerners place on human reason and the corresponding devaluation of emotion, intuition, and experience is called rationalism.**

Western conservative Evangelicals are regularly told not to base their relationship with God on their experience, but on the truth! Who would not agree that we ought to base our relationship with God on the truth? But why would anyone implicitly assume that our experience would not be a vehicle for communicating the truth to us?

> **Experience and feelings are so often called into question that one might begin to believe that only human reason was left untouched by the Fall.**

But every part of our being, including our reason, has been corrupted as a result of the fall. Nevertheless, the idea persists in Evangelical circles that feelings, experience, and intuition are, by definition, suspect while reason is not.

"Bibliolatry" is another word related to rationalism. Daniel Wallace, assistant professor of New Testament Studies at Dallas Theological Seminary, has said that "while Charismatics sometimes give a higher priority to experience than to relationship, rationalistic Evangelicals give a higher priority to knowledge than to relationship. Both of these miss the mark."[1]

Wallace goes on to speak of his own brush with Bibliolatry.

> **For me, as a New Testament professor, the text is my task — but I made it my God. The text became my idol. . . The net effect of such Bibliolatry is a depersonalization of God. Eventually, we no longer relate to him. God becomes the object of our investigation . . . the vitality of our religion gets sucked out. As God gets dissected, our stance changes from "I trust in . . ." to "I believe that . . ."**

Since each one of us is a unique being, our reasoning, and therefore our doctrine, is also unique — one of a kind. But a church of one is not very practical or scriptural, so we seek out others with similar views and join ranks with them.

That is how we come up with an excess of 25,000 denominations, each one claiming they alone have the correct interpretation of Scripture. The human tendency is to forget that our goal is transformation, not information.

> **By what authority do we interpret the Bible? Surely, that authority is not "reason alone." We can conclude that we will never find all truth in the Scriptures by reasoning power alone. Surely, the same authority that inspired and authored the Scriptures is the only authority for interpreting Scriptures. In other words: the Holy Spirit will instruct us — if we know His voice.**

Over the centuries, cultures changed, languages changed, and, therefore, the human co-authors (with the Holy Spirit) of Scripture changed, **BUT** the Holy Spirit did not change. He alone is what kept the continuity and integrity of Scripture intact. The Holy Spirit still knows what He said, and He alone knows exactly what He meant. Therefore, our best chance of knowing what is true is to ask the Holy Spirit! Here is our text.

26. But the Helper, the Holy Spirit, whom the Father will send in My name, He will teach you all things, and bring to your remembrance all that I said to you. (John 14)

27. And as for you, the anointing which you received from Him abides in you, and you have no need for anyone to teach you; but as His anointing teaches you about all things, and is true and is not a lie, and just as it has taught you, you abide in Him. (1 John 2)

9. Just as it is written, Things which eye has not seen and ear has not heard, and which have not entered the heart of man, all that God has prepared for those who love Him.
10. For to us God revealed them through the Spirit; for the Spirit searches all things, even the depths of God.
11. For who among men knows the thoughts of a man except the spirit of the man, which is in him? Even so the thoughts of God no one knows except the Spirit of God.
12. Now we have received, not the spirit of the world, but the Spirit who is from God, that we might know the things freely given to us by God,
13. which things we also speak, not in words taught by human wisdom, but in those taught by the Spirit, combining spiritual thoughts with spiritual words [i.e., the gift of knowledge and wisdom, and discerning of spirits?]. (1 Corinthians 2 My insert)

17. [For I always pray to] the God of our Lord Jesus Christ, the Father of glory, that He may grant you a spirit of wisdom and revelation [of insights into mysteries and secrets] in the [deep and intimate] knowledge of Him,

18. By having the eyes of your heart flooded with light, so that you can know and understand the hope to which He has called you and how rich is His glorious inheritance in the saints (His set-apart ones),

19. And [so that you can know and understand] what is the immeasurable and unlimited and surpassing greatness of His power in and for us who believe, as demonstrated in the working of His mighty strength. (Ephesians 1 Amplified Bible)

Even if we ask the Holy Spirit what is true, and we hear His voice, we will still have some diversity in understanding. We will still see in a glass darkly because we are human. We will still see a poor reflection of Jesus through our veil of flesh, until we see Jesus face to face — beyond this veil of flesh.

Until then, we must rely, in all humility, upon the Living Word to reveal as much of the written Word to us as we can comprehend.

Until then, we must accept and observe much of the diversity amongst the brethren today.

Until then, all that Jesus put in place will remain in place until He comes again.

CONTRIBUTION OF THE APOSTOLIC FATHERS

The term *apostolic fathers* is traditionally used to designate the collection of the earliest Christian writings outside the New Testament (that we have copies of today). These apostolic fathers (who wrote between A.D. 70 and A.D. 135) were widely accepted by the church for several hundred years. Some bishops at that time accepted the *apostolic fathers'* writings as being on an equal footing with the epistles.

In some books which were greatly prized by Christians of the first five centuries, among them the *Didache, The Shepherd of Hermas,* and extensive portions of the *Paidagogos of Clement of Alexandria.*[2]

An early Christian document, the *Didache ton Dodeka Apostolon,* or "Teaching of the Twelve Apostles," describes a church organization that knew of traveling apostles and prophets and of resident

prophets and teachers. It instructs the Christians to appoint for themselves bishops and deacons and to hold them in honor, along with the
prophets and teachers. There were several bishops, not just one, and
no presbyters.

It has been suggested that there was a transition from an earlier
structure of the churches to the later one, either in communities apart
from the main centers where old customs lingered, or perhaps mirror-
ing the change in some of the larger urban churches." [3]

The exact date or period when the ***Didache*** was written is not
known. Dating the ***Didache*** is made difficult by a lack of hard evidence and the fact that it is a composite document written by anony-
mous author(s) and edited and stitched together at a later time. The
Didache may have been put in its present form as late as A.D. 150, yet
the original material was probably written in about A.D. 70, give or
take a decade. It was in popular use up to about A.D. 600. [4]

THE KING JAMES VERSION

I must be particularly discreet and gracious on this particular subject because it can be controversial. Therefore, allow me to make this
a history lesson devoid of any personal prejudice or preferences.

Today it is hard to find anyone who is sure that the Apostle Paul
carried a black, leather bound King James Bible with him on all his
travels. Yet, just a few short years ago many people believed that. I do
not wish to poke fun at those people, but while we are still on the subject of Bible manuscript history, a brief history of the most influential
of all English translations might be in order.

The English language was just starting to be developed in the fifth
century [A.D. 449-1100]. Before that time, there was no such thing as
the English language. This earliest form of English was called Old
English, known formerly as Anglo-Saxon, and we would not understand a word of it. If you have ever seen the epic poem ***Beowulf*** in the
original text, you know what I mean.

Then came the Middle English period from A.D. 1100 to 1500.

**Our interest here is in Early and Late Modern English.
King James and Shakespeare spoke Early English [A.D.
1500-1750]. Since we speak Late Modern English, we can**

appreciate the difficulty we have in reading the original printing of the King James translation [A.D. 1611].

Almost nine-tenths of the New Testament portion of the KJV can be found word for word in the Tyndale version of 1525. During subsequent decades the spelling of the KJV has been modernized, misprints have been corrected, and many English words that are no longer in use (or are obscure) were replaced with the modern equivalent. By 1613, the text showed over 300 differences from the original of 1611! Even then we would not be able to understand very much of it due to the archaic words and sentence structure. This was a wonderful translation for the time, but keep in mind that the church went for 1,600 years without the KJV.

The Old Testament rested upon the same Masoretic Hebrew text as all subsequent versions. However, because no ancient manuscripts of the Greek New Testament arrived in England until 1628, those responsible for the greatest of all translations did not have the advantage of the best Greek text.

The King James translators used a Greek text known as the ***Textus Receptus*** ("Received Text"), which came from the work of Erasmus. When Erasmus compiled this text, he used five or six very late manuscripts dating from the tenth to the thirteenth centuries.

Determining which ancient manuscripts are the most accurate is done by taking the oldest manuscripts available and comparing them, letter for letter. The older the manuscript is, and the more manuscripts that are identical letter for letter, these manuscripts are the ones considered to be the most reliable text.

The earliest manuscript, ***Codex Vaticanus*** (A.D. 325), had been in the Vatican's library since at least 1481, but it was not made available to scholars until the middle of the nineteenth century.

In our zeal for defending the infallibility of the Bible, we sometimes loose track of an all-important fact.

When we make our statement of faith that the Bible is the infallible Word of God, we are referring to the original manuscript of each book that was penned. Only the original manuscript of each book of the Bible can be

said to be unchanged. Today only the Holy Spirit can still tell us with infallible certainly what He had those patriarchs write so long ago.

Gaining an understanding of the original Hebrew and Greek that the Bible was written in is the lifelong pursuit of Bible scholars. Finding the most ancient manuscripts that are still in existence today is another worthy scholarly pursuit. That is why Codex W is so valuable today.

The final pursuit is to find scholars who are totally committed to faithfully and accurately translating these ancient manuscripts from extinct languages to modern languages. The two languages the Bible is written in (ancient Hebrew and Greek) are extinct languages today, and only Bible Scholars know them. The Hebrew spoken in modern Israel and the Greek spoken in Greece today are entirely different languages. They are as different from that spoken by the authors of Holy Canon as modern English is from the ***Beowulf*** poem.

No Bible translation is infallible, but the author still is. Never forget that the Holy Spirit is the ***REAL*** author of the Bible. Although the men who penned Scripture, and the animal skins that they wrote their inspired words on are long gone, the Holy Spirit lives on eternally. The Holy Spirit can enlighten our understanding and transform the written Word into the Living Word.

Our focus is always Jesus. And if anything is Spiritual and of God, God had to do it. We are never to focus on a Bible translation, a denomination, a teacher, or anything else. Our focus is always Jesus.

If you want to do your own research, here is what to look for in an encyclopedia: English language translations, and Bible translations. Many Bibles have a section in the back that gives the history of English translations of Bibles. It might be titled, ***The English Bible and Its Development***. I also referred to a book titled, ***The Origin of the Bible***, by Tyndale House Publishers.

CONCLUSION

The testimony of church history contradicts many of our unfounded, traditional views, and demonstrates that the truth can set us free. I hope this will inspire you to read a book on church history this year. If nothing else, read the history of English Bible translations that can be found in the back of many Bibles. This alone can be a revelation.

I can testify that spending eighteen-months studying church history revolutionized my theological thinking. I either bought these history books, or checked them out of libraries and read them at home.

If you don't think that would happen to you, just try it. Prove me wrong, but with this one qualification. The books I read were written by theologians from seven different doctrinal groups. The tendency is to tell only the good stuff about your own boys, but to reveal every deep dark secret about the other guys. After reading the same 2,000 year history from seven different perspectives, you begin to see a more accurate picture of what really happened, and thereby what is going to happen in the future.

> We cannot truly understand what is going on in the church today if we do not understand the line of continuity from the past. And we cannot truly understand the future of the church if we cannot trace that line of continuity from the past and present into the future. In other words, if we don't know where we've been, we can't know with accuracy where we are going. For this reason old mistakes are made over and over, relentlessly conforming and seldom reforming.

> That line of continuity I spoke of is the Holy Spirit endeavoring to bring change into the church. And the purpose of the change is to conform us to the image of Christ. We are not to return to the pureness of first century Christianity, we are to allow the Holy Spirit to build on those beginnings of purity and power.

A thorough knowledge of church history greatly improves our perspective of unfulfilled Bible prophecy. ◆

Kenneth Uptegrove

Spiritual Victory

Victory in our victorious, undefeatable Jesus is our prophetic battle cry! But, victory comes through obedience to the Living Word. And obedience receives ALL of God's provision, promises, and preparation for us. Picking and choosing which of His gifts we will accept amounts to telling God "No."

And those who have insight will shine brightly like the brightness of the expanse of heaven, and those who lead the many to righteousness, like the stars forever and ever. But as for you, Daniel, conceal these words and seal up the book until the end of time; many will go back and forth, and knowledge will increase. (Daniel 12:3-4)

Scripture Reading for Section Three

It is the glory of God to conceal a matter, But the glory of kings is to search out a matter. (Proverbs 25:2)

A natural man does not accept the things of the Spirit of God; for they are foolishness to him, and he cannot understand them, because they are spiritually appraised. (1 Corinthians 2:14)

Chapter 18

Attaining To The Unity
Of The Faith

Too much of our faith comes out of
our experience — our failures —
rather than from God's promises and
omnipotence — and we don't always
know the difference. Sometimes we
don't even have a Biblical understanding of genuine faith that gives
us the authority to become children
of God.

Our text is Ephesians 4:13 where it says: *"Until we all <u>attain to
the unity of the faith</u>, and of the knowledge of the Son of God . . . ."*
My purpose in this chapter is to define "unity of the faith."

First we will define the word "faith." Genuine faith is confident
obedience to God's Word in spite of circumstances and consequences.

> So faith comes from hearing, and hearing by the word
> of Christ. (Romans 10:17)

The Greek word for faith is *"pistis,"* and it means to have "a firm
persuasion that is based upon hearing."

J. Oswald Sanders said: "Faith enables the believing soul to treat
the future as present and the invisible as seen." And Revivalist Manley Beasley said: "Faith is believing something is so even when it is
not so in order to make it so."

189

Kenneth Uptegrove

The truth is that without faith, it is impossible to please God. We receive things — even things God has promised — only if we have faith.

So, in the simplest of terms, faith is defined as "believing **IN** God, and believing **THAT** God is who He says He is." Therefore, unity of the faith is simply defined as "those who find their unity in the common faith they have in God." Brethren, it is that simple.

Even so, let's look at all the things that unity of the faith is not in order to have a better understanding of what it is.

UNITY IN THE SPIRIT

There is a difference between *"unity in the Spirit"* and *"unity of the faith."* Jesus said: "My sheep hear my (Spirit's) voice (Greek: *phone*), and I know them, and they follow Me" (John 10:27), therefore, those Christians who know His voice and are led by His Spirit are in unity of the Holy Spirit of God. (In chapter 7 we thoroughly examined the unity in the Spirit that Jesus prayed for. Here are some excerpts from that chapter.)

> We cannot be in the unity that Jesus prayed for until each one of us (as an individual) comes into unity with Christ, and is hidden with Christ in God (Colo. 3:3). In this state, we will be in unity — not with each other — but with Jesus, even as he is with the Father.

> If every believer knows Jesus' voice as He knows the voice of the Father — and is obedient to His voice, then God's Holy Spirit can speak the same message to every believer in the entire world simultaneously; and each believer would respond to this message with an amen. Jesus said: "My sheep hear My voice," so this is scriptural.

> This demonstrates the "tower of Babel" principle of the one mind and one language of the Holy Spirit, even though this (potentially) incorporates every human language and mind at the same time. Now we can see how each believer can be in unity with God's Spirit and, therein, be in unity with all believers.

190

FAITH IS NOT ABOUT THE PRESENT

Here is Jim Cymbala's[1] picturesque definition of faith.

Faith is the ability of the human spirit to open up and receive impressions from God that are born from his Word and made alive by the Holy Spirit. This brings about a supernatural conviction of certain facts apart from the senses. Andrew Murray put it this way more than a hundred years ago, "Just as we have our senses, through which we hold communication with the physical universe, so faith is the spiritual sense or organ through which the soul comes into contact with and is affected by the spiritual world." In other words, just as our sense of sight or hearing lies dormant until acted upon by light or sound, so our ability to have faith lies dormant until we open ourselves to receive impressions from the eternal, invisible God.

Then we simply know that something is going to happen, for God's Word has been received and has activated this spiritual sense called faith. We now bank our life on it. If somebody asks us to prove it, we cannot — but we still know it is coming.

This is what Moses experienced thousands of years ago. "By faith he left Egypt, not fearing the king's anger; he persevered because he saw him who is invisible" (Heb. 11 27). How do you see the invisible? Not with the eyes in your head, but with the more powerful eyes of faith.

The senses — touch, taste, smell, sight, hearing — have to do with present and visible things. They can't pick up anything about the future. They have nothing to do with spiritual realities. But faith has to do primarily with these future and invisible things that God has promised us in His Word. Faith makes them more real to us than the headlines of today's newspaper. This other kind of 'seeing' is what faith is all about, as the apostle Paul says in 2 Corinthians 4:18: "*So we fix our eyes not on*

what is seen, but on what is unseen. For what is seen is temporary, but what is unseen is eternal."

Faith can be likened to a transistor radio. When you turn the radio on, music pours out. Are there any trumpets or guitars inside that little box? Of course not. Yet the room has sound waves all through it. The human senses can't detect them at all, but the radio can pick them up. The music is not actually in the radio at all. The music is coming through the radio from a greater unseen source.

So it is with faith. Faith does not originate within us. It comes from God as we receive His living Word into our hearts. Then a supernatural kind of "music" comes alive in us as the product of this faith. A person filled with faith has an entirely different view of things from the person living merely by the physical senses.

FAITH IS NOT A DENOMINATION

The idea that ***"unity in the faith"*** means ***"unity in my doctrine"*** plagues the modern church.

Have you ever wondered why there are so many denominations and doctrinal groups in the world today? On the other hand, have you noticed that God seems to like diversity? Every snowflake is different and every human is different. Each of the five-fold ministries (Eph. 4:11) are different. Jesus healed blind eyes several different ways.

This shows us that diversity in the Kingdom of God is by His design, so long as that diversity expresses the **ONE** faith — faith that believes God.

> What is faith? It is the confident assurance that what we hope for is going to happen. It is the evidence of things we cannot yet see. God gave His approval to people in days of old because of their faith. By faith we understand that the entire universe was formed at God's command, that what we now see did not come from anything that can be seen. (Hebrews 11:1-3 New Living Translation)

"Faith" does not mean "doctrine," does it? For instance, if someone were to ask, "of what faith are you," what would your answer be? If you are a Christian, there is only ONE faith you can have — faith in the ONE living God. You are of the Christian faith. Denominations and doctrinal groups are but diverse expressions of that ONE faith.

> **Faith believes God . . . agrees with God . . . and does not doubt that we have received. Simply stated, faith means: "to gain God's approval by believing Him unconditionally: no stipulations, or reservations."**

POSITIVE THINKING IS NOT FAITH

Your faith is no better than its object. For instance, faith in faith is just positive thinking with nothing behind it. But faith in Christ has all of the power of the universe behind it. Only God — the object of your faith — can move mountains. Mark 11 says:

> Have faith in God. Truly I say to you, whoever says to this mountain, 'Be taken up and cast into the sea,' and does not doubt in his heart, but believes that what he says is going to happen, it shall be granted him. Therefore I say to you, all things for which you pray and ask, believe that you have received them, and they shall be granted you." (Mark 11:22-24)

Verse 24 shows us clearly that faith is to **"believe that we have received."** Faith is not in believing that we shall receive, or are about to receive, or can receive. All these "wills," "cans," and "shalls" are not faith. There is only one kind of faith in the Bible — the faith that believes that one **has** received.

UNITY IN THE FAITH DEFINED

Unity in the faith does not call for only **one universal doctrine** among Christians. **Unity** — in Paul's definition of faith — calls for the local and universal body of believers to join their faith to believe God's promises and prophecies to the universal body of Christ, thereby gaining God's approval.

Paul's definition seems so self-evident-to-be-true that it makes you wonder why ***unity in believing God's promises*** has not happened yet.

> We need to understand that Jesus provided the key to "unity of the faith" when He sent his Holy Spirit to reside in every Christian. This "key" has been available for 2,000 years because the Holy Spirit has resided in every Christian since the day of Pentecost.
>
> If we are in the unity of the Spirit and have faith in God, we are also in unity of the faith. False definitions have effectively separated and weakened us for decades. The truth will set us free and bring power for a great harvest.

Until now we didn't know we could have "unity in the faith"! But now, we do! What will we do with this newfound knowledge?

> One universal doctrine this side of glory is unobtainable in Christ's Church, but "faith in God" — as defined by Jesus — is most certainly obtainable. Therefore, we find our unity . . . our common faith . . . in God the Father!

If faith in God was not obtainable, Hebrews 11:1-3 and Mark 11:22-24 would not be in the Bible.

It is time for every local assembly to state in their bylaws and in their public prayers: **"Our Father which art in heaven, we agree with all that You have said and done (to the best of our limited understanding) as recorded in Your Holy Bible. We unite our faith with the faith of every fellow Christian in the world who likewise agree with all that You have said and done."**

A PRAYER FOR UNITY OF THE FAITH

Would you pray this prayer?

> Lord God, by faith I invite your Holy Spirit to manifest Himself in my life so that I may experience the unity of the Holy Trinity. I implore you to add me to that ever-growing number of believers who are now walking in "the unity of the faith." May that number increase until

a great multitude of Christians — worldwide — manifest this "unity of the faith." Amen!

THE GIFT OF FAITH

While we are on the subject of defining different aspects of faith, we also need to look at "the gift of faith."

It takes a sovereign act of God to accomplish what only God can do, because if anything in the church today is of God, whether it be salvation or the indwelling of the Holy Spirit, or a healing, it is because God did it — in us and through us! It never is ours . . . it is always God in us.

We can no more possess faith than we can possess God.
We can only gain God's approval by believing Him.

But He can reveal His will to us (concerning a specific situation) so that we can have confidence and trust in His will.

Paul said, ***"To each [Christian] is given the manifestation of the Spirit for the common good"*** (1 Cor. 12:7).

This word "manifestation" means: An obvious exhibition, or expression, or bestowal of God's power to the senses. In other words, "the manifestation of the Spirit" is a public demonstration of God's ability — for the common good.

Emphasis should be placed on the fact that since God is sovereign, He will manifest His gifts through us when and where He chooses. He may choose to manifest Himself rarely or frequently, but it's His choice, not ours.

One of "the manifestations of the Spirit" is faith that the Holy Spirit manifests through us. (1 Cor. 12:7, 9). This is divine faith of such an immeasurable magnitude that it far surpasses what any human is capable of. We are talking about an unquestioning knowledge, an unshakable trust and confidence in what God has revealed to us what He is going to do. You are as confident as God is — so to speak — that what He has said is true.

GNOSTIC FAITH

What is sometimes referred to as being "God's faith" goes beyond any faith spoken of in the Bible. For God to NEED anything would be for that thing to exist separately from Him, and He would be dependent on it. For God to have or need faith would be to make Him dependent on faith. Faith would have power over God, and God would not be totally omnipotent and omniscient. He would be like us — still developing. That is a heretical Gnostic teaching.

Gnosticism is a philosophical system, and although the word "gnosis" means "knowledge," their definition of knowledge is far different from ours (see more on Gnostic faith in the endnotes). [2]

On a lighter note, when telling a friend about Gnosticism, he commented: "I take it that the Gnostic philosophical system has an agricultural branch called the agnostics."

I retorted: "No, agnostics are unbelieving farmers."

Seriously though, spiritual knowledge and truth can be elusive.

WHAT IS GODLINESS?

To be godly does not mean to be God-like, or like God. That is a Gnostic[4] or New Age notion that is prevalent in some "Christian" groups.

To be Godly, we need God's Holy Spirit resident in us so that He can manifest Himself through us. And that happens only to those who have accepted Jesus Christ to be the Lord and Savior of our life.

Only God's presence can be manifested as godliness, as indicated so many times in Biblical accounts such as in the book of Acts, the picture and model for the present day church to build on.

Godliness comes through a personal, intimate relationship with Jesus Christ, and through dying to self. Prayer, Bible reading and Bible memorization are commendable, and we all should be doing that.

But godliness comes through relationship, relationship, relationship! And an intimate relationship with Christ comes through dying to self, dying to self, dying to self! And dying to self comes by anguishing over our sin and repenting for it.

Dying to self requires coming to the end of our own ability (which is God given) and anguishing over your inability to glorify Him in all that we do and say.

I hope that statement is emphatic and emotional enough for all of us to get the point. And the point is, Jesus:

11. . . . . gave some as apostles, and some as prophets, and some as evangelists, and some as pastors and teachers,

12. for the equipping of the saints for the work of service, to the building up of the body of Christ;

13. **Until we all attain to the unity of the faith**, and of the knowledge of the Son of God, to a mature man, to the measure of the stature which belongs to the fullness of Christ. (Ephesians 4, emphasis added)

Oh Lord, Help us to join our faith to believe your promises and prophecies to the universal body of Christ! ♦

QUOTES FROM CHAPTER 19

Because divinity indwells us, we can do divine things. Rather, the Divine can manifest Himself through us, the Divine being the Spirit of Jesus. Jesus is in us — collectively — continuing His ministry, and doing (as always) what He sees the Father doing (John 5:19-21). Since there are millions of us, His accumulative work through us certainly can exceed what He did in person.

We do not need to strive to do the things that Jesus did because Jesus is in us to do the things that He did (prior to Pentecost) through us!

Chapter 19

Jesus Prophesied "Greater Works"

Truly, truly, I say to you, he who believes in Me, the works that I do shall he do also; and greater works than these shall he do; because I go to the Father. (John 14:12)

If we accept this prophetic commandment from Jesus as being for us today, we must confess that (for the most part) we have fallen short of doing the works, much less, *"greater works"* than Jesus did. This exposes our limited faith and understanding of who Jesus is, and our need for a sovereign end-time move of God.

How are we to define "greater works?" Are these "greater works" qualitatively or quantitatively greater? Or did He mean conversion alone? Jesus didn't specify, but He *did* say "greater works." Therefore, we are to be expectant, and must refrain from explaining away "greater works."

> **Raising the dead is not a greater or lesser work for us to accomplish than winning souls for Christ. We simply are to be available for God to do either — or both — through us, as He wills and when He wills.**

There is no proof that everyone who received a miracle became a convert. Jesus gave out of His pure heart to reveal Himself as our loving Messiah and not because He could get converts by exhibiting miracles. He never uses cheap gimmicks and "God tricks" to promote Himself. Jesus loves — period!

WHAT ARE GREATER WORKS?

Some theologians interpret "greater works" in this verse to mean the accumulative works of the greater body of Christ over the last 2,000 years. Some cessationists believe the "greater works" applied only to the first century church. But notice that Jesus' statement was made to "He . . . who believes in Me," not to "My Apostles who believe in Me," or "the first century Christians . . . who believe in Me," or "the accumulative works of all those . . . who believe in Me."

In context, the implied definition of "He who believes" is . . . every individual believer from the day of Pentecost to the day of His Second Coming.

The word "shall" in John 14:12 makes this a prophecy and a commandment to every generation until the Second Coming of Christ.

Why? Because in context, "shall" is as "present tense" as Jesus — the great I AM — is (John 8:57-58).

Paraphrased, Jesus said: "If any Christian in any century believes in Me, then all these Christians can do the works that I (Jesus) did, and even greater!"

But, how can that be when our experience verifies that no such thing has happened to us, or to anyone we know?

Let me prove to you — from the Bible — why and how we can do the works that Jesus did.

THE SPIRIT OF JESUS

This may shock you, but the Bible makes no distinction between Jesus and the Holy Spirit, and God and the Holy Spirit — as these verses point out.

5. Test yourselves to see if you are in the faith; examine yourselves! Or do you not recognize this about yourselves, that Jesus Christ is in you — unless indeed you fail the test? (2 Corinthians 13)

17. The Lord and the Spirit are one and the same, and the Lord's Spirit sets us free.

18. So, our faces are not covered. They show the bright glory of the Lord, as the Lord's Spirit makes us more and more like our glorious Lord. (2 Corinthians 3 The Promise Bible version)

20. In that day you shall know that I am in My Father, and you in Me, and I in you. (John 14)

Thinking in terms of the Trinity, the three are ONE, and the Holy Spirit is as much the "Spirit of Christ" as He is the "Spirit of God" the Father. The Holy Trinity cannot be separated.

We are not gods, but divinity resides within us. The New Agers have it all backwards. Because they think they *are* gods, they miss God altogether.

This same Holy Spirit is called "the Spirit of Jesus Christ" in Philippians 1:19, and Acts 16:7. Many older Bible manuscripts say, ***"the Spirit of Jesus."*** This title — ***the Spirit of Jesus*** — emphasizes the unity of action between Jesus and the Spirit that permeates the book of Acts and its companion volume, the Gospel of Luke.

During the days of Jesus' earthly ministry, Jesus directed the disciples. Now, after His resurrection and ascension, "the Spirit of Jesus" directed them. This is why Jesus told us that after His ascension and the coming of His Spirit to indwell us, we would be able to do the things He did and even greater.

Is it not this aspect of "Jesus in us" that will do the works that He did, and even greater, when He walked on the earth? (John 14:12)

Because divinity indwells us, we can do divine things. Rather, the Divine can manifest Himself through us, the Divine being the Spirit of Jesus. Jesus is in us — collectively — continuing His ministry, and doing (as always) what He sees the Father doing (John 5:19-21). Since there are millions of us, His accumulative work through us certainly can exceed what He did in person.

201

We do not need to strive to do the things that Jesus did because Jesus is in us to do the things that He did (prior to Pentecost) through us!

The following is a panoramic .word picture, an impressionistic, idealistic painting that will thrill you as you begin to grasp the depth and breadth of what it means to be *IN* Christ Jesus.

We Christians gained our common salvation in Christ Jesus because Jesus sought us and bought us, and His Spirit indwells us. We did nothing — God did everything. Therefore, if anything is of God, it is because God alone *CAN* do it and *DOES* do it.

DEFINING THE BODY OF CHRIST

When we speak of Jesus as being the head of the body of Christ, we are speaking of the mystical Church — or the body of believers whose Lord and High Priest is Jesus Christ.

When we speak of the blood of Jesus as being our covering and our righteousness, we are speaking of being *IN* the body of Christ where the blood and the headship flows. Furthermore, we are speaking of being *HIDDEN* in Christ so that our unrighteousness is covered by Christ's righteousness (Col. 3:3).

When we speak of the *living stones,* or body members, that make up the vibrant Church of Jesus Christ, we are speaking of brethren that God has fitly joined to work together in complimentary and mutually supportive roles. We are formed, shaped, chiseled, and placed into the image of Christ. This picture should compel us to take a closer look at the stones that God has fitted adjacent to us.

When we speak of our hand doing as our head tells it to, we are talking about a nervous system process where the hand flows with the head. The head does not tell the hand to do thus-and-so, and the hand does not decide to obey or disobey. The hand just flooooooows with the head.

Carrying this analogy to the body of Christ, we — the hand of Christ — can just flooooooow with the indwelling Spirit — the Head of Christ — because the Spirit and the Head are *ONE*. I believe this means that the sovereign Holy Spirit can either speak *to* us or flow *through* us — as He chooses.

That explains why a sermon can suddenly turn into an anointed oracle. I think that is what Stephen experienced on the day he was martyred. Daily, I warmly invite the Holy Spirit to flow through me. My invitation is the "on" switch (so-to-speak), but my unbelief and my sin nature all too often works as a filter — the "off" switch that blocks out some of the blessings that could have been mine.

When we speak of our hand being a body member, we are speaking of our hand being *IN* our circulatory system where the blood flows — *IN* the body. If my right hand were to be amputated and placed on a table, my hand would be out from under the blood and headship of my body, and it would soon die. What's more, I would be in great pain and deep grief over the loss of my beloved hand.

If the hand were to be grafted back onto my wrist soon enough, the hand would recover and be under the flow of the blood and the nervous system again. Our covering is *IN* Christ, and we must take every precaution to never remove ourselves from His presence.

Instead of amputation, let's look at paralyzation. If I were to have a serious spine injury and lost control of my right hand (or whole body), the hand would be in the body and under the blood, but not under headship. Brethren, some of the body of Christ are unwitting quadriplegics.

Being **IN CHRIST JESUS** is a powerful, compelling picture! Reduced to five points: *IN* the body of Christ we are . . .

- *In* the blood, and *in* the headship of Christ;
- *In* the church, living stones being fitly joined with adjacent stones/brethren;
- *In* the mold, being conformed to the image of Christ;
- *In* the unity of the Spirit and, therefore, *in* the faith;
  Indwelled by Christ, therefore, we can do the things He did, and even greater . . . all **IN** Christ Jesus! ♦

QUOTES FROM CHAPTER 20

Since it is God's desire to conform each of us to the image of Christ, it seems to me that alone should be THE Christian's goal in life. Overcomers shoot for that goal . . . that purpose . . . that life. After all, life is short and eternity waits for no man!

Just as holy matrimony between a man and a woman is a union that makes the two ***ONE-in-the-flesh***, so does betrothal to Jesus make us ***ONE-in-the-Spirit***.

If we are born again Christians, the union is already there. Jesus is IN you, pursuing your inner man. And even as the lover of your soul is IN you, you are IN Him! But this union must transcend from passive mental agreement to active spiritual involvement in order to actually accomplish God's purpose for the union. This is faith in action.

Chapter 20

Overcomers and the Bride of Christ

There is but one purpose for life — to prepare for eternity. Life is measurably brief. Eternity is immeasurably endless. Ignorance alone compels us to trifle with our eternal destiny.

Personally, I don't want to get over on the other side of eternity and then find out what I **SHOULD** have known — what I **COULD** have done — on **THIS** side of eternity to lay up treasures in heaven. How about you?

In Christendom, when it comes to the concept of laying up treasures in heaven, the common misconception is that we all enter eternity on an equal basis. One size fits all, they say. Therefore, doing good works, or gaining crowns to cast at Jesus' feet often gets passed over (Rev. 4:10).

It is ridiculous to assume that those who do the minimum and just squeeze by will receive the same rewards in eternity as the patriarchs (like Moses and Paul) who did great exploits. God forbid!

Furthermore, it is unkind to rob naive saints of potential rewards by not teaching them the clear Word of God. That is what discipleship is all about.

We are being robbed if we are not being discipled, and we are robbing the next generation if we are not discipling them.

We know about the Great Commission and the gifts of the Spirit, and all that. The question here is: How can we learn what other "treasures" we can "lay up," if they are not being talked about enough in our churches? For example, I believe that we need to hear more about becoming overcomers.

OVERCOMERS: THE THREE VIEWS

The subject of "overcomers" is somewhat controversial because we are challenged with three basic schools of thought, or theories, or factions.

It's the old story where each of the three factions makes the identical statement of faith and then draws diverse conclusions. But since we are stuck with three theories, rather than one clear-cut absolute, they should be open to discussion.

In the Revelation letters to the seven churches (chapters 2 and 3), Jesus made special promises to *"he who overcomes."* Here is what the Nelson Study Bible's commentary says about these "overcomers."

> "There are three main views about the nature of the overcomer in vv. 7, 11, 17, 26; 3:5, 12, 21:
>
> "**The first view** states that the promise to the overcomer is experienced by all believers. In other words, all genuine believers are overcomers, and failure to overcome means that there was no true salvation in that person's case.
>
> "**The second view** holds that the promises are experienced only by those believers who are faithful and obedient, and failure to overcome means there has been a loss of salvation.
>
> **The third view** contends that the promises are experienced only by believers who are faithful and obedient, and failure to overcome means a loss of rewards, not salvation (see 1 Cor. 3:15).
>
> None of these is without difficulties, but the correct interpretation would be the one that most consistently handles the details of all seven "overcomer" passages. This means the third view is most likely.

John is telling the Ephesian believers that they have spiritual obstacles to overcome. ***The problem in the church at Ephesus was a lack of fervent love for Christ.*** The church is commanded to 'repent and do the first works' (v. 5), which suggests a lapse in Christian living.

"The reward for those who obey is the promise that they will eat of the tree of life. Eating of the tree of life is a promise of special intimacy with the Lord, a promise of renewing the fellowship lost before the fall (see Rev. 22:14; Gen. 2:9; 3:22, 24; Prov. 11:30). The privileged access once denied Adam (see Gen. 3:24) will be enjoyed by the overcomer."

[End of quote/Emphasis added]

Now, back to Christ's message to the seven churches and the three main views.

CHRISTIANS AND OVERCOMERS

Since Jesus was speaking to churches, He therefore was speaking to the Christians in those churches, not to unbelievers. It is obvious that He differentiated between ***ordinary*** Christians and ***overcomer*** Christians. Otherwise there was no point in Jesus calling on the Christians in each of these churches to become overcomers.

Here is my own synopsis of the shortcomings found in those churches. (1) Various kinds of heretical teachings and teachers were tolerated. (2) They left their first love. (3) They were devoid of spiritual life and power, and (4) were lukewarm in their zeal. To tell the truth, that sounds like a lot of our churches today.

Overcomers are not some special class. They are simply people from every generation who overcame the shortcomings found in these churches. They are promised wonderful privileges, special and exceptional rewards — treasures in Heaven — that are not promised to other Christians.

ONE OF THOSE DIFFICULTIES

As the Nelson Study Bible's Commentary says: "None of these (three main views) is without difficulties." Here is one of those difficulties:

Does Christ want you to believe **ALL,** accept **ALL** that God has said (in the Bible)? If you do not believe **ALL** or accept **ALL** that Christ offers, are you rejecting a part of Christ?

Here is the Scripture reading that compelled me to ask these hard questions:

> 7. He that overcometh shall inherit ALL things; and I will be his God, and he shall be my son.
>
> 9. And there came unto me one of the seven angles...and talked with me, saying, come hither, I will shew thee the bride, the Lamb's wife. (Revelation 21 KJV)

Notice that no mention is made in these verses of those Christians spoken of in the seven churches who were ***not*** overcomers (Rev. 2-3). Only overcomers and the bride are mentioned here.

What would you do with Christians who are not counted among the overcomers? One alternative that is often used to identify these Christians can be found in the parable of the ten virgins (Matt. 25:1). Virgins are said to be a typology for Christians. Five had oil in their lamps, a typology for the Holy Spirit, and five did not. These five "Christians" were not invited to what appears to be the wedding of the bride of Christ.

This is a most uncomfortable subject, but it is one that must be resolved. Again, what would you do with this class of Christians who are not counted among the overcomers?

THE GOD CHASERS

John's Revelation tells us what overcomers shall receive. But, what is characteristic of an overcomer, and what other terms can be used to describe them? Let's look at some alternate terms used for "overcomers."

Tommy Tenney, in his popular book, ***The God Chasers,***[1] says:

> A God chaser is an individual whose hunger exceeds his reach. A God chaser is a person whose passion for

God's presence presses him to chase the impossible in hopes that the uncatchable might catch him.

A child chases a loving parent until, suddenly, the strong arms of the father enfold the chaser. The pursuer becomes the captive, the pursued the captor. Paul put it this way: "I chased after that I may catch that which apprehended me." [Tenney's eloquent paraphrase of Philippians 3:12]

Tommy Tenney's **God Chasers** is a unique and picturesque view of "overcomers." By combining the essence of these two expressions, we get a larger and more exciting picture of what I think this brother described so beautifully. Maybe we could combine the two in this way:

Overcomers radically pursue the mountaintop presence of God, even as Moses did.

CHASED BY GOD

If you are a Christian today, it is because Jesus first pursued you. God foreknew all He would provide before the foundation of the world, and then was released to us at the Cross. For us, **ALL THINGS** are available and possible; we just haven't allowed God to release them in our lives . . . yet.

By faith we may pursue so that we may receive all God has given.

Paul is the most remarkable example in the New Testament of one who pursued Jesus Christ. But Paul (Saul) first pursued and killed Christians. *It took a sovereign act of God* to strike Paul blind on the Damascus road in order for him to gain *spiritual eyes* to see the Truth. Then he pursued Jesus with a perseverance and passion that was nothing short of heroic! Saul, the Christian killer, became Paul, the Christian martyr!

When Paul was whipped, stoned, jailed, or shipwrecked, he could hardly wait to get well enough again to hit the dangerous streets and preach again. Safety and comfort meant nothing to him. Proclaiming Jesus Christ as his Lord and Savior was his life, his passion!

What love!

Moses is the most remarkable example in the Old Testament of one who pursued the face of God. But Moses didn't have any such inclinations until **after his burning bush experience.** It took a sovereign act of God, in which He pursued Moses, for Moses to get all fired up in his quest to see Him. Then Moses had his mountaintop experiences.

Moses longed for more than visitation; his soul longed for habitation. He wanted more than just seeing God's finger or hearing His voice speaking from a cloud or a burning bush. He had gone beyond fear to love, and God's abiding presence had become his consuming desire. That is why he begged God in Exodus 33:18: **"I beseech Thee, show me Thy glory."**

This is the consuming desire of every overcomer!

Do you long for habitation?

A CAUTION FLAG

Before you start asking God for an extraordinary encounter like Paul and Moses experienced, remember; when much is given, much is required. In their case a **colossal** amount was given and a **staggering** amount was required. They (like Jesus) are our models because they were among **the most exceptional examples of overcomers** in the Bible. Be careful in what you ask for or expect in your quest to become an overcomer.

OVERCOMERS DEFINED

Since it is God's desire to conform each of us to the image of Christ, it seems to me that alone should be THE Christian's goal in life. Overcomers shoot for that goal . . . that purpose . . . that life. After all, life is short and eternity waits for no man!

Many Christians claim the redemption of the blood of Christ, but they go on living their lives for themselves, not as a true overcomer or bond-servant of the Lord. They may attend services every week, pay their tithes, and even be highly involved in their church or ministry, but they live for, and base most of their decisions on what they want or need, not on the purposes of the Lord. American Christians tend to believe the purpose of life is to be happy and have fun. This is hedonistic Christianity. There is a profound difference between the way overcomers or bondservants live and the majority of those who may profess to be bondservants.

There is no motivation to devote our lives to becoming overcomers until we understand that. . .

MOST Christians minister without the Holy Spirit MOST of the time; and MOST Christians are NOT overcomers.

Oh, they are saved for eternity in God's Kingdom — and that is wonderful — but there is **MORE** to achieve in life besides salvation and eternal life.

We can serve God in all these ways:

- Fasting and praying
- Bible reading
- Bible memorization
- Flowing in the gifts and fruit of the Spirit
- Offering up praise and worship
- Preaching and winning souls
- Establishing churches

More could be added to this list, but such commendable feats are not what really pleases God (2 Cor. 5:9)!

Overcomers seek His face to worship and serve and bless Him with all their being.

The politically correct seek His hand for His blessings. But the Bible urges us to seek Him who blesses, not His blessings. Seek Him who revives, not revival! Seek the Giver, not the gifts! Seek to know Him, not just about Him! Seek His face, not His hands!

Salvation is a free gift, but God's glory will cost us everything. We are going to have to lie down and die, and the more we die to self, the closer Jesus will press in. And He wants us to press in and live in His perpetual habitation of glory. He wants us to be so saturated with His presence and glory (as Moses and Paul were) that we carry His presence with us everywhere we go in this life, living out there on the edge as a holy saint of God. This may be the only way the unspeakable glory of God will find its way to God's house, the White House, and every house.

BRIDE OF CHRIST

All Christians are called to be kings and priests to rule with Christ, but because so many of us think like slaves, we get "rained *on*" instead of "reigning *with*" Christ.

Overcomers think like those in the *royal* priesthood, like a bride-to-be who is riotously in love with the King of Kings.

Think about this for a little bit: royalty marries royalty, and King Jesus is coming for His royal bride.

Some theologians make a good argument for believing that "the bride of Christ" is a synonymous term for "overcomers." This subject can get complicated and controversial. The late Jim McKeever presents this view for us. Here is a brief reiteration of what his book on this subject says:

> Some theologians tell us that Abraham was a type of God the Father, and Isaac was a type of Jesus, the Son of God, and Eliezer, Abraham's servant, was a type of the Holy Spirit. If this is a valid typology, then it is logical to conclude that Rebecca was a type of the Bride of Christ, and her family was a type of the family of God. Isaac did not marry Abraham's family — just Rebecca.
>
> You will recall that Abraham said to Eliezer (in Gen. 24:4): "You shall go to my country and to my relatives, and take a wife for my son Isaac." Now, allow me to ask some obvious questions and then reiterate this passage using this typology. Who are God's relatives in this passage? Is the Bride of Christ in the midst of God's relatives? What country is God's? What are the countries that are **NOT** God's? The lost?
>
> In this typology God might be saying to the Holy Spirit: "You shall go to the sons of God in the Kingdom of God, and take a wife from amongst them for my son Jesus." In other words, the Bride of Christ is chosen from among Christians in the Kingdom of God. It is the Over-

comers who have made themselves ready for their Bride Groom — King Jesus. Judge the accuracy of this teaching.

If McKeever and these other theologians are wrong, forgive them and let's go on. Mckeever sure missed God in some other things. If they are right though, consider what you and I will need to do to become an overcomer.[7] Just a thought!

> **Many of the truths of God — His original plan — are waiting to be organized in men today. In fact, Martin Luther said (in reference to Rev. 19:7), "We can expect God to restore truths to His church until we become a Bride acceptable to the Bridegroom."**

Brethren, as Oswald Chambers might have said, we are called to achieve to His utmost!

EMBARRASSED BRIDE

When we read The Song of Solomon and are told that this is a picture of Jesus and His bride, we may be turned off, offended, and embarrassed. Yet, this book is as inspired as any other book in the Bible. This might be a good time to ask again, do you believe the Bible?

If you have forgotten just how steamy the Song of Solomon is, stop for a minute and read a few verses from chapter seven.

Let's face it, we get uncomfortable when we hear the term "the bride of Christ" because to us it has sexual overtones. For men, this whole bride thing seems very unmasculine.

Have we forgotten? There will be no marriage or sex on the other side of eternity.

> **God uses concepts that we understand to symbolize the Spiritual application.**

Although we know this, we still have a hard time getting past our fleshly perspective and seeing the spiritual.

To us the reality and the thrill of spending eternity in the presence of Jesus is as impossible to comprehend as asking Albert Einstein to explain his theory of relativity to us one more time — in German. That is why this overcomer concept can seem to be over our heads.

We should not be surprised that it takes spiritual eyes and ears to grasp the concept.

If you have ever had a genuine spiritual experience, you know that it can be wonderfully fulfilling. Such an encounter with the Holy Spirit can be ***more fulfilling and memorable*** than any human experience. Emotions and cherished memories go hand in glove with a meaningful relationship.

To say that we are to base our relationship with Jesus on the Bible alone and not on an experience is theologically correct. However, that is like a wife asking her husband if he still loves her, and he sternly orders her to read those old love letters he wrote when courting her. READ THE LETTERS! READ THE BOOK!

But, won't you tell me one more time that you love me?

The truth is; most of those who say that have never had a spiritual experience actually would never ***allow*** themselves to have one. The motive behind their stern stand may be to discourage some of us from seeking a real relationship with Jesus.

So, how do we get a spiritual, Biblical view of the Bride? First we need to understand that there is nothing sexual about the Christian experience. But gender traits are observed in the attributes of God. For instance, Jesus exemplified the feminine qualities of gentleness and — at the same time — the masculine qualities of a powerful, commanding presence.

We cannot comprehend the **ONENESS** of the Trinity (even from the symbolism of marriage), but even so, we are called to come by faith into that same **ONENESS** with Jesus.

If these sexual overtones make you uncomfortable, do spiritual experiences that are rapturous also embarrass you? Do the experiences that Paul and Moses had with the Lord sound unreal and unobtainable today? Does the picture of David dancing ecstatically before the Ark of the Covenant fill you with contempt as it did his wife? Is that what the Bible tells you, or is it the limitations your flesh and traditions impose upon you?

I hope you are as uncomfortable and embarrassed as I am right now in making this comparison between sex and a spiritual experience, but it is worth the distress — **IF** you are understanding the point of all this. However, I'm not through yet...

RED HOT FOR CHRIST

The Spirit of Christ wants to do more than just passively indwell you; He wants to *actively* be **ONE** with you. God created us for the sole purpose of loving us with His perfect love, and to encourage us to return that love! Call this a relationship, fellowship, or a spiritual experience, but . . .

> **If your relationship with Jesus is not intimate, intensive, and passionate, you are lukewarm.**

In the letters to one of the seven churches, Jesus told us to either be hot or cold towards Him, because when we are lukewarm it makes Him vomit. Certainly the overcomer, the bride of Christ is **RED-HOT**.

> **How hot are you?**
> **How cold are you?**

I wonder what percentage of Christians fall into each of those three categories? Hot, lukewarm, or cold?

> **One thing is crystal clear; you cannot be a lukewarm or cold Christian and be counted among the overcomers.**

ALL HAS BEEN GIVEN

Jesus loves those who date Him every Sunday morning, but He really gets excited over those who pursue Him — day in and day out. Jesus will chase . . . pursue . . . woo you until you stop running from Him. When you stop, turn, and embrace Him, you are allowing a courtship that can culminate in everlasting marriage. Courtship, as you and I understand it, is not a two-hours-on-Sunday-morning religious obligation; it is a lifestyle, a foreshadowing of married bliss.

Just as holy matrimony between a man and a woman is a union that makes the two *ONE-in-the-flesh*, so does betrothal to Jesus make us *ONE-in-the-Spirit*.

> **If we are born again Christians, the union is already there. Jesus is IN you, pursuing your inner man. And even as the lover of your soul is IN you, you are IN Him! But this union must transcend from passive mental agree-**

215

ment to active spiritual involvement in order to actually accomplish God's purpose for the union. This is faith in action.

Lovers find it a real joy to give and to receive gifts from each other. Will you receive **ALL** the gifts the Bridegroom has given to His prospective bride? Will you give your all to Him? We must transcend from betrothal (the engagement) to marriage.

YOU ARE CORDIALLY INVITED

When we are invited to a banquet my wife always has to show me what all those fancy utensils are called, and what I am supposed to do with them. I even have to be shown **HOW** to use them. And I always have to be reminded to place that beautiful linen napkin on my lap. My lack of couth and culture really embarrasses her. Will we be like that at the wedding feast?

"Lord, what is this cute little unity thingy here by my goblet? Lord, what am I supposed to do with this peculiar gift of healing anyhow? Lord, why is the deacon board at my church not seated at the table today (Matt. 25:1-13)?"

I doubt that such questions will be heard, because the Bride's spiritual etiquette will be impeccable.

Over and over, we keep pointing out the fact that **ALL IS GIVEN, ALL IS PROVIDED.** The hard question is, are we flowing in . . . are we using all of God's provisioning all of the time?

I suppose I am presently a part-time overcomer, but with God's help I am determined to be counted among the full time, red-hot, bride of Christ overcomers! How about you? ♦

Chapter 21

A Vision of Recovery

— Revisited —

Consider what an embarrassing and sad day it would be if the redeeming blood of Jesus — very God — could only save and secure a small fraction of mankind. Is it possible that Satan will take the Lion's share?

Never! Never! Never!

Thanks be to God, who ALWAYS leads us in His TRIUMPH in Christ, and manifests through us the sweet aroma of the knowledge of Him in every place. (1 Corinthians 2:14)

Omnipotent God is *perpetually* victorious, and the Lion of Judah is *absolutely* victorious.

The problem is, if we keep on doing what we've been doing, we're going to keep on getting what we've been getting — limited revival! Therefore, the question arises: *why* do we keep on doing what does not work? And *why* do we lose so many battles when our Lord is undefeatable? Isn't it sad that so many Christians just don't get it?

When Jesus was on trial before Pilate, Pilate asked Jesus the old philosophical question, "What is truth?" Pilate was so spiritually inept that he was unaware of the fact that Jesus had just answered that question.

WHAT IS TRUTH?

Jesus had just told Pilate, *"for this I have been born, and for this I have come into the world, to bear witness to <u>THE TRUTH</u>. Everyone who is of the truth hears My voice"* (John 18:37, emphasis added).

So, what is truth? Here is the definition. Truth is a Person, not a concept. Jesus said He was the truth (John 14:6).

Truth is a divine attribute of God the Father, God the Son, and God the Holy Spirit! Psalms 31:5 says God IS Truth!

In John 14:6 Jesus said, *"I am the way, and the truth, and the life; no one comes to the Father but through me."* And John 16:13, says the Holy Spirit is *"the Spirit of truth."* Even God's Word, whether written or spoken, is "truth" according to John 17:17b (Titus 1:2).

As for Satan, *"Whenever he speaks a lie, he speaks from his own nature; for he is a liar, and the father of lies"* (John 8:44b). And no matter what, *"let God be found true, though every man be found a liar"* (Rom. 3:4).

And even though God is Truth, that does not presuppose that we comprehend (or *want* to comprehend) all His Truth revealed in the written Word or in His glorious creation.

> 17. That the God of our Lord Jesus Christ, the Father of glory, may give to you the spirit of wisdom and revelation in the knowledge of Him.
>
> 18. I pray that the eyes of your heart may be enlightened, so that you may know what is the hope of His calling, what are the riches of the glory of His inheritance in the saints,
>
> 19. and what is the surpassing greatness of His power toward us who believe. These are in according with the working of the strength of His might. (Ephesians 1:17-19)

218

"The knowledge of Him" (vs. 17) can come only by revelation. Or maybe you prefer to say "spiritual insight" rather than "revelation." Either way, our understanding is thwarted when we apathetically presuppose that we already know *enough* truth and are not in need of any enlightenment.

Such presumption stymies all spiritual enlightenment and progress in our lives. Although we may believe that all of God's truth is in the Bible, and that we believe in God's truth, that does not mean that *our understanding* of the Bible is "truth" or infallible. Let's be honest and admit that our understanding of God and His Holy Word is subject to error.

TRUTH IS DIVINE

An old saying tells us "truth is where you find it." God's creation is packed with truth, but Christians (as well as evolutionists) stumble all over the clear evidence.

We humans loathe believing the evidence of God's truth in His creation when it contradicts our belief system. Too often we do not want "truth." Instead, we want our belief system defended and confirmed at any cost.

What is truth?

Truth is divine. Only God is absolute truth. And, only God can reveal truth. His creation is a revelation of His truth in itself. But, in intimate moments, when He opens our Spiritual eyes to a truth that is "new" to us, oh, those are very special moments!

Since it is reasonable to believe that God has placed the desire to know the truth that is Jesus within ourselves, He will fully satisfy that desire — and in a manner that will provide certainty to every sincere seeker (Jer. 19:13). Such has been His way from the very beginning.

UNBELIEF AND LACK OF VISION

We can resist the Holy Spirit with our unbelief and lack of vision and understanding, thereby not allowing Him to manifest Himself through us. Or, we can ask Him to open our spiritual eyes to "see" what He wants to do through us — if we will only submit to Him and say, **"Yes, Lord!"**

Lack of vision, lack of understanding, and lack of faith has stymied the church's conclusion for almost 2,000 years.

But I believe these hindrances are being removed at an accelerated rate of reformation and restoration in these last days. As our generation grows in unity and faith in Christ, we will see Him glorified by a great end-time harvest that we — and His angels[1] — shall gather for Him.

DEFEATIST THEOLOGY

We serve a victorious Lord, but we believe a defeatist theology. Brethren, that does not compute.

We need a victory theology that is in keeping with our Lord and His written Word to us. It's in there! We just haven't had the Word revealed . . . come alive to us yet. And I do say "Yet," because His living Word is coming. Oh, it is coming!

One does not have to be a prophet to foretell this wonderful news. The Bible is chock full of proof that the very nature of God is victorious. In fact, He doesn't even have any competition. It is we who have an opponent, but the Bible says Jesus defeated Satan and made that victory available for all who serve Him.

THE PROPHESIED SOLUTION

As I have said throughout this series of chapters:
- The unity Jesus prayed for (in John 17:20-23) is a prophecy that will come to pass.
- Unity of the Spirit means knowing — and being led by — God's voice and the Bible (John 10:27, Rom. 8:14).
- Unity of the Spirit will bring spiritual power and authority.
- This power and authority will release the Spirit of Jesus in us to manifest His Spiritual gifts.
- The manifestation of these spiritual gifts will build our faith in the gift giver, resulting in unity of the faith, which means total confidence in God.
- This unity of the faith will release the Ephesians 4:11 ministries as unprecedented in history.

- All of the above — and God's sovereign intervention — will release upon the world a harvest that will fulfill God's promise to Abraham.
- All Christians are called to be overcomers. Overcomers do not allow heretical teaching or teachers in their churches, they are on fire for Christ, and they are full of spiritual life and power.
- A bride is being prepared for the Bridegroom.

Let's develop this line of thought.

MAKING DISCIPLES OF
ALL THE NATIONS

The Great Commission — or evangelism — is but one tool, one commands that God has given us, but there are other commandments to obey as well. To obey what we consider *The Great Commission,* and thereby excuse ourselves from obeying what we consider *lesser commands* is still disobedience. Because of our disobedience, we fail miserably at fulfilling the Great Commission because the "lesser commands" are part and parcel of fulfilling the Great Commission.

So long as we do not have either the strong arm of "unity of the Spirit" or of "unity of the faith" we appear to be fighting the good fight with both hands tied behind our backs.

To make disciples of multitudes in every nation is a command . . . a promise . . . a prophecy — the heart's desire of our Lord and Savior!

But there is a problem. Too often we unwittingly substitute the word "disciple" for the word "evangelize."

Charles Schism, who wrote the preface to this book, defines *evangelism* as the act of getting people saved, and *evangelization* as the discipleship process.

In most Evangelical circles, if we are asked to define the word "disciple," we will give an accurate definition. But the way we practice discipleship is another matter.

> We err in believing we have discipled a person whom we have led to salvation. These new converts are saved, but not discipled.

This is an unconscious trap we fall into because we extravagantly desire spiritual success. This is success measured by, and patterned after, the form set by the religious age we live in now.

THINKING GOD-SIZED

This *religious* pattern is that of a congregation (i.e., the act of *congregating* in one hall for the purpose of conducting a church service).

Preachers who think small are more *possessive* than *scriptural* in their definition of a local church assembly. They think more in limited terms of *their loyal following* than in unlimited terms of *God's Kingdom people*.

> When we don't think big enough — God-sized — we diminish God.

When we look at the big picture we see that salvation is more than just getting individuals saved. Salvation, in the largest sense of the word, gains citizenship for us in the eternal Kingdom of God. Since this is a spiritual Kingdom, made up of saints, it is also referred to as the Church. Out of this Kingdom come self-disciplined and well-trained Soldiers under the command of our King.

COMMERCIALIZED VIEW

Here is what we are not. We are not notches in some evangelist's podium that show how many he has saved. We are not admiring spectators under the headship of some charismatic preacher. We are not left out in the cold, alone and obscure — saved and shelved.

Here is what we are! We are joint participants in a massive endeavor to take the world for Christ. The good news is . . . God is always 100 percent victorious and in the end Satan loses 100 percent.

We are never to seek after anything other than the approval of God, and we should always be willing to go "outside the camp, bearing His reproach" (Heb. 13:13).

Here are Oswald Chambers' convicting comments on Luke 10:20, where Jesus said to His 70 disciples: *"**Do not rejoice in this, that the spirits are subject to you** . . . ."*

> Jesus told the disciples (in Luke 10:20) not to rejoice in successful service, and yet this seems to be the one thing in which most of us do rejoice. We have a commercialized view — we count how many souls have been saved and sanctified, we thank God, and then we think everything is all right.
>
> Yet, our work only begins where God's grace has laid the foundation. ***Our work is not to save souls, but to disciple them.*** Salvation and sanctification are the work of God's sovereign grace, and our work as His disciples is to disciple others' lives until they are totally yielded to God.
>
> One life totally devoted to God is of more value to Him than one hundred lives that have been simply awakened by His Spirit. As workers of God, we must reproduce our own kind spiritually, and those lives will be God's testimony to us as His workers.
>
> God brings us up to a standard of life through His grace, and we are responsible for reproducing that same standard in others.
>
> [My Utmost for His Highest, April 24]

Brethren, only God can save souls, we can't. But not only can we disciple those God has saved; we are commanded to make disciples of **ALL** the nations. He will save them, we will disciple them, because He has **ALL** power and authority, even to the end of the age, to save souls.

And when does "the end of the age" end? No matter what our answer might be, the end of the age — potentially — will come in our lifetime.

THE ENEMIES OF REVIVAL

We can never fulfill the Great Commission until we use **ALL** the tools Jesus provided, and avail ourselves to fulfill **ALL** the prophecies inspired by the Holy Spirit.

Bible prophecies are divine promises that God — who is omnipresent in time and space — has already fulfilled, or is a liar.

For these reasons it may well be that ours is the generation that God (in His foreknowledge and planning) knew would fulfill the Great Commission.

If we Evangelicals are as red-hot to fulfill the Great Commission as we say we are, why would we balk at equipping the saints for the work of this holy commission?

The answer is simple. We don't really want revival. We are comfortable and apathetic. We are saved and going to heaven and that's enough. Until then we are just sitting around, waiting to be taken out of this mess. We plan on the minimum of good works and the maximum of the good life. Bottom line is number one, sorry about the rest.

If that weren't bad enough, history shows that when revival does come, something like two out of three Christians oppose it because it is not like the last revival. Again, history shows that every revival is different. Revival is a progression, a restoration/reformation process that is conforming us to the image of Christ. Therefore, the next great move of God will be a new thing that God is doing.

And again, history shows what killed all prior revivals. The killer was the act of turning revivals into a doctrine and a denomination. New wineskins don't stay new, they mature . . . they age . . . they become old wineskins over the years.

> We must break out of our own little world of experience into abandoned devotion to Him. Think who the New Testament says Jesus Christ is, and then think of the despicable meagerness of the miserable faith we exhibit by saying, 'I haven't had this experience or that experience!' Think what faith in Jesus Christ claims and provides — He can present us faultless before the throne of God, inexpressibly pure, absolutely righteous, and profoundly justified. Stand in absolute adoring faith 'in Christ Jesus, who became for us wisdom from God — and righteousness and sanctification and redemption . . .' (1 Cor. 1:30). How dare we talk of making a sacrifice for

the Son of God! We are saved from hell and total destruction, and then we talk about making sacrifices!

[Oswald Chambers, My Utmost for His Highest, November 13]

SPIRITUAL VICTORY

"Victory in our victorious, invincible Jesus" needs to become our
prophetic battle cry! But victory comes through obedience to the Living Word. And obedience receives **ALL** of God's provision, promises, and preparation for us.

If we are going to pursue the victory God has promised, what
other gifts or tools — besides those already discussed — must we become skilled in?

One of these tools is . . . *the authority in Jesus' name.* Another
tool is *God's promise to overcomers.* These are realistic, practical
goals that you and I are able to attain.

THE PRAYER OF AUTHORITY

**There are two kinds of prayer: the ordinary prayer of
petition, and the authoritative prayer of command.[2]**

Ordinary prayer is praying or petitioning from earth to heaven.
Authoritative prayer is not petitioning, it is commanding.

Commanding prayer is praying from heaven to earth. In Isaiah
45:11 God said, "Command (*appoint, charge, commit*) ye me."

Jesus explained why He could curse a fig tree and see it already
withered and dying the very next day. He said:

> 23. Have faith in God. Truly I say to you, whoever
> says to this mountain, "Be taken up and cast into the
> sea," and does not doubt in his heart, but believes that
> what he says is going to happen, it shall be granted him.
> 24. Therefore I say to you, all things for which you
> pray and ask, believe that you have received them, and
> they shall be granted you. (Mark 11:23-24)

We are to command what God has already commanded; we are to
decide and agree on that which God has already decided and decreed.
Due to the possibility and need of fully knowing God's will, such

faith as this is possible, or Jesus would not have instructed us in how to speak to the **mountain.**

The *"therefore"* in Mark 11:24 shows us that verse 23 also deals with the subject of prayer. Yet nowhere in verse 23 are we told to pray to God. Instead, it simply says, "Say unto this mountain." In other words, we are to command the mountain that hinders. This is authoritative prayer that does not **speak to** God, it **agrees with** God.

David, when he was just a boy, stood in front of Goliath and boldly announced that he was going to roll his head — then and there. Was David just a cocky, arrogant kid? No, he was speaking out of a **sure** conviction that God **TOLD** him to kill this defiant giant. So he did — plain and simple. He didn't just utter an optimistic statement of faith and then hope for the best. He spoke God's command into existence.

> Here is a spiritual truth. Having giant-killing faith comes from a sure knowledge of God's perfect will, and authoritatively speaking His will into existence. "Mountain, be taken up and cast into the sea — in Jesus name!"

YOU HAVE THE LEGAL RIGHT

God has made this authority available to us to command what He has already decided. The power of attorney — the legal right to this authority — is granted to us in Jesus' name. For instance, when we pray to the Father, we invoke the authority Jesus gave us to pray in His name.[3]

> When we do ANYTHING that is according to His will and instruction, we are to use His name — to make it legal — to make it His.

All things are in subjection under His feet because He is the Head of the body of Christ . . . the living stones . . . the church . . . us. And if we — being in the body of Christ — use the authority of God, we may bring all things under His feet — which in fact are our feet as well.

May God teach us how to use the authority of Jesus in these last days. Is there a mountain in your life that you need to speak to today?

Here are some Scripture verses to back up this claim.

18. Truly I say to you, whatever you shall bind on earth shall be bound in heaven; and whatever you loose on earth shall be loosed in heaven. (Matthew 18)

17. And the seventy returned with joy, saying, "Lord, even the demons are subject to us in Your name."
18. And He said to them, "I was watching Satan fall from heaven like lightning.
19. Behold, I have given you authority to tread upon serpents and scorpions, and over all the power of the enemy, and nothing shall injure you.
20. Nevertheless, do not rejoice in this, that the spirits are subject to you, but rejoice that your names are recorded in heaven.
21. At that very time He rejoiced greatly in the Holy Spirit and said, "I praise Thee, O Father, Lord of heaven and earth, that Thou didst hide these things from the wise and intelligent and didst reveal them to babes. Yes. Father, for thus it was well pleasing in thy sight. (Luke 10)

18. And Jesus came up and spoke to them saying, "All authority has been given to Me in heaven and on earth.
19. Go therefore [using the authority in My name] and make disciples of all the nations . . . (Matthew 28 Insert added)

God has hidden these truths (Luke 10) from the wise and intelligent and has revealed them to Christians such as you and me. The question is, although these truths are revealed to us, are we using them?

YOU ARE BLESSED

19. God is not a man, that He should lie. He is not a human, that He should change His mind. Has He ever promised and not carried it through?

20. I received a command to bless; He has blessed, and I cannot reverse it! (Numbers 23:19-20)

Balaam was commanded to speak this blessing to Israel. The Jewish people historically understood the importance of "hearing" a blessing by making the **Shema** the central prayer of Judaism: "Hear, O Israel, the Lord our God, the Lord is one" (Deut. 6:4).

Jesus had a favorite expression to accentuate His message, sometimes crying out in a loud voice after an especially important discourse: "He who has ears to hear, let him hear!" The first and most extensive parable in Mark's Gospel is the parable of the sower. You may recall that chapter 4 was devoted to that parable.

OUR ACCOUNTABILITY FOR NEWLY ACQUIRED KNOWLEDGE

HE WHO HAS EARS LET HIM HEAR. We are to place a very high premium on the true knowledge of God. The treasure of the Knowledge of God that is hidden within the Word of God is of far greater value than any earthly fortune. And, it also requires that we search for it.

This heavenly treasure is purposely hidden, because it is not intended for those who are halfhearted or indifferent.

Yea, if thou criest after knowledge, and liftest up thy voice for understanding; if thou seekest her as silver; and searchest for her as for hid treasures, then shalt thou understand the fear of the Lord, and find the knowledge of God. (Proverbs 2:4-5 KJV)

In the Gospel of John there is a lengthy allegory that concerns the Shepherd and His sheep. The chief characteristic of the sheep is that they hear the Shepherd's voice. Everything, it seems, hinges on hearing His voice.

Three times the phrase is repeated, "He who has ears, let him hear!" It is a story about being able to hear a spiritual insight that only God's Spirit can reveal to our spirit. Are you ready?

In the parable of the sower in Matthew 13:1-23 Jesus said, **"For whoever *has*, to him shall more be *given*."**

In context with the parable of the sower, Jesus reiterates vs. 11 in vs. 12, saying something like this:

> Since it has been granted to you to know the mysteries of the kingdom of heaven, to you shall more of the mysteries of the kingdom be given, and you shall have an abundance of knowledge of these mysteries.

> On the other hand, anyone who does not have knowledge of the mysteries, even what he has heard, (vs. 19a) shall be taken away from him because he does not understand.

This gives the evil one opportunity to come and snatch away what has been sown in his heart (vs. 19b).

We all need to ask ourselves, "Do I understand what God may be revealing to me as I read this book?" None of us want to give "the evil one opportunity to come and snatch away what has been sown in (our) heart."

If you have come into a new understanding while reading this book, please remember that God will hold you accountable for it. With that exhortation in mind, meditate on the following verses.

> There is no prophetic teaching found in Scripture that can be interpreted by mans unaided reason; for no prophetic teaching ever came in the old days at the mere wish of man, but man moved by the Holy Spirit, spoke direct from God. (2 Peter 1:20-21 20th Century N.T.)

> When you assemble, each one has a psalm, has a teaching, has a revelation . . . Let all things be done for edification. (1 Corinthians 14:26b)

> I pray . . . that the God of our Lord Jesus Christ, the Father of glory, may give you a spirit of wisdom and of revelation in the knowledge of Him. (Ephesians 1:17)

AS WE ENTER THE FULLNESS OF TIME

As we approach the end of this age, I believe the Father's heart is fervently working to train people who will represent Him in these later last days. Thus, as no other time in history, we must become people who truly and accurately reveal Jesus Christ.

> **There is no truth more profound than this: God's expressed will for us is nothing short of the fullness of Christ! All that Jesus did, all that Jesus was in His earthly character, and all that Jesus purchased — Christ in divine fullness — is the mandate spoken by God for the church.**
>
> **Francis Frangipane**

At the core of our destiny is one source of fulfillment and power: Christ in us. John confirms this when he says, *"As He is, so also are we in this world"* (1 John 4:17). And again, *"By this we know that we are in Him: the one who says he abides in Him ought himself to walk in the same manner as He walked"* (1 John 2:5c-6). Jesus himself said that we were to be students whose goal is to be *"fully trained,"* until we become *"like [our] teacher"* (Luke 6:40).

In whatever study or course of training we embark upon in our spiritual life, we should ask ourselves one question: Will I become more Christlike in the process? Our goal should be to present the singular source of our destiny: Christlikeness.

God's goal with us is not merely that we prepare anointed teachings, but anointed people — disciples who shall reveal the fullness of Christ as we enter the fullness of time.

THE RISK OF RECOVERY

In one word the message of this book is "RECOVERY." God is calling upon the church to RECOVER all that was lost in the first three centuries. God never changes, and the Bible never changes, but a whole lot changed in the church. Only RECOVERY; only restoration of first century Christianity can prepare the church for these latter last days. But RECOVERY requires change; a word that invokes *fear* in us all.

God may not be asking you and me to change churches (denominations or doctrinal groups), but God is asking us to take the *risk* of allowing His Holy Spirit to *bring change to EVERY church*. After all, just as no individual is perfect, neither is any church.

Each person's life is written in risk — the ones taken and the ones avoided.

John Maxwell
Running With The Giants

If we take no risk, there is no need for faith. Will Jesus find courageous faith, or comfortable traditions in your church and mine when He returns?

Take the risk of recovery . . . Amen. ♦

End Section

Directory of Names
End Notes
Selected Bibliography
Meet The Author

A mind that has been stretched will never return to its original dimension.

— Albert Einstein

Directory of Names

Beasley, Manley: 189.
Blackaby, Henry: 162, 165, 246, 249.
Boone, Wellington: vii, viii, 35, 245
Bright, Bill: 42, 158, 162-170, 246, 249.
Chambers, Oswald: 213, 223, 225.
Coleman, Robert: 139, 245, 249.
Colson, Charles: 62.
Cymbala, Jim: 97-98, 129, 171, 191, 240, 243, 246-247, 249.
Duplessis, David: 70.
Einstein, Albert: 213, 234.
Floyd, Ronnie: 90, 163, 166-170, 246, 249, 252.
Frangipane, Francis: 11, 36, 66, 68, 230, 239.
Graham, Billy: 10, 139-140, 158, 240, 245.
Hitler, Adolf: 75, 239.
Josephus: 30.
Joyner, Rick: 16, 17, 30, 171, 237, 239.
Kennedy, John F.: 22.
Kennedy, John: 87-88, 240, 249.
King, Claude: 162, 165, 246, 249.
Lenski, R. C. H.: 108-109.
Lucado, Max: 28, 84.
McKeever, Jim: 212-213.
Miller, Craig: 32, 238.
Murray, Andrew: 191.
Nee, Watchman: 248.
Paine, Thomas: 64.
Pasteur, Louis: 86.
Ravenhill, Leonard: 14-15, 155, 237, 249.
Rosenthal, Marvin J: 53, 56, 238.
Ryrie, Charles: 5, 88-89, 106, 116, 175.
Sanders, J. Oswald: 189.
Semmelweis, Ignaz: 86.
Schism, Charles: viii, 221.
Spurgeon, Charles: 131, 243.

End Notes

Chapter 1: A Vision of Recovery

1. One of the bright shining stars of the Puritan movement, Pastor **John Robinson**, gave his farewell address, which he delivered at the time the Pilgrims fled England for America. In that message the Holy Spirit gave him a prophetic word, which is still a challenge to the church four centuries later. John Robinson wrote:

   "I charge you before God and before His blessed angels, that you follow me no further than you have seen me follow the Lord Jesus Christ. If God reveal anything to you by any other instrument of His (another ministry), be as ready to receive it as ever you were to receive any truth by my ministry: *for I am verily persuaded, I am very confident, the Lord hath more truth yet to break forth out of His Holy Word.* For my part, I cannot sufficiently bewail the condition of the reformed Churches, who are come to a full stop in religion and will go at present, no further than the instruments of their first reformation. The Lutherans cannot be drawn to go beyond what Luther saw: whatever part of his will our good God has imparted and revealed unto Calvin, they will rather die than embrace it. And the Calvinists, you see, stick fast where they were left by that great man of God who 'yet saw not all things.' This is a misery much to be lamented; for though they were burning and shining lights in their time, yet *they penetrated not into the whole counsel of God: but were they now living, they would be as willing to embrace further light, as that which they first received.*" (Editors emphasis)

   Quoted from John Fletcher's *History of Independence*, Vol. 3, 69.
2. Arthur Wallis, The Radical Christian (revised), Colombia, Cityhill Publishing, 1987, 161.

Chapter 2: The Next Great Move of God

1. **Charles Dickens.** *A Tale of Two Cities*, Book 1, Chapter 1.
2. **Leonard Ravenhill,** *Why Revival Tarries*, Minneapolis, Bethany House Publishers, 101. Evangelist and orator Ravenhill conducted huge outdoor revivals in England before World War II and wrote several bestseller books on revival.
3. Ibid, P. 106
4. **Rick Joyner,** *The Morning Star Journal*, Vol. 8, No. 3, excerpts from article: Church History Part VIII — Persecution and Perseverance, P. 67-74.
5. Ibid.

Chapter 3: The Coming Glorious Harvest

1. This teaching was borrowed from **Reuven Doron**, Embrace Israel Ministries, PO Box 10077, Cedar Rapids, IA 52410-0077, www.embraceisrael.org
2. **Biblical Archaeology Review**, July/August 1999, Vol. 25. No. 4., Pinpointing the Temple, by David Jacobson. This scholarly article demonstrates that

Herod's Temple sat precisely within the parameters of the Dome of the Rock, al Sakhra.
3. **Marcus J. Borg and N.T. Wright,** *The Meaning of Jesus — Two Versions*, Harpers San Francisco, 1989, 73, 84, 96, 98, 100, 101, 117, 262.
4. The First Temple was built by Solomon in the tenth century B.C. and was destroyed by the Babylonians in 587 B.C. When the exiles returned from Babylonia in the sixth century B.C. they rebuilt the Temple — the Second Temple. Herod's later rebuild (19 B.C.-A.D. 64) is also regarded as the Second Temple in Jewish tradition.
5. **Craig Miller** is a dynamic, world-traveling evangelist that is as bold as John the Baptist. Contact him at 501-855-3433 or 501-636-8400, P.O. Box 874, Rogers, AR 72757; CMMGLOBAL@aol.com; www.globalimpact.info.

Chapter 4: The Coming Sovereign Manifestations of God

1. The word "angel" means "messenger." It can refer to spirit beings, or human beings (e.g. John the Baptist, disciples — Luke 9:52), or God Himself (The Lord becoming His own messenger [e.g. the phrase, "the Angel of the Lord" in the OT]). However, in Matthew 13:39 the in-text meaning is "spirit beings."

Chapter 5: Old and New Testament Confirmation

1. **Dale Rumble,** *The Glorious Harvest*, Fountain of Life Publications, 71 Old Kings Highway, Lake Katrine, NY 12449
2. **Tares:** This plant is the bearded darnel or rye grass, and resembles wheat so closely that it can prosper in the Cornfields and be almost indistinguishable until fully grown. It flourishes in quantities in countries along the Mediterranean Sea. To the farmer it is one of the most destructive of all weeds, and in Eastern countries women and children are employed to pick out these tares before they can ruin the good crop. As soon as the ears are formed, it is possible to recognize them, but both the wheat and the tares are usually left intermixed until after reaping. Then fanning is used to blow away and separate the lighter and smaller seeds of the tares. And after threshing, all seeds are shaken in a sieve. Thus any darnel seeds still remaining will usually pass through and leave the larger wheat behind. The inner coats of these seeds often harbor seriously poisonous fungus growths that, if eaten by humans or animals, will cause dizziness and vomiting and sometimes even death. Virgil the historian calls it the infelix lolium, and the Arabs siwan.

— All The Plants Of The Bible, Winifred Walker
3. **Marvin J. Rosenthal,** *Zion's Fire Magazine*, March-April 1997, P.O. Box 690909, Orlando, Florida, 32869.
4. References to the Kingdom of Heaven: Matt. 3:2; Matt. 6:10 and 33; Luke 22:29; John 3:1-8; Acts 8:12; Acts 14:22; Rom. 14:17; Col. 4:11; 1 Thess. 2:12; 2 Peter 1:10-11.
5. **Marvin J. Rosenthal,** *Zion's Fire Magazine*, March-April 1997, P.O. Box 690909, Orlando, Florida, 32869.

Chapter 6: Reviving the Fallen Away

1. **David Wilkerson** wrote a two book series contending that a depression is coming. He bases his prediction on Old Testament history and not on an oracle from God. Even if you do not believe a depression is coming, these still are important books to read. The principles he presents are right, even if his prediction proves to be wrong. The two books are titled: America's Last Call — On the Brink of a Financial Holocaust and God's Plan To Protect His People in the Coming Depression. World Challenge, Inc., P.O. Box 260, Lindale, TX 75771.
2. **Francis Frangipane's** article: "Open Letter to Ed Tarkowski," found on the Internet at http://www.frangipane.org.
3. **Francis Frangipane.** This quote came from an email news letter dated September 14, 2000. Arrow Publications, RiverofLifeMailer@InChristsImage.org.
4. **Francis Frangipane's** article: "Open Letter to Ed Tarkowski," found on the Internet at http://www.frangipane.org.

Chapter 7: The Unity Jesus Prayed For Will Come

1. This information was edited from several sources, but the main one was from **Rick Joyner** literature.
   Adolph Hitler: The cruel, demented leadership of Adolph Hitler probably directly resulted in more death and destruction than any other single individual in history. The name Hitler will forever be one of the most ugly scars on human history. However, even Churchill acknowledged that if Hitler had died in 1938, he would have been considered one of the greatest leaders of all time.

   When Hitler came to power, Germany was suffering under some of the worst economic and political conditions a nation has suffered during modern times. There was between fifty and seventy-five percent unemployment. The government was bankrupt and the German mark actually fell to an exchange rate of four trillion to a dollar before it was declared totally worthless. Mobs ruled the streets, perversion was rampant, and the whole nation tottered on the brink of becoming a Soviet state. In just four years, Hitler not only balanced the budget; he paid off the national debt while building the most powerful economy in the world. He brought employment to near one hundred percent. He restored Germany's national dignity, and built the most powerful army in the world. He also drove pornography and other forms of perversion from the land. There has never been such a transformation of a country in the history of the world.

   Most of the church in Germany was so fooled by Hitler that they helped establish his power base, with some church leaders actually calling him "a messiah." Are we doomed to keep repeating history because we fail to study history?

Chapter 8: Does God Speak To Us Today?

1. Most Pentecostal denominations have very conservative doctrinal statements regarding the inspiration and authority of the Bible. Thus, most Pentecostals are Evangelicals.

Alister McGrath, an English theologian, listed six characteristics of Evangelicalism. In his opinion, these include: 1. the supreme authority of Scripture, 2. the majesty of Jesus Christ, 3. the Lordship of the Holy Spirit, 4. the need for personal conversion, 5. the priority of evangelism, 6. the importance of Christian community. Mainstream Trinitarian Pentecostals clearly fulfill these six criteria. [Alister McGrath, Evangelicalism and the Future of Christianity, London: Hodder and Stoughton, 1994, 51. Nevertheless, in popular usage, conservative Evangelicalism generally refers to that portion of Evangelicalism that is noncharismatic. In the United States, the leadership of Billy Graham and Carl Henry would represent conservative Evangelicalism.

2. **John Kennedy** is a precious brother in the Lord, and I highly recommend this very affordable, and easily understood book on church history, The Torch of the Testimony, Auburn: Christian Books, 1965, 30. I can assure you that it is on my bookshelf along with many other books on church history, and the margins are crammed with my scribbled notes.

Chapter 9: When The Perfect Comes

1. **Charles Carrin, *The Edge of Glory*,** published by Charles Carrin Ministries, P.O. Drawer 800, Boynton Beach, Florida, 33425-0800, 1999, 99. Used by permission of Charles Carrin.
2. Similar words, such as boat, vessel, and ship, can be either neuter or feminine in gender. Even so, I believe the corollary behind comparing a ship to "the perfect" is very descriptive and appropriate in this setting.
3. I believe that my definition of the perfect and the partial, as used in 2 Cor. 13:10, will hold up under any eschatology.
4. The argument that "not only has 'knowledge' not passed away, but it has greatly increased this century, therefore the gifts are still valid for today," has a fatal flaw. Knowledge has increased today, that is true. However, this "knowledge" in verse 8 is in reference to, and in context with "the word of knowledge" in 1 Corinthians 12:8.
5. **Jim Cymbala, *Fresh Wind, Fresh Fire*,** Grand Rapids, Zondervan, 1997, 147. Jim Cymbala is Pastor of the Brooklyn Tabernacle. Used by permission of Zondervan Publishing House.
6. **Jim Cymbala, *Fresh Faith*,** Grand Rapids, Zondervan, 1999, 204. Used by permission of Zondervan Publishing House.

Chapter 10: The Partial Will Be Done Away

1. **William Law, *The Power of the Spirit*,** Fort Washington, PA: Christian Literature Crusade, 1971, 23.
2. Part of the insight for this chapter came from the book: *Empowered Evangelicals*, by **Rick Nathan** and **Ken Wilson**, Vine Books.

Chapter 11: Do You Believe The Bible?

1. **John Maxwell** conducts lay ministry training seminars across the country, and is a frequent speaker at Promise Keeper rallies.

2. **Dr. Lee W. Woodard, DBA,** *Kodex W: Old and Holy*, Printed by Lee W. Woodard, P. O. Box 1605, Sallisaw, Oklahoma 74955, www.lasalle monument.com. Dr. Lee W. Woodard has a forty plus years background of in Biblical, Paleographical, Historical, and linguistic studies, and presently pastors a Christian church in Sallisaw.

   Since the Latin-English expression "Codex" is dealing with documents written in ancient Greek, which has no "C," as such the author chose to change "Codex" into a combined Anglican-Greek-Germanic "Kodex." Thus becoming part of the book title, "Kodex W."

2a. In 1981 while attending Phillips University Graduate Seminary, Enid, Oklahoma, Dr. Woodard was studying the "Infancy Narratives." He became convinced that there was a recognizable poetic rhyme within Joseph's dream about the miraculous conception of Jesus. His professor, Dr. Boring, suggested that he look at some photographic facsimiles of the actual pages of some of the oldest known manuscripts to further his study. He was looking for manuscripts with line arrangements or some sort of small scribal notations or markings of rhyming words. Most manuscript facsimiles had very little by way of scribal notes or markings, which would apply to what he was studying, until he came to Codex Washingtonensis, or Codex W for short. Then he realized that he had discovered something potentially far more important. Strangely, no one prior to him had noticed the marvelously informative Aramaic notes.

2b. Washingtonensis is Latin for Washington, the city where that old Codes came to be housed. It is on display at the Charles Lang Freer National Gallery of Art, which is a significant portion of the Smithsonian Institution and Museum complex in Washington, D.C.

2c. On December 19, 1906, Cheikh Aly Arabi of Gizeh, Egypt sold codex W and other old Bible manuscripts to Charles L. Freer. Freer was a wealthy man who made his fortune manufacturing railroad passenger cars. Cheikh Aly probably got these manuscripts from an illegal artifacts digger, so the exact location of the find is unknown. But the digger said he found this Codex in a wooden housing buried in the sand in the ruins of an ancient Christian Church-Monastic community in Medinet Dismay, Egypt.

2d. Codex is a formal Latin expression for an old and important collection of historically valuable manuscript(s), or, in this case, a bound, velum (sheep and goatskin) paged "book:" composed of four old codices, or originally separate manuscripts, bound together within that larger book. These four codices were composed of the four Gospels of Matthew, John, Luke, and Mark (bound in that order),

2e. We know from history that a scribe did not sign an author's signature, but the scribe would write, "signed by Levi Mark." Sometimes patriarchs (such as Mark) would dictate to a scribe. Then the author would proof the work and sign it. One time Paul said, "signed with my own hand." John signed his gospel this way, "I Jesus' John sign this." There may well have been a class of professional scribes, such as Fortunatus, Sylvanus, Tertius, etc, who did part of the tedious scribal and manuscript reproduction duties.

All four of the gospels and Acts were progressive works that took years to complete. The first edition of Matthew's gospel did not contain the genealogy, nor the birth and escape into Egypt. Copies of it were made and passed around. Then years later Matthew pinned the beginning we know.

It would take pages to explain all the history behind the gospels. The historians of the time, and other letters and records tell us these things.

Since the authors signed their names in both Greek and Aramaic, and since their personal seal is by their name, and since the date it was signed is usually in Aramaic and a special coding method, this proves that Codex W is an original. No other gospel manuscript has a signature in both languages, just a scribal notation of who signed it.

Most commentaries date Codex W to about A.D. 400, but the dates on the manuscripts and in the pictures — written in Aramaic — are all first century. The scholars who estimated the date at A.D. 400. could not read Aramaic, and hesitantly made their estimate on other factors.

Some of the Old Testament scholars will probably think of the Dead Sea discoveries as being just as important (at least to them). But this discovery needs some of those Dead Sea scholars to issue agreements to some of the Aramaic on Codex W.

2f. It may seem outlandish to claim that a First Century codex containing the four Gospels has been found that is in the actual handwriting — in whole or in part — of Matthew, Mark, Luke and John. But in all areas of science and academia the validity of EVERY discovery and theory is disputed, and ALL GREAT DISCOVERIES are rejected for a few years before they are accepted.

As a result of Dr. Woodard's research, this discovery is being recognized by an ever-growing number of scholars, but is virtually unknown outside of this small circle of academics. There may be folks who will want to argue with some aspects of Dr. Woodard's claim (at least for a while); but he predicts that eventually all of the academic community will recognize Codex W as being an original.

Once this discovery becomes fully recognized there will be a lot of interest in those samples of first century A.D. Aramaic, even though most of them are of small script and some of them smudged and difficult to read. Additionally, there are those who might be searching for the latest in New Testament studies.

2g. On the last page of Mark's Gospel three endings are visible, along with his seal after each of them, and his signature and date at the bottom. Shorter endings were copied and passed on before the longer endings were added. The Codex W ending was Mark's last extension while living in Egypt. Although Jerome quoted part of it, this ending did not get passed on. Perhaps that ending was added not very long before this collection of the four Gospels was bound and then buried. Dr. Woodard believes that the ending within the KJV is from the first century A.D., and from Mark himself in A.D. 72.

Dr. Woodard is of the opinion that Mark himself authorized and approved the various endings for his Gospel; and he may very well have penned them himself. It should be kept in mind, however, that there were trained Scribes and penmanship experts who often did the final versions of those Manuscripts; but in such cases Mark (and other Gospel namesakes) would still have affixed their own seals and signatures, approving what they had authorized for the text.

It is unreasonable to believe that scribes invented the Text. They just rewrote it in fine script to fit what the gospel namesakes were intending and approving; and it is reasonable to believe that the endings of quite a few Gospels and Epistles were altered by the namesakes — witness Mark, John, Paul.

The wooden book cover on the front and back of the manuscripts helped preserve the codex. The front cover has a portrait of Matthew and John painted on it, and the back cover has a portrait of Mark and Luke. Their names are painted into the pictures in Aramaic and Greek, so there is no missing who the pictures represent. Dates and location are also encoded into the pictures. Except for John, the paintings are in fair condition, giving us some idea of what these great men looked like. The manuscripts of the four gospels were assembled in this order: Matthew, John, Mark, and Luke.

Chapter 12: Not False . . . Just Fallible

1. Much of the material under the heading: "We also need the gifts of the Spirit," was excerpted in edited form from Steve Thompson's article titled: The Lies That Bind. The Morning Star Journal, Vol. 7, No. 2, Charlotte, North Carolina, P. 47-53.
2. **Jim Cymbala with Dean Merrill**, *Fresh Faith*, Grand Rapids, Michigan, Zondervan Publishing House, 1999, 68-70. Used by permission of Zondervan Publishing House.
2a. The Works of **John Wesley** — CD, Franklin, Tenn.: Providence House, 1995; see also The Character of a Methodist, The Works of John Wesley, 3d ed., Vol. 8, 339, London: Wesleyan Methodist Book Room, 1872; reprinted Grand Rapids: Baker, 1996.
2b. **Charles Spurgeon** sermon entitled The Eternal Name, preached on the evening of May 27, 1855, at Exeter Hall, London.
3. A reference: **Dr. Neighbor** teaches (in his book: *The Seven Last Words of the Church: We've Never Done it That Way Before*), that our enslavement to tradition can cause us to miss the present leading of the Holy Spirit.

Chapter 13: Peter's Definition of the Last Days

1. Verses 19 and 20 in Acts 2 reads a lot like verses 29 and 30 in Matthew 24.
   29. But immediately after the tribulation of those days the sun will be darkened, and the moon will not give its light, and the stars will fall from the sky, and the powers of the heavens will be shaken,
   30. and then the sign of the Son of Man will appear.
2. It can be argued that Peter reluctantly quoted verses 19 and 20 only because he was trying to get to verse 21. Here we are in the middle of one of the most important days in church history. The Holy Spirit has 120 people simultaneously

preaching in a language they don't know. And Peter is telling us all about something he had no way of knowing anything about. Obviously, the Holy Spirit was using him as an oracle to proclaim a great new revelation to the church. Due to the importance of this momentous day in history and the unprecedented anointing on Peter and the 120, it seems ridiculous that anything that happened that morning was fumbled or bumbled or done in the flesh. Therefore, I believe that there is nothing misleading or erroneous in this passage of the inerrant Word of God. Surely everything Peter said that morning was a completely clear and straightforward oracle of God.

3. The following confirmation was copied from Parousia . . . The Sign Ministries Newsletter, Spring 1998, by **Charles Cooper**. P.O. Box 113, West Olive, MI 49460. Article: Dispensational Foundations, Acts, Joel, and Revelation, Part 2 of 2, 3, and 4.

Peter's quotation of Joel 2:28-32 evidences several changes from its Old Testament counterpart, the most important being the phrase "in the last days." The original phrase "after these things" is very broad and offers no clue as to when the event would occur from Joel's perspective. However, with the alternative phrase "in the last days" the timing became crystal clear. The outpouring of the Holy Spirit marked the entrance into a period called "the last days" (the church age), the period proceeding the day of the Lord. The gift of the Spirit is thus a token that the last days foretold by the prophets have arrived. This period is characterized by prophetic utterances (2:17).

Unlike the previous generations, both male and female, the young and old, slave and free will reveal God's will. Secondly, heavenly wonders and earthly signs will mark the beginning of the eschatological Day of the Lord (2:19-20); and thirdly, salvation is available to anyone requesting it (2:21).

The book of Acts does contain prophecies, visions, and miraculous signs. However, there are no cosmic disturbance on a magnitude prophesied by Joel listed in Acts. Therefore, the Pentecost experience is a beginning of the fulfillment of Joel 2:28-32, but it certainly is not the total fulfillment.

A second significant change by Peter of Joel's passage is the phrase "and they shall prophesy" at the end of verse 18. Peter's insertion of this sentence in Joel's prophecy at the beginning of verse 19 underscores the fact that as prophetic activity marked the beginning of "the last days," the end of "the last days" will be characterized by prophetic activity as well. God's servants shall announce the coming Day of the Lord. The time period between these two events is called "the last days," "the church age," and "the dispensation of mystery."

4. It can be argued that while the Spirit is certainly inspiring the sermon, it may be one of the things He brings to mind that Jesus taught. Some say a "word of knowledge" usually does not refer directly to a Scripture. But, since opinions are a dime a dozen, here is my nickel's worth. When God speaks knowledge to us in word form . . . how are we to restrict, define, or dictate His source? When the Holy Spirit tells a Christian a "word of knowledge," the message usually addresses (reveals, defines) a problem that the ministering Christian had no

way of knowing about. In like manner, a "word of wisdom" usually gives God's answer to the problem. And the problem and answer most probably are both addressed in Scripture. That is both an academic and an experiential answer.

5. See note 1.

6. A teaching borrowed from **Wellington Boone**, as recorded in The Morning Star Journal, Vol. 9, No. 3, P. 59; under the heading: Visions and Dreams.

7. **Billy Graham** wrote the introduction to **Robert Coleman's** book, *The Coming World Revival*, Wheaten, Crossway Books, 1989, 1995, P. 154-159. Coleman, among his other credits, is also director of the Institute of Evangelism at the Billy Graham Center in Wheaten, Illinois, and serves as Dean of the International Schools of Evangelism.

8. Water and rain can be symbolic of the Holy Spirit, but only if the context supports this symbolism. In John 7:37-39, the context supports the symbolism, but in James 5:7-8 and Joel 2:23 some believe that the rains may simply be an analogy, but Billy Graham used it symbolically (see Billy Graham quote above).

Chapter 14: Observing All The Lords Commandments

1. This could refer to a certain level of maturity attainable in this age (1 Cor. 2:6; 14:20; Phil. 3:15; Heb. 5:14).

2. The explanation for the four goals (Eph. 4:13) was borrowed from the paper that **Charles E. Powell** (a graduate student at Dallas Theological Seminary) read at the 48th annual meeting of the Evangelical Theological Society, November 21-23, 1996, in Jackson, Mississippi. The paper is titled: Questions Cessationists Should Ask: A Bible Examination of Cessationism.

3. This is "selective unbelief," or believing what we want to believe, and blotting out the rest. Several Scriptures warn us about adding or omitting words to the Bible, such as Rev 22:18-19; Deut. 4:2; 12:32; Prov. 30:6. These warnings tell us what our unbelief will cost us — in a word — VICTORY. If there is anything we don't have in the church, it would be . . . victory. Oh, we have salvation and successes, but victory has eluded us because belief . . . faith . . . obedience has eluded us. It is time to start believing ALL of the Bible, and believing God, and start disbelieving some of our old, die-hard traditions that came into existence sometime after A.D. 1520.

4. The Scriptures mention twenty-three apostles. Some of these apostles were not Jews. In addition to calling Jesus Christ an Apostle, and naming the original twelve Apostles, the Bible also calls these men apostles:

> Barnabas and Paul (Acts 14:14)
> James, the Lord's brother (Gal. 1:19)
> Andronicus and Junia (Rom. 16:7) *
> Silvanus and Timotheus (1 Thess. 1:1: 2:6) *
> Apollos (1 Cor. 4:4-9)
> Two unnamed brethren (2 Cor. 8:23) **
> Epaphroditus (Phil. 2:25) **

> * Interpretation is debated by scholars.
> ** The word translated "messenger" in these verses is the same Greek word translated "apostle" elsewhere.

5. Obviously not all the pastors, evangelists, and teachers in that day were recorded in the Bible, so — in all probability — not all apostles and prophets were recorded either. These prophets are mentioned in the New Testament:

> Agabus and other prophets (Acts 11:27-28).
> Barnabas, Simeon, Lucius, and Manaen (Acts 13:1).
> Judas and Silas (Acts 15:32).
> A prophet of their own (Titus 1:12).
> The four sisters who were prophetess' (Acts 21:9).

6. The Scripture reference for these thirteen points: (1) 1 Cor. 9:1-2; 2 Cor. 3:1-3. (2) (2 Cor. 1:12; 2:17; 3:4-6; 5:11; 6:3-13; 7:2; 10:13-18; 11:6; 23-28. (3) 2 Cor. 4:7-15; 5:4-10; 11:21-23; 13:4. (4) 2 Cor. 10:3-4, 8-11; 13:2-4, 10. (5) 2 Cor. 11:1-6. (6) 2 Cor. 11:6. (7) 2 Cor. 11:7-11. (8) 2 Cor. 22:20,21. (9) 2 Cor. 12:1-6). (10) 2 Cor. 12:7-9, 11. (11) 2 Cor. 12:10. (12) 1 Cor. 4:15. (13) Acts 1:22. This research and these Scripture references were borrowed from the paper that Charles E. Powell (a graduate student at Dallas Theological Seminary) read at the 48th annual meeting of the Evangelical Theological Society, November 21-23, 1966, in Jackson, Mississippi. The paper is titled: Questions Cessationists Should Ask: A Bible Examination of Cessationism.
7. Books on this subject are listed in the Selected Bibliography.
8. Much of the material under the heading: **THE RENEWAL OF OLD WINESKINS**, was excerpted from **Dutch Sheets'** article titled: ***Divine Disorder — the Paradox of Revival***. The Morning Star Journal, Vol. 9, No. 4, Charlotte, North Carolina, P. 8.

Chapter 15: On The Cutting Edge Of What God is Doing Today

1. **Dr. Bill Bright, *The Coming Revival*,** America's Call to Fast, Pray, and "Seek God's Face", Orlando, NewLife Publications, 1995, 35-39, P. 41-42.
2. **Henry T. Blackaby and Claude V. King, *Experiencing God*,** Nashville: Broadman and Holman Publications, 1994, P. 31.
   Author's Note: Amos 3:7 says: "Surely the Lord God does nothing unless He reveals His secret counsel to His servants the prophets."
3. **Dr. Ronnie W. Floyd, *The Power of Prayer and Fasting*:** 10 Secrets of Spiritual Strength, Nashville, Broadman and Holman Publishers, 1997, P. 31-37.
4. **Jim Cymbala, *Fresh Wind, Fresh Fire*,** Grand Rapids, Zondervan, 1997, 97. Used by permission of Zondervan Publishing House.

Chapter 17: The Reformation's Greatest Weapon

1. **Daniel Wallace, *Who's Afraid of the Holy Spirit?*,** Christianity Today, September 12, 1994.
2. **Kenneth Scott Latourette, *A History Of Christianity*,** Vol. 1, Beginnings to 1500, Revised Edition, Harper San Francisco, 1975, P. 215.

3. Ibid, P. 117,118.
4. Excerpted from *the Apostolic Fathers — Second Edition*, translated by **J.B. Lightfoot and J.R. Harmer**, published by Baker Book House.

Chapter 18: Attaining To The Unity Of The Faith

1. **Jim Cymbala with Dean Merrill, *Fresh Faith***, Grand Rapids, Michigan, Zondervan Publishing House, 1999, P. 200-201. Used by permission of Zondervan Publishing House.
2. Gnosticism is a system of belief that combines ideas derived from Greek philosophy, Oriental mysticism, and, ultimately, Christianity. The purest modern form of Christian Gnosticism is Mormonism. One of their statements of faith is . . . as man is, God once was; as God is, man may become — a pure Gnostic statement. Gnosticism dates back to the Garden of Eden when Satan told Eve, " . . . you will be like God, knowing good and evil" (Gen. 3:5b).

Those that believe that God has faith, or is faith, or needs faith, believe a Gnostic doctrine. God does not **HAVE** faith because He does not **NEED** faith — He is absolute. Let me explain.

Nowhere in Scripture does it say that God **HAS** faith or that God **IS** faith. The Bible does say that "God is love," but it never says "God is faith."

For God to NEED anything would be for that thing to exist separately from Him, and He would be dependent on it. For God to have or need faith would be to make Him dependent on faith. Faith would have power over God, and God would not be omnipotent. He would be like us — still developing.

Since God is omniscient (knows all things), omnipotent (has all power and authority), and omnipresent (present in all space at the same time), He does not **NEED** faith. This is mind boggling to us, but God does not **HAVE** faith or belief or confidence because He doesn't **NEED** anything.

There is no such thing as "God faith" or "the faith of God." Since He has all power and all knowledge and foreknowledge, He never has to wonder if He can do as He wishes. He speaks and His will is fulfilled — He is supreme.

God told Moses at the burning bush; "I AM that I AM." In other words, God does not HAVE anything; He IS all in all! God IS eternally omnipresent in the present tense! There is no yesterday or tomorrow or beginning or end to Him, only the present tense, but present in all of time and space . . . the Alpha and the Omega.

Chapter 20: Overcomers and the Bride of Christ

1. **Tommy Tenney, *The God Chasers***, Shippensburg, PA, Destiny Image, 1999, back cover.

Chapter 21: A Vision Of Recovery — Revisited

1. See "Ministry of Angels" in Chapter 4, The Coming Sovereign Manifestations of God.

2. Teachings taken from **Watchman Nee's** book, ***God's Plan and the Overcomers.***
3. In the mystery of the Holy Trinity, the Father and the Son are ONE. Therefore, Jesus cannot have any more power over the Father than He has over himself. Jesus said He simply said and did what He saw the Father doing (John 5:19). He also said He was equal with the Father (John 10:29-30). So the absolute power and authority that Jesus claims and gave to us (Matt. 28:18-20) was given to Him by the Father. In short, we have no power over Jesus and He has no power over the Father. And, like the Son, we are to obey and submit to the Father.

SELECTED
BIBLIOGRAPHY

Blackaby, Henry T., and Claude V. King, *Experiencing God*, Nashville: Broadman and Holman Publications, 1994.

Bright, Bill, *The Coming Revival, America's Call to Fast, Pray, and "Seek God's Face"*, Orlando, NewLife Publications, 1995.

Bruce, F.F., and Henry, Carl F.H., and Packer, J.I., and Harrison, R.K., *The Origin of the Bible*, Wheaton: Tyndale House, 1992.

Coleman, Robert E., *The Coming World Revival*, Wheaton: Crossway Books, 1989, 1995.

Cymbala, Jim, *Fresh Wind, Fresh Fire*, Grand Rapids: Zondervan, 1997.

Cymbala, Jim, *Fresh Faith*, Grand Rapids: Zondervan, 1999.

Floyd, Ronnie W., *The Power of Prayer and Fasting: 10 Secrets of Spiritual Strength*, Nashville, Broadman and Holman Publishers, 1997.

Kennedy, John W., *The Torch of the Testimony*, Auburn: Christian Books, 1965.

Kydd, Ronald A.N., *Charismatic Gifts in the Early Church*, Peabody, Massachusetts: Hendrickson Publishers, 1991.

Lightfoot, J. B. and Harmer, J. R., *The Apostolic Fathers*, Grand Rapids: Baker Book House, 1989.

Nathan, Rich, and Wilson, Ken, *Empowered Evangelical*. Ann Arbor: Servant Publications, 1995.

Ravenhill, Leonard, *Why Revival Tarries*, Minneapolis: Bethany House, 1991.

Tenney, Tommy, *God's Dream Team, A Call To Unity*, Ventura: Regal Books, 1999.

Vedder, Henry C., *A Short History of the Baptists*, Valley Forge: Judson Press, 1907.

Woodard, Lee W., *Kodex W: Old and Holy*, P.O. Box 1605, Sallisaw, Oklahoma 74955, 2002.

Kenneth Uptegrove

ABOUT THE AUTHOR

Kenneth Uptegrove

Kenneth Uptegrove is a Christian writer who desires to speak to the entire Christian community. Ken is the founder and sole operator of ArkHaven Ministries and Publications.

Ken uses the apologetic style of writing, and is well known for being academic, thorough, and gracious. His prior career as a computer professional influenced this style of writing.

In 1987, at age fifty, he went into full time ministry, concentrating his efforts on writing a newsletter, articles for a local paper, and working on a book. Since going into ministry work, he has studied church history and related subjects extensively, such as Bible manuscript history, Bible translations, and Holy Land archeology.

He also is conversational in such subjects as psychology, philosophy, cosmology, archaeology, astronomy, geophysics, paleontology, anthropology, Egyptology, naturopathy, and horticulture. He is his own Webmaster, and has designed websites for other ministries as well. His website is www.arkhaven.org.

At the turn of the twentieth century, the author would have been called a gentleman scholar. Today we would say his training was in God's University of Silence. Simply stated, he holds no degrees and has no seminary or Bible school training, but is described by some as being didactic. Although his writing style is formal and serious, in real life Ken is warm and humorous, and is well known for his perpetual smile.

Ken was an honor student and all-conference basketball center in his high school years (1953-56). Then he spent three years in the Army (1957-60), two of which were spent in Germany. In 2002 Ken and his wife, Joyce, celebrated their 39th wedding anniversary. They have three sons, two of whom are married. They have seven grandchildren.

Ken's father was a first stringer at the University of Nebraska Cornhuskers football team in 1932-1934, and was a successful educator and coach. Ken's mother turned 93 in February of 2003, and still lives alone.

The Uptegrove's are active members in a 13,000 member Southern Baptist Church in Springdale, Arkansas. Millions see this church service every week on national TV and over the Internet. Their pastor, Dr. Ronnie Floyd, is a major leader in the Southern Baptist Convention.

ArkHaven Ministries

www.ArkHaven.org

NOTES

Printed in the United States
1549400003BA/286-309

9 781410 740113